Iconic architecture at the University of Leicester: In the background is the Attenborough Tower, designed and constructed by Arup and opened in 1970. *Photo: Paul C. Whitehouse*

T0306976

What People Are Saying About

Shaping for Mediocrity

Do you think business schools should be helping to produce a low carbon, high inclusion, high democracy economy? Or should they be sacking academics who work towards these goals in order to produce a business-as-usual b-school that makes big profits? This urgent and beautifully written book shows why universities need to change, and what happens to free speech when higher education becomes a product.

Martin Parker, author of *Shut Down the Business School: What's Wrong with Management Education* and *Against Management: Organization in the Age of Managerialism*

Gibson Burrell, Ronald Hartz, David Harvie, Geoff Lightfoot, Simon Lilley and Friends have provided the academic community with a comprehensive narrative of the most shameless and blatant violation of academic freedom I have ever personally witnessed. The authors were all made redundant as a result of Leicester University's 2021 "Shaping for Excellence" – the vision of vice chancellor Nishan Canagarajah – which pitted management's "right" to "disinvest" from an area of research against academics' freedom to pursue an autonomous program of enquiry.

Critical management studies had been a beacon of success at Leicester and the international reputations of its exponents were beyond question. Canagarajah felt, however, that CMS didn't attract the right kind of customer, and so its perceived adherents were targeted for redundancy on the flimsiest of assumptions. What placed them at highest risk, though, was a history of union organizing.

The authors expose the moral dissolution of a university's leadership team in an era of competition, marketisation and managerialism where everything including research must be 'governed'. In an era where university management seems impervious to accountability, Burrell et al. name names, including who was silent, who lent support and who were "the enforcers". Their reflexivity and honesty stand in contrast to the deviousness and cynicism of the managers they encountered. Other administrators, they note, carried a weight of shame for the shabby scheme they were obliged to participate in, and resigned.

This is a book that should be read by every academic and trade unionist. What happened at the University of Leicester in 2021 could happen anywhere. Indeed, we see an escalation of "restructurings" which target arts, humanities and social sciences which are traditionally home to the kinds of critiques that irk the managerial cadre. *Shaping for Mediocrity* is a call to resist, to take back control of the university, and, above all, recognise the power of solidarity against the implacable tyranny of managerialism.
Liz Morrish, co-author of *Academic Irregularities: Discourse and Neoliberalism in Higher Education*

No area of existence is exempt from exploitation, including the acquisition of knowledge. State authority decides the matter, with particular regard to the needs of Global Capital. Our universities were thrown to the wolves many years ago; now students are being thrown too. There is no "right to education". An ignorant public is the preferred option. The difficulty with "thinking" is that it leads to asking questions. The authors of this book expose the cynicism, the hypocrisy and the appalling cowardice of the British education authorities.
James Kelman, author most recently of *God's Teeth and Other Phenomena* and *The State Is the Enemy: Essays on Liberation and Racial Justice*

This most welcome book uses an act of intellectual vandalism perpetrated by management at Leicester University as its springboard. This is part of a growing trend in the UK and US, where centres of critical thinking are dismantled as universities resemble corporations, using "market forces" as an alibi, in order to treat staff and support-service workers as disposable entities. The authors analyse this trend superbly while providing an intellectual basis for countering dismal developments such as the one at Leicester.
Kenneth Surin, professor emeritus, Duke University

Next generations will read *Shaping for Mediocrity* as a "future archive" of what we could have done collectively to save public higher education, and how those who fought the hardest battles were failed

not just by the system but by the movement itself. Yet, the book is written with a humour, hope and humility that defy bitterness and defeatism. It documents forensically how small leaks of individual mediocrity sink large vessels built on collective hard work and benevolence. It teaches us important lessons about what can still be done to stop the toxic spread of neo-managerial capitalism in our public universities, before it is too late.
Mariya Ivancheva, author of *The Alternative University: Lessons from Bolivarian Venezuela*

Shaping for Mediocrity is an exposé of what neoliberal university management does when academic workers passionately promote a rigorous and useful critical education. Without fear or favour, the authors journey through a notorious seven-month battle at one university, which ended in bitter defeat with tragic personal and professional costs. While it is a saddening and emotional read, their experiences are invaluable hard lessons for all education workers engaged in struggles everywhere. I've read nothing like this book in five decades. I salute those involved.
Alpesh Maisuria, co-author of *Life for the Academic in the Neoliberal University*

Anyone who works in a university business school should read this book. No, anyone who works in a university should read this book. Actually, make that anyone who is interested in the abuse of power, rampant neoliberalism and how employees can be treated as mere resources, to be disposed of on baseless, knee-jerk, reactionary managerialist whims. It's an absolute tour de force, a perfect example of parrhesia in a context where speaking truth to power is becoming more and more risky. I salute my friends and former colleagues for writing it.
Jo Brewis, Professor of People and Organisations, The Open University

While we have a lot of literature on the hypocrisy of the university as a supposed place of critical thinking, we have nothing so forensic and stinging as this real-time account of mass redundancies at one of the leading centres for critical scholarship and teaching in the UK, and perhaps the world. And yet despite the viciousness and brutality of the University of Leicester's hostility to thinking, this is the story of fierce and creative resistance, common courage and care, and the ultimate victory of collective critique over capitalist perfidy at work in the university. In other words, you are reading the last word on the University of Leicester.

Stefano Harney, co-author of *The Undercommons: Fugitive Planning and Black Study*

By the same authors

Gibson Burrell and Gareth Morgan, *Sociological Paradigms and Organisational Analysis Elements of the Sociology of Corporate Life* (London: Routledge, 1979; 978-1857421149)

Gibson Burrell, *Pandemonium: Towards a Retro-Organization Theory* (London: Sage, 1997; 978-0803977778)

Matthew Higgins, **Geoff Lightfoot**, Martin Parker and Warren Smith, *Science Fiction and Organization* (London: Routledge, 2001; 978-0415215886).

Stephen Linstead, Liz Fulop and **Simon Lilley**, *Management and Organization: A Critical Text* (London: Palgrave, 2004; 978-0333947500)

Geoff Lightfoot, **Simon Lilley** and Paulo Amaral M.N., *Representing Organization: Knowledge, Management, and the Information Age* (Oxford: OUP, 2004; 9780198775416)

David Harvie, Keir Milburn, Ben Trott and David Watts, eds. *Shut Them Down! The G8, Gleneagles 2005 and the Movement of Movements* (Leeds: Dissent! and Brooklyn, NY: Autonomedia, 2005; 978-0955206504)

Karen Dale and **Gibson Burell**, *The Spaces of Organisation and the Organisation of Space: Power, Identity and Materiality at Work* (London: Palgrave, 2007; 978-0230572683)

Peter Case, **Simon Lilley** and Tom Owen (eds), *The Speed of Organization* (Copenhagen: Copenhagen Business School Press, 2007; 978-8763001885)

Ronald Hartz, *"Dieses Anderssein aufzuheben…": Grundlagen einer dialektischen Theorie der modernen Arbeitsorganisation* ["Abolishing this otherness…": Foundations of a dialectical theory of modern work organisation] (Münster: Westfälisches Dampfboot, 2009; 978-3896917584)

Peter Armstrong and **Geoff Lightfoot**, *'The Leading Journal in the Field': Destabilizing Authority in the Social Sciences of Management* (London: MayFly Books, 2010; 978-1906948085)

The Free Association [Alex Dennis, **David Harvie**, Nette Humphries, Keir Milburn and David Watts], *Moments of Excess: Movements, Protest and Everyday Life* (Oakland, CA: PM Press, 2011; 978-1604861136)

Turbulence Collective [**David Harvie**, Keir Milburn, Tadzio Müller, Rodrigo Nunes, Michal Osterweil, Kay Summer, Ben Trott and David Watts], eds. *What Would It Mean To Win?* (Oakland, CA: PM Press, 2011; 978-1604861105)

Carl Rhodes and **Simon Lilley**, eds. *Organizations and Popular Culture: Information, Representation and Transformation* (London: Routledge, 2012; 978-0415692380).

Gibson Burrell, *Styles of Organizing: The Will to Form* (Oxford: OUP, 2013; 978-0199671625)

Ronald Hartz and Matthias Rätzer, eds. *Organisationsforschung nach Foucault* [Organisation Studies after Foucault] (Bielefeld: Transcript, 2013; 978-3837621716).

Ronald Hartz, Werner Nienhüser and Matthias Rätzer, eds, *Ästhetik und Organisation: Ästhetisierung und Inszenierung von Organisation, Arbeit und Management* [Aesthetics and organisation: aestheticisation and staging of organisation, work and management] (Wiesbaden: Springer, 2019; 978-3658219772)

Camille Barbagallo, Nicholas Beuret and **David Harvie**, eds. *Commoning with George Caffentzis and Silvia Federici* (London: Pluto Press, 2019; 978-0745339405).

Gibson Burrell, *Organization Theory: A Research Overview* (London: Routledge, 2022; 978-0367713638)

Rainer Diaz-Bone and **Ronald Hartz**, eds. *Dispositiv und Ökonomie: Diskurs- und dispositivanalytische Perspektiven auf Märkte und Organisationen* [Dispositive and economy: discourse and dispositive analytical perspectives on markets and organisations], 2nd edition (Wiesbaden: Springer, 2023; 978-3658315320)

SHAPING FOR MEDIOCRITY

THE CANCELLATION OF CRITICAL THINKING AT OUR UNIVERSITIES

Gibson Burrell, Ronald Hartz, David Harvie, Geoff Lightfoot, Simon Lilley and Friends

zer0 books

London, UK
Washington, DC, USA

CollectiveInk

First published by Zer0 Books, 2024
Zer0 Books is an imprint of Collective Ink Ltd.,
Unit 11, Shepperton House, 89 Shepperton Road, London, N1 3DF
office@collectiveinkbooks.com
www.collectiveinkbooks.com
www.zero-books.net

For distributor details and how to order please visit the 'Ordering' section on our website.

Paperback ISBN: 978 1 80341 796 7
eBook ISBN: 978 1 80341 797 4
Library of Congress Control Number: 2024932953

A CIP catalogue record for this book is available from the British Library.

Design credit(s): Lapiz Digital Services

UK: Printed and bound by CPI Group (UK) Ltd, Croydon, CR0 4YY
Printed in North America by CPI GPS partners

CONTENTS

PREFACE

> The past is never dead. It's not even past.
> – William Faulkner, *Requiem for a Nun*[1]

Shaping for Mediocrity was written in the aftermath of a seven-month struggle against mass redundancies at the University of Leicester in 2021, a struggle which saw 145 employees targeted and an eventual exodus from the university that likely exceeded 200.[2] The book's authors were all involved in that dispute in the most intimate way – we were amongst those being made redundant, in our case from the university's School of Business. We have written the book as part of an effort to make sense of the struggle, to understand the reasons why we lost. It was written partly for ourselves – an act of catharsis, a search for closure. It was also written for the wider world, for those who care about universities and perhaps especially those who labour within them, to hopefully offer lessons that might inform them in their own conflicts against the powers that ultimately defeated us. In this sense, our book is not merely *about* the redundancy struggle, it is a *part* of redundancy struggles. In this sense too, our book is less about closure, than about seeking to open up, to make possible other outcomes.

This is much more than a story of some university lecturers – business school lecturers at that – being sacked. Our story and our book are about questions that we hope will resonate far more widely. Are university scholars free to write and teach what they think is right? Is it OK for university scholars to be sacked for publishing in the 'wrong' journals (journals that have the word 'critical' in their title, for instance)? Is it right that universities have been taken over by business people, people who bow to the logic of finance? (How did this happen?) Should employees be able to organise in trade unions and to question those people in charge of their institution?

These questions should matter for everyone. Universities matter. In the UK, around half a million people work in a university – only the school system and the National Health Service are larger employers. In Britain more than one 18-year-old in every three starts a full-time university undergraduate course – at any one time, almost three million people are engaged in the labour of studying. The ideas and knowledges that are produced within universities and that emanate from them shape – though they do not fully determine – society. And as a society facing myriad intersecting crises – of democracy, inequality, xenophobia, global heating, and mass extinction, to name just a few – we need critical thinking more than ever. We need thinking that asks difficult questions, that offers answers that might be uncomfortable (at least to some), thinking that is brave and imaginative. If it is not possible – if it is not permitted – to be critical at university, then the future is dark indeed.

Shaping for Mediocrity has also been written as an act of remembrance. University of Leicester's bosses have done everything in their power to expunge the 2021 dispute – and their own part in it – from the official records. Even the restructuring programme, *Shaping for Excellence*, in whose name the wholescale sackings were executed, has been quietly dropped. And so too has our very existence been erased. Between us, the five named authors have 75 years' experience working at the University of Leicester. Two of the named authors – Gibson Burrell and Simon Lilley – were heads of school for a total period exceeding a decade. Yet we and our contributions no longer appear in the School's official history.

Just as our redundancy struggle stretches forward in time to encompass the writing and publication of this book, so too does it stretch backward. To situate our 2021 fight against redundancy, we found it necessary to revisit the history of the School of Business and, in turn, to place this history against its wider context of the neoliberal reforms of higher education of the past four decades and the often tense relationship between schools of management, or business, and the university itself. Temporally, then, our account overflows the seven months of the redundancy dispute, January–August 2021, encompassing much of the era of modern higher education. In this overflowing, we explore issues surrounding university governance, professional autonomy, academic freedom, trade unionism, and leadership.

Three intertwined questions permeate *Shaping for Mediocrity*, though they are not made explicit on every page: *who makes the university* and *how?* And, *what is the university for?* Although we lost our battle – we were made redundant from the University of Leicester – we have continued to think collectively and critically about these questions and possible answers. We hope that this very book is evidence of that. We have not completely given up on the university as an institution, though we are also hedging that bet. We hope that those who believe with us that the university must be a critical institution can make use of our account of the policy of the cancellation of critical thinking at the University of Leicester and its wider implications for our profession.

Who are *we* and who are our friends?

We first conceived the idea of this book in February 2021, just a few weeks into the redundancy struggle. Both Matteo Mandarini, our editor, and Tariq Goddard, Zer0's co-founder, were supportive. Our intention was that we write the book contemporaneously with our campaign against the redundancies. We have little idea now what such a book would have looked like. Probably it would have been more of a chronology of those seven months of 2021, also containing numerous documents from that struggle. Perhaps it would have looked more like *Warwick University Ltd*, the book assembled (in just one week) by staff and students at that institution to document their struggles of the late 1960s.[3] In fact, we do have something like that – chronology, documents and other materials – on our website: ulsb16.com.[4] But, as it turned out, we had no time to put together a book in 2021: the immediate demands of the campaign were (too) many and always took precedence. What we have produced – with continued support, advice and encouragement from Matteo and Tariq – is the product of 18 months' reflection on what happened at University of Leicester. It's the product of far wider reading on and deeper engagement with many of the issues our particular struggle was about and the contested histories of universities. It is probably a more valuable book for this.

We write in the first-person plural because this is our story and we are several. But throughout the book our use of *we* is fluid. It shifts from the narrow *we the authors*, or perhaps *we who were targeted for redundancy*, through the *we who were and are workplace organisers and activists*, to the *we who were and are university staff*, whether University of Leicester employees or university employees more generally. This slippage is intentional, though we (the authors) have tried to clarify where the meaning is ambiguous. All transformative political projects must involve the construction and maintenance of a *we* – an *us* that is often in antagonism to an explicit or implicit *them* – and the struggles against mass redundancies at University of Leicester were no exception. We – those of us threatened with redundancy, those of struggling against redundancies – failed to prevent these redundancies because the more expansive *we* that we sought to construct was insufficiently large and resolute to counter managers' *they*. There were also times in the campaign when we activists and organisers misjudged the extent and resolve of this more expansive *we*, assuming allyship and solidarity that did not, in fact, exist. If the meaning of *we* is not always clear then, that's because this lack of clarity reflects political reality.

Three principles inform our perspective. First, Karl Marx's idea, in *The Eighteenth Brumaire of Louis Bonaparte*, that we make our own history, but not in circumstances of our own choosing. Second, that universities are sites of conflict, of antagonism, of struggle. Third, that these are class struggles – though these struggles are also intersectional, often taking racialised and gendered forms. There is an *us* and there is a *them*.

But the identities of 'us' and 'them' are not so straightforward. It's easy, of course, to point to the vice-chancellor and say, "there is the boss"; and to the porter, cleaner, and hourly paid seminar teacher and say, "and there are the workers". But it quickly becomes more ambiguous. Many university employees have or have had some sort of managerial responsibility, even limited rights to hire and fire: grant holders vis-à-vis research assistants; module leaders vis-à-vis teaching assistants; departmental heads vis-à-vis 'rank and file' members, some of whom might be on higher-paying and higher-status contracts. This is certainly the case with us, who have 'enjoyed' line-managerial responsibilities of one sort or another in our careers. In some respects, then, we have been 'them'. Or, at least, we have been partially them. But this characterisation is still too crude.

Every day, in the modern university, individuals make choices, both as individuals and as part of larger collectives. They act either to reproduce and even deepen relations of domination. Or they act to undermine and sabotage these relationships. Most of us, most of the time, act in both ways in the course of a single day. The capital relation is an internal relation, 'the class struggle… is something that runs through us, individually and collectively. Only if we were fully class-ified could we say without contradiction "we are working class" (but then class struggle would be impossible).'[5] In our view, this is a reworking of the claim that class 'is a historical phenomenon. I do not see class as a "structure", nor even as "category", but as something which in fact happens (and can be shown to have happened) in human relationships.'[6] We think that class has been 'happening' in and to a lot in British universities (hence the many books and articles discussing the 'proletarianisation' of academics): this is 'an active process, which owes as much to agency as to conditioning.' Another way of saying this is that the university is a site – possibly a frontline – of value struggles. The site of contestation between competing and antagonistic conceptions of the university, of education, of study. This process, these struggles, and the impacts of human agency, are often clarified during periods of open conflict, such as our redundancy struggle in 2021 and earlier struggles at the University of Leicester.

But if 'us' and 'them' (or 'we' and 'they') are slippery concepts, we at least know who our friends are. In March 2022 the University of Leicester's media team announced the institution's intention to end the use of Non-Disclosure Agreements 'when dealing with student and staff complaints of sexual misconduct, bullying and other unacceptable behaviour'. The official tweet heralding the announcement included the hashtags #CantBuyMySilence and #BuildTrustNotSilence.[7] A worthy commitment. But in 2021, University bosses bought a hell of a lot of silence – as well as destroying a lot of trust. Many staff took voluntary redundancy for fear of being left only with meagre statutory compulsory redundancy pay-outs. Others, disgusted with bosses' behaviour, negotiated a financial package to leave. Of the 15 employees made compulsorily redundant in August 2021, many accepted financial payments following their dismissal in return for dropping claims for unlawful dismissal via employment tribunal. In all of these cases the individuals concerned were obliged to sign non-disclosure agreements. Such NDAs prohibit them publicly discussing the University of Leicester or the manner of their departure from it. At least seven of our former colleagues in the School of Business signed such agreements – always as a result of economic necessity – and are thus unable talk or write of their experiences. They are our friends.

We also want to thank the many friends and comrades who supported us in our struggle against redundancies – who were *part of* the struggle against redundancies and for another type of university. The following people, in particular, were there with us in 2021, alongside us and caring for us: Emma Battell Lowman,

Armin Beverungen, Peter Bloom, Jo Brewis, Gavin Brown, Steve Brown, Rob Clarke, Cara Dobbing, Helen Eborall, Jo Edge, Marta Gasparin, Dan Hamilton, Emi Mise, Mike Mulheran, Martin Parker, Alex Patel, Martin Quinn, Sarah Seaton, Charlie Smith, and Deborah Toner. Plus our families and some others we cannot name.

We want to extend our thanks to the people who read this manuscript and provided invaluable feedback. They are: Peter Armstrong, Jo Brewis, Peter Fleming, Becca Harrison, Effie Harvie, Mariya Ivancheva, Alpesh Maisuria, Robert Ovetz, Martin Parker, Deborah Toner, and David Watts. Finally, we thank our editor Matteo Mandarini and the 'behind-the-scenes' people at Zer0, in particular, Adam Jones and Frank Smecker. Needless to say they share no blame for any of the book's weaknesses.

INTRODUCTION

> Mediocre, *adj.*: Of middling quality; neither bad nor good, average; (hence contextually) indifferent, of poor quality, second-rate.
> – *Oxford English Dictionary*

In April 2021, the following extraordinary, one-sided exchange took place. It concluded an individual redundancy consultation, part of a business case framed as a plan 'to disinvest from research and scholarship in critical management studies and political economy'. The main speaker is Gareth Brown, then employed as a lecturer in the University of Leicester School of Business (ULSB) and also – a significant part of our story – a prominent official in our local union branch. The first person he addresses – 'Alex', a pseudonym – was a human resource professional at the University of Leicester. Brown then turns to Professor James 'Jim' Devlin. At the time, Devlin was dean of ULSB, that is, Brown's boss. He was architect and executor of the business case, which saw 16 members of ULSB faculty – Gareth Brown, Gibson Burrell, Joseph Choonara, Sam Dallyn, Valérie Fournier, Fabian Frenzel, Oz Gore, Chris Grocott, Ronald Hartz, David Harvie, George Kokkinidis, Hugo Letiche, Geoff Lightfoot, Simon Lilley, Keir Milburn and Martin Wood – put at risk of redundancy in January 2021. Brown also mentions Gary Dixon, chair of the University of Leicester Council, the university's supreme governing body.

Alex, you are a highly competent, decent human being, you don't have to have this on your conscience, and you are very, very aware of what is going on here. I would implore you to use the whistle-blower policy, to join UCU [the University and College Union], and we will do absolutely everything within our power to defend and support you against anything bad that might happen as a result of that.

Jim…

Yes.

There are countless backdoors, loopholes, various other means by which you can fly under the radar, get rid of the people you want to get rid of without detection. Frankly it is beyond insulting that we have been presented with this utter shambles of a business case, had to watch you going through these ridiculous contortions, week after week, obfuscations, lies, contradictions: utterly absurd. You will be hammered on academic freedom when this goes [to] court. You will be hammered on the issue of job similarity. You will be hammered on the failure to provide crucial information when asked. Your use of 'primarily' is likely to be something that is talked about for years in legal circles and in the HRM [Human Resource Management] literature. And you will be hammered on the issue of union victimisation. For the eleven of us in scope [for redundancy] there are at least two separate law cases, legal cases. For most of us there are three. That's likely to be over a million pounds in terms of payout, between the eleven of us. Your reputation at this point is unsalvageable. And if you think for one second that when this all goes further south you are not going to be thrown to the wolves in order to save those on larger salaries, then that is hopelessly naïve. However, you can still act in such a way to ensure that vulnerable deans in the future can't be exploited in the same way that you have, by giving us the list of names that was given to you by Gary Dixon on November 12 [2020], or on one of three other possible dates during the end of last year. You may have been discreet about it, but Gary Dixon is alleged not to have been discreet about it. We will have that list at some point. It's better if it comes from you.

I have no knowledge and never have seen any such list.

Thank you. I call this meeting to a close.

Two of these sixteen individuals targeted for redundancy in January 2021 accepted so-called voluntary redundancy payouts. Four were removed from the pool of those targeted, though two of them subsequently resigned anyway. One accepted a transfer to a role he considered inferior. The remaining nine – Brown, Burrell, Dallyn, Fournier, Hartz, Harvie, Kokkinidis, Lightfoot and Lilley were eventually dismissed – 'by reason of redundancy' – in August 2021.[1] The total exodus from that School, as a result of the plan Devlin executed, numbers at least forty – and is still rising.

The redundancies in the business school were part of wider restructuring across the University of Leicester, which its bosses called *Shaping for Excellence*. In total 145 colleagues were targeted, across five academic departments – English; Informatics; Mathematics & Actuarial Science; Neuroscience, Psychology & Behaviour; and Business – and three professional services units – Education Services; Library User Services (frontline library staff); and Estates & Digital Services. By the end of year, at least 200 people had exited the university, a result of dismissal, 'voluntary' redundancy or resignation. Gareth Brown's remarks in his redundancy consultation touch on many of the issues that we explore in this book – the attack on academic freedom, the targeting of trade unionists, managerial prerogative and its limits.

Brown's monologue, above, was prescient. The situation did indeed go 'further south'. Two weeks after this consultation, the University and College Union applied a global academic boycott to the University of Leicester, a rare and serious sanction, which was not lifted until the end of 2021. As we write these words two years later, the University's reputation remains in ruins, possibly having passed a tipping point. We have seen no evidence that our former bosses have a strategy for reversing this reputational disaster.

After a year of doing the bidding of 'those on larger salaries', as well as that of Gary Dixon, chair of the University Council (its supreme governing body), it appears that Devlin was indeed 'thrown to the wolves'. Just three weeks after the effective dismissal of those he had made redundant, his immediate superior, Professor Henrietta O'Connor, pro-vice-chancellor and head of the College of Social Sciences, Arts and Humanities, announced that Devlin too would be leaving the University of Leicester. His tenure at the institution lasted only two years. The notice that he was leaving failed even to gloss over the manner of his departure by saying that he had resigned. His replacement as dean was Professor Dan Ladley. Ladley had been Devlin's deputy throughout the redundancy process and indeed its co-executor. At the time of writing, he remains in post, as do O'Connor, now deputy vice-chancellor, and the University's president and vice-chancellor, Professor Nishan Canagarajah. The then-deputy vice-chancellor, Professor Edmund Burke, who was also a major cast member, especially in our chapter on academic freedom, has been rewarded for his part. He is now the vice-chancellor of Bangor University. (The elevations of Ladley, O'Connor and Burke are symptomatic of wider structural issues within the sector: senior managers perceived by ordinary staff to have failed are frequently promoted. Of course, there is more on this later in the book.)

It is this set of academics and a few other senior university managers that form the group of actors upon our stage. There are many other *dramatis personae* in our tale of a university aspiring to – or shaping for – mediocrity, but in our account we only name those further up the hierarchy. Younger, more junior members of staff make fewer appearances in our account, not because they are irrelevant to the unfolding of events – far from it – but because we wish to protect them as best we can. Thus, the individual whom Gareth Brown first addresses is pseudonymous. 'Alex' was a human resource professional at the University of Leicester. They are indeed a decent human being and they exited the University of Leicester a few months after this exchange, without, as far as we know, any other job to go to.

On mediocrity

The title of our book is *Shaping for Mediocrity*. 'Shaping' obviously echoes the name of the university leadership's 'Shaping for Excellence' programme. The word 'mediocrity' we use with intention. We're not simply being rude about university senior managers; it's a way of understanding their behaviour. Why should any university's leaders seek to be 'of middling quality' or 'ordinary'? Why would they aspire to be average? In the years before 'Shaping for Excellence', Leicester had been a city on the up and far from average. In 2016, its football team won the English premiership, and King Richard III's body was discovered and reinterred in the city's cathedral. Both drew international attention. But the university's leaders have not capitalised on the achievements of its archaeologists, historians, and scholars of English who collaborated in the discovery of Richard III's remains. In fact, its specialists of Medieval English were amongst those made redundant in 2021, whilst historians, classicists and archaeologists who remain employed there report feeling increasingly beleaguered.

The University of Leicester has never been recognised as one of Britain's 'best' universities. Established in 1921 as a 'living memorial' to those who had lost their lives in the Great War, the university's motto is *Ut Vitam Habeant* ['that they might have life']. It is obviously not one of the 'ancient' institutions (Oxford, Cambridge, St. Andrews, Glasgow, Aberdeen, Edinburgh). Nor is it a member of the self-selected Russell Group of twenty-four 'leading' UK universities.

But it was a good university. Its scholars provided a decent higher education to its students; they conducted decent research. Many still do, of course. The university could even boast of scholarship of world-class brilliance: Alec Jeffreys, for instance, who, with co-workers, developed techniques for genetic fingerprinting and DNA profiling; sociologists Norbert Elias and Anthony Giddens; The Sir Norman Chester Centre for Football Research; the space research which still thrives; the Stanley Burton Centre for Holocaust and Genocide Studies, which is also ongoing; finally, dare we say it, for Critical Management Studies Leicester was internationally renowned. The University of Leicester was respected. It was distinctive – that is, not average, not ordinary, not mediocre. It accommodated scholars and allowed them to carry out teaching and research to the best of their ability. Why the turn to mediocrity?

Within the field of strategic 'management' there is a concept known as *mimetic isomorphism*. Applying this concept to higher education, many institutions, 'faced with an increasingly complex, competitive and uncertain operating environment, have mainly resorted to the isomorphic strategy of mimicking fellow universities which are perceived to have the highest degree of legitimacy among peer institutions. As a result, conformity among universities and their organisational structures has intensified'.[2]

But mimicry is unlikely to lead to any new forms of excellence nor the maintenance of existing ones. It's a strategy of hiding amongst the 'normal', of setting 'the sector norm' as a target – an explicit aspiration of several University of Leicester leaders in recent years. It's 'run of the mill'. Essentially, mimetic isomorphism is a 'middling' strategy. Mediocrity as strategy is a result of a lack of confidence, a failure to dare to be different, and a failure of leadership. This strategy, that university officers at Leicester have pursued from 2014 onwards, is captured perfectly in Thomas Docherty's witty aphorism about 'the exceptional and the ordinary' in university leadership: '"Thinking outside the box" is precisely what everyone inside the box does; and, indeed, it is precisely now the qualification for getting into the box in the first place'.[3]

Mimetic isomorphism is the institutionalised belief that other, 'better' institutions must know what they are doing and should thus be quietly shadowed. The Russell Group plays an exaggerated role in this process and the sector more broadly. Its revolving chair often appears in TV studios purporting to represent the 'system' and its interests as a whole. Subtly and not so subtly the Russell Group imposes uniformity of strategy.[4] It helps to create an institutionalised fear that the consequences of standing out in almost any way are dangerous to longevity and survival. And despite their best efforts, the quest to join the Russell Group engaged upon by Leicester's current and previous two vice-chancellors tells us not only something about the Russell Group's allure, but also about why an aspirant vice-chancellor would engage in mimetic isomorphism for fear of standing out.

What forces do a vice-chancellor and their senior management team have to bend to? It is true that vice-chancellors face the trials and tribulations of turbulent environments and turbulent chairs of university councils. It is also true that they have agency: a damn sight more agency than their staff, for sure. Should we regard and present these 'senior' characters as malign or disturbed or weak, as careerist, or as mere personifications of forces and logics outside of their control, as unable to act against the machine as their less well-remunerated staff? This, in turn, raises a further question: who or what is 'the machine'? There is evidence that, at the University of Leicester, senior staff regarded campus trade unions as a block to their freedom of action. As we shall reveal, the senior management team certainly saw Leicester UCU and UCU nationally – of which we were all more-or-less active members – as an especially difficult trade union.

What of our 'evidence', which we use to bring our story to life? We have at our disposal a huge database of recorded material, transcripts, emails, documents, 'clarifications', and other texts. It would not make an interesting narrative for you, dear reader, to present all of this material. But the exchange with which we opened this book—in which Gareth Brown addresses first 'Alex', the HR professional, and then ULSB's then-dean James Devlin—gives a flavour of one type of interaction. There were several other types, which we will discuss as our account unfolds. Individuals like Alex will appear in our tale in the role of 'extras'. They may speak a line or two, appear in more than one scene, but for our purposes their role is not a central one. That Alex walks across our stage so briefly, uttering no words of their own, might be seen as insulting to a professional colleague. This is not our intention. Any narrative drive places some actors centre-stage, whilst others remain on the periphery, in the wings.

This leads us to our treatment of other *dramatis personae* who, in the hierarchy of the institution, are neither above nor below us – our peers. We were sorely disappointed by many of our professorial colleagues and their silence in the face of our redundancy. Some of these individuals had made careers from espousing critical orientations to their subject matter, from speaking critically of the politics of institutions and from their involvement in progressive struggles. Nearly all were union members. Their lack of public engagement; their failure to speak to more 'junior' colleagues in open ways about the necessity of resisting; their failure to open up spaces in which such discussions might be had; their failure to even support us privately – all this shocked us. We name very few of these characters who were once our colleagues, who are also extras in our story. A few we refer to by their office alone. Many we will not mention at all. At the same time, many erstwhile colleagues, many of them relatively junior – both academics and professional service staff among them – were outspoken in their support for us. Their solidarity made a difference and we thank them for it. Since most are still employed by the University of Leicester we feel it better not to name them. But they know who they are, and so do we.

The *dramatis personae* will also include, as extras, a number of university administrators who have no formal academic role. These individuals' particular roles were various, but they can be best described as *enforcers*. In redundancy consultations they attempted to police our behaviour, keeping things 'professional'. In the electronic realm, they monitored social-media activity as we sought to garner support for our struggle, reporting their observations back to their superiors. These individuals played a not insignificant part in the redundancies and a few were subsequently rewarded by the university's vice-chancellor. We will tell more about this later – the more senior of these individuals we will mention by name as well as role.

About our book

There is a large and still-growing genre of critical writing about universities. The tenor of many of these books and articles is one of loss and decline, succinctly captured in titles such as *The Decline of Donnish Dominion*, *The Fall of the Faculty*, *The University in Ruins* or, more recently, *Dark Academia: How Universities Die,* and *The Hopeless University*. It is somehow convenient to dismiss such attempts as pure nostalgia and, in consequence, demean the critical analysis and reflection about the current state of universities that they contain. Moreover, as one observer puts it: 'when it comes to nostalgia in higher education, outsiders are often more guilty of sentimentalism than those on campus'.[5]

Our narrative is different for a number of reasons. We tell the story of a single institution during a period of intense struggle – a narrative of 'us' and 'them' set in a provincial university – but it is set against the backdrop of wider university politics across the sector in the first decades of the twenty-first century. What happened at University of Leicester in 2021 was particularly egregious. But it was also fully within the realms of the 'acceptable' – when all was said and done, it was accepted – of the 'normal' even. As we've already remarked, Leicester's vice-chancellor, Nishan Canagarajah, rewarded many of those individuals who executed our redundancies (with the notable exception of James Devlin, of course). The governing body of Bangor University saw fit to appoint Canagarajah's deputy Edmund Burke to their top job. Gary Dixon, the chair of Leicester's governing body, is simultaneously a director of the University Superannuation Scheme (USS) pension fund, another key player on the stage of UK higher education. In other words, these individual managers and their practices are fully integrated into the broader system of British university governance. Aspects of what we narrate – authoritarianism, curtailment of academic freedom, subordination of the university towards business logics, financialisation, the assault on trade unions – have taken place at many other higher education institutions. What happened at University of Leicester in 2021 could have happened – could happen – at almost any university.

Our story, which we also situate within a longer period of neoliberal reforms, and an even longer period of capitalist and patriarchal university governance, thus reveals much about the wider picture. We had better than front-row seats to the spectacle of the shaping of mediocrity: we were in the ring. Two of us were principal officers and negotiators of the University of Leicester branch of UCU. (We believe, in fact, that this is the principal reason for our targeting.) As such, we attended multiple meetings with key members of the university's executive board and knew more of the way in which redundancies were prosecuted across the university than all but a small handful of managers. Our number includes several early members of what was first the University of Leicester Management Centre and later the School of Management, who long pre-date the redundancies and the arrival of Dixon, Canagarajah and Burke. This early history is important too – for its own sake and for what it tells us about criticality in British universities, but also for the way in which it established the conditions that led to 2021's attack on critical thinking, academic freedom and trade union organisation. In short, ours is a story which invites us, and you, to think about the wider context in which universities are created, and recreated, and for whom.

We begin our story (Chapter 1) by explaining how our union branch came to be described as 'the most intimidating and disruptive in the country', before recounting the seven months of intense struggle which ended with our dismissals (Chapter 2). We conclude the first half of the book by examining the broader turn to authoritarian leadership within universities (Chapter 3). In the book's second half we situate our struggle in its historical context. In Chapter 4 we explain how, in the context of Thatcherism and the 'massification' of the business school such bodies came, perhaps paradoxically, to afford considerable space for critical thinking. Many of the higher education reforms of the past four decades have proved to be key elements of the 'great moving right show'.[6] They revolve around university governance and have enabled the increasing financialisation of universities: we shine a light on these trends in Chapter 5. The declared reason for our redundancy – a plan that involved 'disinvest[ing] from research and scholarship in Critical Management Studies and political economy' – looked very much like an attack on academic freedom. We explore this contested issue in Chapter 6, concluding that, both in law and in practice, it is actually subordinate to the freedom to manage of university bosses.

In our concluding chapter (Chapter 7), we pose some vital questions: could the university be ours – and what would that mean? And, in a crisis-ridden world, what is the future of critical thinking in universities?

CHAPTER 1

THE COUNTRY'S MOST INTIMIDATING AND DISRUPTIVE UCU BRANCH

I won't forget this.
– Deputy Vice-Chancellor Edmund Burke to Leicester UCU negotiators, following the conclusion of talks in September 2018, at which university bosses conceded they would make no compulsory redundancies.

Leicester UCU is the most intimidating and disruptive branch in the country.
– Vice-Chancellor Nishan Canagarajah to striking University of Leicester workers, November 2019[1]

Just 273,000 working days were lost to labour disputes in the UK in 2018, the sixth-lowest annual total since records began in 1891. But two-thirds of these working days were lost in the education sector, mainly universities.[2] These figures certainly underestimate the numbers involved in university strikes that year: up to 42,000 members of the University and College Union (UCU), employed at sixty-four 'pre-92' or 'old' universities struck for 14 days in February and March, as part of a dispute over reductions to pension entitlements through the Universities Superannuation Scheme (USS).[3] The 2018 USS disputes were a pivotal moment for the union and Leicester UCU organisers played a key part. Leicester UCU fought a second, local dispute later in the year, and 2018 probably represented a zenith in the branch's power to limit managerial prerogative and articulate its own alternative vision for the University. These battles also established a grudge between management and the union, one which festered for two years before managers struck back with their 'Shaping for Excellence' programme, disproportionately targeting union organisers. In this chapter, we explore how the local branch established itself as a fighting force, setting the scene for Chapter 2, in which we recount its dismemberment under the aegis of 'Shaping for Excellence'.

A new militancy on campus

In the UK, as in many other countries, the education sector is a frontline of capitalist development, a frontline of struggle. In universities, metrics, rankings and league tables have become ubiquitous. Students are encouraged to see themselves – and behave – as consumers. Vice-chancellors are making increasing use of precariously employed workers for both teaching and research. They are intensifying workloads for everyone. At the same time that academic and professional services (administrative) staff alike are expected to identify with our employer and its 'values' and 'mission', we are also expected to behave as entrepreneurial neoliberal subjects, managing our own careers and CVs. Poor physical and mental health are the inevitable result. The university has become an 'anxiety machine'.[4]

But capital has been exploring this frontier for several decades now. Marxist and other critical scholars have been writing about the 'global entrepreneurialisation of the universities', 'academic capitalism', and the 'proletarianisation' of academics for at least a quarter of a century. Why has our resistance only seriously erupted in the past few years? Some observers have used the fable of the boiled frog to explain the failure of university workers to resist the deterioration of their wages and working conditions over these decades. That is, the deleterious changes have been imposed incrementally so that, though we might grumble, we have acquiesced.[5] If this is true, then 2018 represented the moment that 'the frogs' suddenly became more active in our attempt to escape the heating water – and to 'arrest the incremental turning up of the heat that is threatening our extinction'.[6] But we think there's more to it than this, with at least part of the reason for university workers' increased militancy lying with demographic shifts and associated changes in university workers' subjectivity.

In 1980, only 15% of British 18-year-olds remained in full-time education following school or college. This figure includes those participating in any kind of training as well as those attending further education colleges, polytechnics and universities. The proportion attending university – from which almost all future university lecturers have been drawn – was even smaller. In that year 68,150 people obtained a first university degree in the UK, with fewer than 19,000 obtaining a higher degree.[7]

Of course, these individuals were – for the most part and almost by definition – academically gifted. Certainly, they had succeeded at school and in examinations, probably as a result of hard work. They were used to being praised by teachers. Mostly – because that has been the nature of British social mobility (or lack thereof) – they came from middle- or upper-class backgrounds. By the time (some of) these individuals became university academics, they had been fully socialised into a particular form of subjectivity, a subjectivity which valorised individual studiousness and hard work, characteristics that yielded individual success. The desire to please one's teacher transmuted into desires to please one's professor, one's head of department, the journal or book editor, the vice-chancellor – and, correspondingly, not to make trouble, not to rock the boat. Even today, you do not need to scratch a senior academic very hard to reveal the attitude that another academic in difficulty (struggling to find or keep a job, for instance), must carry at least a share of the blame for their difficulties and that *it's always possible to publish your way out of a bad institution.*

In 2010 – the year in which David Cameron's Conservative government tripled university tuition fees to £9,000 per year for UK students – 330,720 students obtained a first degree, a fivefold increase over the preceding three decades. The increase in numbers obtaining a higher degree was even more dramatic: that had risen almost tenfold, to 182,610. By 2017/18 – the academic year that included the 14 days of USS strikes – a reported 50.2% of young people went into higher education.

The marked increase in the number of university students is important. Over these decades, British higher education had moved from being an 'elite' system to a 'mass' system to a 'universal' system.[8] As participation in higher education widened, so too did the social background of those who ended up working as university teachers, lecturers, and researchers. That new generation of university workers carried with them a new, much more varied set of subjectivities. Notably, 2018's USS pension strike was the first involving young workers who'd participated in the UK's student movement of 2010 – which erupted in response to the government's decision to triple tuition fees. Eight years later, this cohort had graduated, completed a post-graduate degree and were old and qualified enough to have waged jobs in universities. They brought with them their experiences of student militancy and ongoing struggles against systemic oppression (such as patriarchy and white supremacy) that until recently had excluded them from working as academics.

A second – complementary – reason for the new militancy of university workers in 2018 is that British higher education is far more international than it was a few decades ago. Of the 430,000 staff working in UK universities in 2017/18, more than one in five were not UK nationals.[9] For academic staff, the most represented group within the union, the proportion of international migrants was even higher: 45%. Migrant workers carry with them experiences of political and workplace struggle from other places and such diversity can obviously only enrich movements. Indeed, struggles in other countries have frequently been more militant than those in Britain, and in both 2018 and 2019, migrant comrades frequently remarked on the hesitancy, caution, and conservatism of British workplace struggle. As we turn our attention to University of Leicester and to Leicester UCU, it's worth remarking that in the period we're discussing it became a running joke that one necessary ingredient for a successful strike was the involvement of Italian militants.

We are the University of Leicester!

To understand the changes that Leicester UCU underwent in the years running up to 2018, and how it was that an 'intimidated' management began to see the local branch as a 'problem' to be solved, we need to go back to October 2014. In that month, Paul Boyle was appointed as vice-chancellor, replacing the retiring Bob Burgess. Just shy of 50 years old when he took on the role and very ambitious, Boyle was an academic who had leveraged a modicum of scholarly ability to advance his own career in university leadership. Like many 'disruptive' leaders, Boyle arrived in Leicester with preconceived ideas of what a 'good university' should be like and soon started trying to transform the University of Leicester to match his vision. Boyle's schemes included the creation of a School of Business through the forced merger of the School of Management and the Economics Department (discussed in Chapter 4), ambitious capital spending plans (which we explore in Chapter 5), and a programme of 'institutional transformation', announced in summer 2016, which involved mass redundancies and the closure of several departments, including the respected Vaughan Centre for Lifelong Learning, an institution older than the university itself. All provoked ongoing dissent amongst staff.

One of Boyle's early gestures was to sign up the university to a UN campaign called 'He For She', intended to encourage men and boys to advocate for gender equality. The irony was heavy, given Leicester's position as the university with the widest gender pay gap, a gap which hardly shifted during Boyle's tenure as VC. One anonymous riposte was an ironic postcard promoting an alternative initiative 'All For Paul'. In 2018, in a particularly ill-judged act, Boyle appointed to the ceremonial role of University Chancellor Conservative peer David Willetts, who, as universities minister, was architect of the tripling of tuition fees to a maximum of £9000 per year, and who had blamed feminism for Britain's lack of social mobility.[10] That new fees policy, approved by MPs in December 2010, triggered an angry student movement involving mass demonstrations, along with occupations of the Conservative party's Millbank headquarters and several universities' administration buildings. Willetts's appointment as Chancellor of University of Leicester provoked similar fury amongst both staff and students – from that point on every picket and campus demonstration included its share of 'Willetts Out' placards and chants.

'All For Paul': Several thousand of these anonymous A6 postcards appeared across the University of Leicester campus in late 2016. *Photo: the authors*

Opposition to Boyle and his planned 'institutional transformation' had several features, which, over the next few years, came to define the branch and its approach. They're important as they have a crucial role in both the prosecution of the action against *Shaping for Excellence* and, perhaps, also in its failure.

First was humour and an irreverent attitude to management, both as individuals and as a cadre. There is a long history of social movements deploying humour, both to advance their message to external audiences and internally, and to help establish and strengthen collective identity. But, although workplace humour is pretty much ubiquitous as a form of 'organisational misbehaviour', we don't think it's much used as part of trade union organising and mobilising, certainly not in Britain. We might extend to the majority of British trade unionists sociologist Hans Speier's characterisation of 'the revolutionary and the scientist' as 'humourless'.[11] Humour manifested itself in many ways, the 'All For Paul' postcard being just one obvious example of this.

A second feature of Leicester UCU's approach was its attempt to articulate a clear separation between university management, on the one hand, and employees and unions, on the other, with an insistence that *we* – and not them – were/are the university. In their communications, both internal and external, University of Leicester bosses, like most bosses, always identified their own persons and perspectives with 'the University', thereby implicitly situating any opposing or alternative views – such as those of unions or other critics – as outside and less legitimate. Leicester UCU consciously attempted to invert this formulation, portraying executives as external to, and parasitic upon, the organisation.

We asserted our separation from management and its claim to (be) the university in a quite material way – this is the third feature. During the 14 days of strike action in early 2018, for instance, the usual business of picketing was supplemented by rallies. As the strike progressed, these campus marches and rallies became increasingly noisy. On the morning of the first day, a single drum and its drummer arrived for picket duty. By the strike's final day, the ensemble included a dozen percussion instruments, one saxophone, one euphonium, one (purple) trombone, two guitars, a dozen or so vuvuzelas, a legion of whistles, and a cowbell. As one comrade expressed it, the sound of drums is the sound of winning. We know that Leicester UCU's cacophony was responsible for recruiting at least one now very active member to its ranks and we also know that it was disruptive to those staff members who wished to continue working. In this way, we staked our claim to the university and its territory – as well as disrupting business as usual. The decision to march on campus and to demonstrate loudly in front of the administration building was taken both for affective reasons – to express our ownership of the university – and for the disruptive power of these actions. It also underscored the third of our branch's features, a targeted and well-informed antagonistic stance towards management that articulated an alternative vision for the university.

Leicester UCU banner. Commissioned in December 2019 and designed by Cath Long, the banner features the purple trombone as well as the 'goose of solidarity'.

Photo: Leicester UCU

Whose university? Our university! Left: International Women's Day 2018, which fell on one of the 14 days of the USS strikes. *Photo: Steve Brown* Right: Four Fights strike, December 2019. *Photo: Jacob Drew @jxdphoto*

Fourthly, whilst some of us already had long-standing research interests in the political economy of higher education and some of its attendant issues like academic publishing, from around the time of Paul Boyle's arrival as vice-chancellor, a number of us began turning our scholarly attention to the University of Leicester's management. Our intent here was unashamedly partisan. We were undertaking studies *against* management. And these studies were, more often than not, published under the auspices of Leicester UCU.[12] In fact, much of the material we present in Chapter 5 first saw light of day in reports circulated to members of the union branch. As a branch, our criticism of management was informed, and informed by, the focused application of our particular research expertise.[13] These studies against management uncovered managers' differing value systems, ethical frameworks and priorities. And, perhaps more damningly, in many cases they brought to light actions or decisions that we interpreted as evidence of managerial incompetence and/or willing obfuscation. What we discovered when we focused our expertise on our employer was that in many cases senior managers were misrepresenting the situation and the facts. UCU's research delegitimised university managers, revealing not only their problematic ethics and a deficit of imagination, but a basic lack of competence. We don't doubt that this work helped develop and maintain more widespread antipathy towards management amongst employees and, instead, support for Leicester UCU and its objectives.

The final distinguishing feature of Leicester UCU that emerged during the period was its articulation of its own vision for the university. As well as opposing management's agenda it was able to express compelling alternatives. During the February–March 2018 pension strikes, for instance, one 'Free University of Leicester' teach-out invited participants to reimagine the University [of Leicester] of the Future, repurposing its physical infrastructure in more equitable and socially useful ways. Another action of those strikes took place on March 8, International Women's Day, when every building on campus was renamed in honour of a woman.

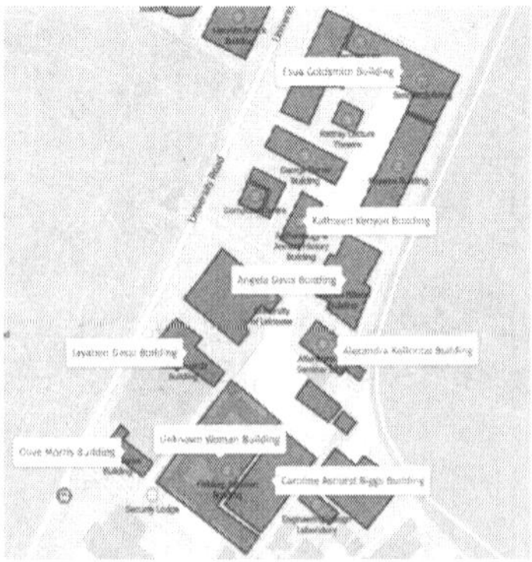

Reimagining the university campus. Buildings renamed on International Women's Day 2018. *Image: Leicester UCU* Banner for the renamed Kathleen Kenyon Building, International Women's Day 2019 *Photo: Leicester UCU*

At many moments, the branch, usually as a complement to analysis that criticised senior management's stewardship of the institution, proposed alternative priorities, such as diverting resources from investment in new infrastructure (rarely a student priority) to investment in staff, and shifting the balance of wage spending away from 'bullshit jobs' (whether carried out by academics and researchers or administrators) towards work that facilitated teaching and scholarship.[14] This alternative ethos for the university was encapsulated in the slogans we adopted to oppose Paul Boyle's second attempt to make large-scale compulsory redundancies, which he announced in May 2018: *Workers Not Widgets* and *Brains Before Buildings.* Our ability to put forward a credible vision for the university – breaking the neoliberal mantra that *there is no alternative*, demonstrating that another University [of Leicester] was possible – helped cohere support for the branch in opposition to management. On this occasion, the branch made a credible strike threat and managers were forced to concede that no one would be made compulsorily redundant. It was at the conclusion of this dispute that Burke uttered to Leicester UCU negotiators those words we used in the chapter's epigraph: "I won't forget this."

Poster and leaflet designs for campaign against compulsory redundancies, June–September 2018. *Image: the authors*

'The most intimidating and disruptive branch in the Country'

We don't know if Leicester UCU really was 'the most intimidating and disruptive branch in the country' as incoming vice-chancellor Nishan Canagarajah declared in November 2019. But we are convinced the five features we describe above combined to make us *one of* the UK's most effective UCU branches. Leicester UCU was effective, that is, in constraining management prerogative. It's certainly the case that the branch grew in size over this period – the number of members rising from 600 or so to around a thousand – despite the number of eligible staff remaining more or less constant, whilst the proportion of members participating in ballots for – and voting for – industrial action also grew. We should not be surprised that Canagarajah, Burke and Council chair Gary Dixon considered us troublesome. We should not be surprised that they made it part of their mission to destroy us.[15]

But, after 2018, the branch's power – as with that national union – appeared to wane. In the spring of that year, the national UCU emerged from the 14 days of USS strike action with the upper hand; in the late summer Leicester UCU forestalled all compulsory redundancies. When, nationally, we were forced into further strike action in late 2019–picking up the unfinished business of USS pensions and also advancing claims on pay, gender equality, more manageable workloads and against casualisation – we felt the loss of advantage and momentum. Twenty-two days of further strike action between November 2019 and March 2020 failed to secure any concessions from employers on any issue, leaving members – nationally and in Leicester – feeling frustrated, demoralised and disempowered, not to mention considerably out-of-pocket.

The COVID-19 virus appeared just as we were concluding ineffective strike action in March 2020. As the UK reeled from the worst pandemic in a century, with Leicester one of the country's worst-affected cities, university staff put their all into moving teaching provision online. For the next two years or so, encounters in shared air became difficult, rare and, during the many months of various lockdowns, impossible. Leicester UCU struggled to adapt to and effectively organise in the changed situation. An early indicator of our weakness was our inability to reverse the university leadership's decision in spring 2020 to cancel the contracts of around 150 teaching staff employed on casualised contracts. The incongruity between bosses' actions and their 'Citizens of Change' 'all pulling together' rhetoric was, of course, glaring and this was also a harsh demonstration of the academic unfreedom of the higher education precariat, discussed in our coda to Chapter 6.

A later challenge materialised in the summer of 2020, when planning was underway for the new academic session, starting in September. The dispute here concerned face-to-face or shared-air teaching. Some departmental heads, including James Devlin, the dean of our school, adopted a particularly gung-ho approach, insisting that seminars should continue almost as normal, making no allowances for any individual's personal circumstances, unless that individual was able to provide medical evidence of their own vulnerability. Despite dogged work by two of the branch's health and safety officers, Leicester UCU proved unable either to force Devlin to change his policy or to persuade the executive board to do so. Many members of business school staff – including several subsequently made redundant and one of this book's authors – took stress leave from work as a result of the injunctions to do face-to-face teaching, individual responses to a collective and public health problem.[16] These genuine mental health issues were perceived as malingering by managers, a presumed extension of the antagonistic industrial relations outlined above.

And then, in October 2020, as out of touch as a Number 10 lockdown party, Vice-Chancellor Nishan Canagarajah declared, "With our centenary approaching and a new strategic plan underway, this is the perfect moment to secure our second century". As we would soon learn, what felt like 'security' for bosses was, in fact, a prelude to mass compulsory redundancies – and years of related emotional, financial and intellectual insecurities – for many of us and our wider university community.[17]

CHAPTER 2

PERFECT MOMENTS: THE COVID-INFUSED STRUGGLES OF 2021

A profound strategic miscalculation and lack of awareness as to the prospective role of Business Schools for addressing urgent 'grand challenges' facing the world.
– Open letter from 2500+ scholars to Vice-Chancellor Nishan Canagarajah, 26 January 2021.[1]

Once again, the university's vice-chancellor, Nishan Canagarajah, has declined our request for an interview, as he has done ever since the dispute began.
– Peter Bearne, ITV Central, 9 June 2021.[2]

It's not easy being made redundant. It's a process of violent severance. We were not surprised to be threatened with redundancy, especially given that Canagarajah's 'perfect moment' announcement of autumn 2020 was swiftly followed by news that our department was one of those to be shaped for excellence. But it is nevertheless a visceral shock to open the emailed letter telling you that your job is at risk. Moreover, the particular form of the attack – the purported plan to 'disinvest from research and scholarship in critical management studies and political economy' – was startling. After all, the University of Leicester School of Business (ULSB) had an international reputation for research in Critical Management Studies and for critical scholarship more generally. And, as we explore in Chapter 6, such a rationale also seemed an obvious attack on academic freedom, so much so that at first we hoped that the good ship *Excellence* was holed below the waterline.

Across the University of Leicester a total of 145 colleagues received similar letters on 18 January 2021. What followed were seven months of intense and bitter struggle, as we fought both for our own livelihoods and to make more real a different vision of the university. The initial shock never subsided – and its effects still linger more than two years later. In fact, this initial trauma was only aggravated with each indignity delivered by bosses – although those moments were punctuated by many of optimistic excitement, euphoria even, when our own counter-offensive appeared to strike home. We were finally forced to concede defeat on August 11 when our dismissal notices, received three months earlier, were enacted. We cannot recount here every (less than perfect) moment of this struggle. In what follows in this chapter we seek to summarise some of its key aspects.

Dear Vice-Chancellor...

'Shaping for Excellence' attracted immediate and considerable attention in the academic world – attention that was unwelcome for the university's leadership. Scholars outside the university signalled their protest in the form of open letters and statements to the vice-chancellor, the university's de facto chief executive officer (CEO). It took only eight days before the first such letter was published. It 'strongly requested' Canagarajah to 'reconsider' his decision which, the signatories informed him, demonstrated a 'profound strategic miscalculation and lack of awareness as to the prospective role of Business Schools', putting the University of Leicester 'in danger of looking backwards'. By the end of April 2021, this letter had been signed by around three thousand academics. A day later, on 27 January 2021, alumni of the School of Business published another open letter. Theirs declared that '[y]oung people know that the world needs to change, and are desperately seeking ways to make that change a reality. Critical management studies and political economy education can be a part of that change, as it has been for all of us who have signed this letter.' These two letters were just the first of dozens, with Canagarajah's plans condemned by many professional associations, journals, and individual scholars.[3] The letters emphasised the importance of critical thinking for addressing current and future social challenges such as gender and racial inequality, global poverty, and environmental devastation. Many letters voiced concerns about academic freedom at the University of Leicester.

How were these letters received? Their recipients – the vice-chancellor, Nishan Canagarajah, along with James Devlin, the School's dean – failed to engage with a single one of the arguments presented to them. They responded with a box-ticking mentality and boilerplate responses. The following from the vice-chancellor – or, most likely, an underling – is exemplary:

> Thank you for writing to me about the proposed changes at the University. These proposals are currently being considered as part of a formal 90-day consultation process, and I have asked that the views and feedback you have expressed be considered as part of this consultation exercise.

Managers replied to our own appeals in a similarly formulaic and disengaged way. What is interesting about these (slightly longer) responses is their invocation of what other senior managers referred to in different contexts as the sector norm – and what we have been calling mediocre or mimetic isomorphism: we're only doing what everyone else is doing.

> What we are proposing is not dissimilar to recent developments in many other business schools and such developments are crucial to aligning research to demand and wider economic strategies and which have practical relevance for business research and teaching.

It is clear that neither the vice-chancellor nor the dean considered in any serious way – or perhaps even read – the 'views and feedback [his many correspondents] expressed'. On the contrary, he and his executive turned the strong opposition to their plans into an argument for their right to manage (which we discuss in the next chapter). Moreover, they claimed that their decision had been driven by 'strategic needs' – simply ignoring the fact that the letters also touch upon strategic issues.

> It is important to note that the vast majority of communication received asked us to reconsider the decision to disinvest from Critical Management Studies and political economy. Decisions relating to areas for disinvestment are within the purview of the senior leadership team and are taken in the light of strategic priorities for the institution. While we respect the views shared by academic colleagues and welcomed their feedback the decision made has been driven by the needs of the business and the future strategy of ULSB.

It's also notable that even Canagarajah's boilerplate responses were sent only with considerable delay. Some correspondents waited two months before receiving a reply. Moreover, it was not uncommon that, where they had opened their letter with the salutation 'Dear Vice-Chancellor' or 'Dear Professor Canagarajah', he addressed them by given name only, omitting any honorific or reference to academic position. This tone of disdain echoed with our experience, whereby those of us at risk of redundancy were frequently referred to or addressed by our given names, rather than title and family name. One of the authors of this book – Gibson Burrell, at the time of his redundancy one of the university's longest-serving professors – wrote to Canagarajah three times. In each of his three replies Canagarajah spelled Burrell's name a different way, all of the spellings incorrect. These aspects of *Shaping for Excellence* are particularly ironic given that one weapon university managers sought to wield against those critical of their plans was the university's Dignity and Respect Policy, as we discuss below.

Our focus in this book is the School of Business, but we were not the only part of the University of Leicester to be shaped for excellence. The outpouring of protest against the plans for the business school was replicated across the other threatened departments. The London Mathematical Society, for instance, criticised the proposal to sack the university's pure mathematicians, describing it as 'seriously flawed', while the president of the Institute of Mathematics and its Applications also wrote, explaining why 'mathematics is a continuum', thus making it ridiculous to sever pure maths from applied.

The executive's plans for English attracted particular attention, for they involved making redundant scholars of medieval and early modern literature to allow – in the executive board's messaging – the department to 'decolonise' its curriculum. Far-right media such as the *Daily Mail* predictably denounced the scheme as 'woke'. One honorary graduate of the university, poet Isabel Armstrong, returned her degree in protest and external examiner Catherine Clarke also resigned, excoriating both Canagarajah and Henrietta O'Connor, head of the College of Social Sciences, Arts and Humanities.[4] Professor Clarke charged that the reasoning behind the proposals was 'extremely confused' and that their purported aim to 'decolonise' the curriculum was 'either a cynical exploitation of the language of "decolonisation", or genuine (and appalling) ignorance of the work medieval and early modern subjects can contribute to this endeavour, including the work that medievalists at Leicester are doing right now, tackling complex subjects such as sexuality, migration and identity'. She continued by expressing horror at the way 'the University's glib, fraudulent use of the language of decolonisation has been seized upon by racists', and concluded by condemning the university leadership for its 'dismal failure'.[5] Cambridge professor of postcolonial studies Priyamvada Gopal, in a short thread of tweets, was equally blunt: 'Decolonisation requires Chaucer to be present in class.'[6]

The plans for English are particularly interesting to us because – as Professors Clarke and Gopal both highlighted – they demonstrated the contradictory and arbitrary nature of the executive board's strategy. Clarke and Gopal emphasised the necessity of including medieval and early modern literature in a 'decolonised' curriculum. For our part, we can emphasise that, within business and management scholarship and education, Critical Management Studies and critical political economy, those very areas being purged, are amongst the fields that have done most to uncover the origins of modern management and modern finance in colonialism, imperial expansion, the Triangular Trade and slave-plantation economies.

The many open letters played an important role in focusing wider academic attention on events at the University of Leicester. They boosted our morale – an affect not to be dismissed – and we are certain they caused some worries amongst senior managers and senior academic colleagues about the university's image and reputation. However, their direct impact on the case itself seems negligible. In the end the university's management simply ignored all their arguments, overwriting these by insisting on its own 'right to manage'. In fact, bosses not only ignored the substance of these arguments, they sought to ignore or elide the very fact that they were being questioned: de facto, bosses asserted a right to manage without question. When pushed to comment on the many letters of protest and the many resignations (of external examiners, like Catherine Clarke, say), the vice-chancellor insisted that it was 'normal' and 'expected'. In short, he treated critics as complainers. That is, he did not hear them.

Much of our struggle took the form of complaint. Within the School and the College we complained that definitions of Critical Management Studies and political economy had not been shared with us. We complained that these definitions – when they finally arrived – were not robust. We complained that these definitions had not been clearly or consistently applied. We complained that the initial redundancy screening process was opaque – no minutes or other notes were kept, for instance. We complained that we were not permitted sufficient time in the collective redundancy consultations to ask questions. For all of the above complaints, we complained that our complaints were not addressed either in a timely fashion or adequately.

Within the university, we complained that our academic freedom had been breached. We complained that the procedures for making this complaint about breach of academic freedom were opaque – the procedure stipulated, for instance, that the complaint should be addressed to the university's Staffing Committee, but no information about such a committee existed on the university's website or in any other documentation we were able to find. We complained that these complaints, when we did discover whom to address them to, were not dealt with in a timely manner. We complained that the deputy vice-chancellor, Edmund Burke, who convened and chaired the panels that eventually heard our complaints of breach of academic freedom, was conflicted as he was also a lead architect of the redundancies.

When we appealed our redundancies – following the institution's stipulated policies and procedures – we complained that our appeals were not heard in a timely manner, that is, within the time period stipulated in those same policies and procedures. And we complained that the composition of the panels that heard – and, of course, rejected – our appeals did not conform to the norm, again as stipulated in the policies and procedures. We complained too that the convenor and chair of many of those appeal panels, Gary Dixon, chair of University Council, was conflicted given the role we believed he played as an originating architect of the redundancies and his role as a director of the USS pension scheme, with whom our union, UCU, was in active dispute.

We submitted many so-called data subject access requests (DSARs) to the university's Information Assurance Officer, seeking copies of correspondence that mentioned our names and personnel files. We then complained – repeatedly – to that office about its failure to comply with these requests within the period legally stipulated by the UK's general data protection regulations (GDPR) and to provide all of the unredacted information that we could reasonably expect under those regulations.[7] Outside of the university, we wrote to the UK Information Commissioner's Office, complaining about the failure of the University of Leicester Information Assurance Officer to comply with the law. We further complained to the UK Information Commissioner's Office about *its* failure to respond in a timely manner or adequately to our complaints about the University of Leicester. Also outside of the university, we complained to both the Office for Students, tasked with upholding academic freedom within universities, and to Michele Donelan, at the time minister of state for universities, who had, in other contexts, been vocal in her support of academic freedom and freedom of speech.

For all of the above complaints, we had to keep *pushing*: 'You have to keep pushing, because at each step of the way, you encounter a wall, made up, it seems of a curious combination of indifference and resistance'.[8]

The above passages are inspired by and draw on Sara Ahmed's study of complaints in universities – and what complainers' experiences teach us about power in universities – published in the year of our redundancy struggle. Ahmed hears testimony from academics who have complained – or considered complaining – about sexist, racist, ableist, homophobic or transphobic bullying, abuse or assault, including sexual abuse and assault, or about discrimination during promotion or application processes. She also records and explores the stories of those who have complained about policies and procedures that are supposed to channel such complaints. Our complaints – made predominantly by white, cisheteronormative male scholars – concerned the procedures and processes around our redundancy. But many of the effects we experienced were similar to those that Ahmed chronicles. As one reader of our testimony notes, patriarchy turns on men when they call its structures into question, and survivors of gender-based violence (among other forms of oppression) may recognise some of the institutional tactics wielded against us. Foremost among these is the sense that, by complaining, *we* were the problem. The sense that we were *tiresome*, that by complaining, we were 'distracting somebody from doing "*important* work elsewhere."'[9] The sense that we were always having to push. The way in which complaining and pushing both wore us out and wore us down. 'Making a complaint is never completed by a single action: it often requires you do more and more work. It is exhausting, especially given what you complain about is already exhausting.'[10]

There are three further connections between our experiences and Ahmed's insights. First, she suggests that, 'Making a complaint can require becoming an institutional mechanic: you have to work out how to get a complaint through the system. It is because of the difficulty of getting complaints through the system that complaints often end up being about the system'. Moreover, 'the system is working by stopping those who are trying to transform the system'.[11] As we have emphasised, we are convinced that Leicester UCU activists and organisers were targeted as part of the redundancy programme – *because* they were UCU activists and organisers. Amongst these were three of the branch's six main caseworkers, including Gareth Brown (also branch co-secretary), who, by 2021, had become one of Leicester UCU's most effective staff representatives and was taking on perhaps half of all the cases brought to the branch. We strongly suspect that when James Devlin was offered the job of dean of University of Leicester School of Business in 2019 he was informed that there was one particular person whose removal he should engineer – Brown's.[12] Gareth Brown and other caseworkers had become highly capable institutional mechanics: they had 'work[ed] out how to get a complaint through the system' and, between them, they supported dozens of complainers each year, complainers who were typically making complaints of the type that Ahmed catalogues.

Second, at Leicester UCU, the knowledge of caseworkers and those members whom they supported informed branch strategy and priorities more generally. Those numerous complaints that 'end[ed] up being about the system' shaped the ways in which Leicester UCU activists and organisers sought to 'transform the system'. As we suggested earlier, we should not be surprised that the university's senior managers (probably supported by senior academics not in formal managerial roles) wanted to 'stop' us.

Finally, 'to be heard as complaining is not to be heard'.[13] In our many appeals, complaints and requests for clarification, we were always heard as complaining – that is, not heard. We were frequently *blanked* – made to disappear.[14] The way that an institution and those individuals who constitute it learn to not hear and practise not hearing, learn to blank and practise blanking, is part of its culture. We don't doubt that the ways we were not heard had been practised and perfected – if we can use such a word – over the course of many previous complaints. This is *strategic inefficiency* at work. Or *strategic incompetence*, a term coined by Gareth Brown some years earlier, trying to make sense of his experiences as a caseworker and, in particular, the many 'institutional barriers', the 'blockages' that caused a complaint to become 'bogged down'.[15]

#BoycottLeicester: Twitter's contested terrain and the information war

For several days in May 2021, the Twitter hashtag #BoycottLeicester was trending in the UK. This followed the announcement on May 4, that the University and College Union had decided to make the University of Leicester the object of a global academic boycott, a rare and serious sanction.[16]

The university's managers responded to the announcement ten days later, professing themselves to be 'very disappointed by UCU's decision to endorse the global boycott and the local decision to take continuous action short of strike'. The tweet accompanying our bosses' statement elicited a huge backlash and was *ratioed* on the platform – meaning (critical) quote tweets and replies enormously outnumbered likes and retweets. Its wording – 'we are disappointed' – attracted particular derision. The flurry of Twitter activity around the announcement of the global academic boycott was just one moment in the battle on the social media front and around communications and information more generally – though, from that moment, #BoycottLeicester remained a hashtag that accompanied most critical tweets throughout the redundancy process and beyond.

Social media has become a new contested terrain for workplace struggles. Throughout the redundancy process, we (and our allies) were confronted with the double-sided nature of social media in organisations. On the one hand, it opened up a space for us to share our critique of university management, both inside and outside the university, and to mobilise support for our cause – to circulate our struggle. On the other hand, it is very easy to surveil social media activity, and our antagonists did just this – even engaging the services of an outside consultancy to conduct this surveillance, as well as encouraging enthusiastic middle managers. Bosses were clearly needled by our Twitter and other social media activity and used what measures they could to limit the expression of dissent, leading to a 'chilling effect of social media policies on employee voice and expression in their personal lives'.[17]

Social media activity was typically uncoordinated, with little clear strategy. Individuals' activity overlapped with the UCU branch's official posts, with each sharing and amplifying the other. It was a powerful means by which we drew attention to events at the University of Leicester, with some interesting facets of these activities, encompassing both their content and their form. First and most obviously, Twitter was the main platform by which we shared information, news and analysis. This included many documents marked confidential (sometimes in a redacted fashion), as well as other correspondence from those executing our redundancies. (As the process wore on, managers began to append their communications to us with a line stating that they did not consent to their words being shared on social media, an instruction we ignored.) These documents would not otherwise have seen the light of day. Much of our news, especially concerning key events, gained significant attention. Many of our 'non-affected' colleagues learned more about what was happening from our tweets than from senior managers, who refused all requests for meetings.

A second strand of Twitter activity focused on the communications of the university's marketing department and its senior management. At the height of the dispute, no tweet from the official University of Leicester account escaped critical replies and quote-tweets. Several particularly egregious tweets were singled out. One of these praised the 'game-changing' research of scholars who were at the same time facing redundancy. Following a public outcry, the university's marketeers quickly deleted their original tweet – which led to yet more derision – but could not prevent the incident receiving coverage on the more traditional university news platform, *Times Higher Education*.[18]

There was much *shitposting*.[19] Shitposting clearly carries attendant risks that the form distracts from and devalues the content of the message, but the reception of tweets and other social media communication – as with other forms of communication – is always complex. Our view is that we should not isolate a tweet from its context, from the power relations and discursive struggles it is part of. To pick up on single words, for example, and thereby accuse the author that they are 'bringing the university into disrepute' – as happened on multiple occasions in our case – is a technology of power. In fact, we can say that 'respectful' and 'professional' language is a privilege of the powerful, part of a '"politics of niceness" that seeks to maintain the violent status quo of white capitalist heteropatriarchy'.[20] For those in a position of power, it is easy and cheap to create and uphold the appearance of respectful communication (a point we will return to).[21] Moreover, requests or injunctions by those in power that we communicate in a 'respectful' manner – with invocations of a 'dignity and respect' policy, for instance – can in fact be a tool to undermine resistance and impose silence. In short, given the circumstances – asymmetric power relations and our righteous anger at what was being done to us – shitposting, along with aggression and other 'militancy', were all entirely appropriate ethically – even if not always the best option tactically.

We can illustrate some of these issues with one particular case from the dispute. In April 2021, Peter Armstrong – at that time an emeritus professor[22] – received a letter from Henrietta O'Connor, at that point pro-vice-chancellor and head of the School of Social Sciences, Arts and Humanities, threatening that the university's governing body – Council – would remove his title, 'if [your] social media activity continues in the same manner as I have outlined'. Armstrong would also lose, 'the privileges associated with the title, which include access to the library and the provision of an IT account.' Armstrong was accused of breaching the university's 'Dignity and Respect' policy with his comments on Twitter. When invited to contribute to a *Guardian* article on the case, Armstrong commented: 'I accept that I should not have said that the [University of Leicester] managers who were bullying a clearly distressed young academic "should be slapped across the neck with a stocking full of diarrhea [sic]". I am sure that readers can suggest an appropriate alternative.'[23] That the university's managers threatened to strip Armstrong of his title – a threat the University Council made good on in Spring 2022 – for his language choices but ignored the bullying allegation reveals much about asymmetric power relations in an institution such as a twenty-first-century British university.[24]

Professor Armstrong's case is exemplary of university management's handling of dissent on social media. This and many other instances where it sought to discipline those who stepped out of line created a chilling effect on others minded to voice their own critical views.

More generally managers sought to dampen opposition through two complementary tactics. First, they weaponised the university's existing 'Dignity and Respect' and social media policies, constantly 'reminding' staff members about their 'obligations' within the framework of these policies, 'assuring' colleagues that 'we take any breach' seriously, and persistently reframing critique as falling outside the bounds of acceptable communication – breaching the policies. The Dignity and Respect policy had, in fact, been introduced, with union support, as a mechanism to support victims of harassment and bullying, especially those who had been bullied by those in power; now those in power had turned the policy into a tool to subjugate. Further, this power was obfuscated through managers' articulating *their* objections in the name of 'concerned colleagues', whose sensibilities 'the University' had a responsibility to protect. This reframing was a first move in the devaluing of critique.[25] A second move was to talk down the volume of critical commentary. The communications from bosses alluding to the 'appropriate action' that would be taken against those breaching the policies always spoke of 'a small number of staff' whose posts they categorised this way.

In their communications on unacceptable social media activity, managers typically claimed that 'in each case such posts [had] been reported to the University by concerned colleagues'. In February 2021, Kerry Law, the chief marketing and engagement officer during that time (and now deputy vice-chancellor), insisted that 'we don't monitor staff social media accounts'.[26] The reality was strikingly different. In fact, as we learned following several Data Subject Access Requests (DSARs) and Freedom of Information (FOI) requests, the university's management engaged a social media company – the Birmingham-based WPR Agency – to monitor Twitter, Facebook, LinkedIn and Instagram accounts. WPR then delivered 'Crisis Monitoring' reports, quite possibly daily. This monitoring began with January's announcement of the *Case for Change* so clearly managers expected negative coverage on social media. Perhaps it's quite normal for an organisation's managers to be interested in what is said of them on social media. What is less normal – though perhaps it's the new normal – is when such interest evolves into systematic monitoring of employee accounts and when this monitoring results in sanctions and threats of disciplinary action against some of these employees. A social media agency contracted to monitor employees' activities is not a 'concerned colleague'.[27]

It is true, however, that some of our former colleagues – presumably 'concerned' ones – were also following our communications with keen interest and we must say a few words about them. As we learned from earlier Data Subject Access and FOI requests some form of systematic monitoring was already taking place in 2020, that is, before the redundancy announcement.[28] This monitoring involved, not only social media, but also colleagues' email communications and out-of-office auto-replies. We learned, for instance, that various administrators and human resources professionals were reporting to their superiors content that could be construed as critical of university management. One such administrator who was themself an active poster on Twitter even admonished a migrant faculty member for not being in the United Kingdom, during the period of COVID lockdown: 'we know where you are', was the substance of their later-deleted tweet.

These fragments of evidence are unsettling for at least three reasons. First, we were quite surprised to find them. We had reason to believe that very senior leaders might have been calculating how we might be separated from the university and we hoped that the DSARs might unearth some evidence of this.[29] We did not expect to discover that much less senior employees had been monitoring and reporting on us. Second, we don't know how systematic or widespread such monitoring and reporting was. It certainly seemed to be routine, at least for the individuals we mentioned above, but we don't know how many other mid-level employees were also monitoring and reporting on their colleagues.[30] Finally, we do not know whether such monitoring and reporting was ordered, possibly by the then-Chief Marketing and Engagement Officer, or whether the individuals who carried it out were acting on their own initiative. Certainly, even our fragmentary evidence is sufficient for us to confidently conclude that this monitoring and reporting was sanctioned and even welcomed and rewarded by the university's most senior figures.

Clearly our social media activities drew attention to events at University of Leicester and mobilised solidarity – and university managers' authoritarian reaction to our social media activity also attests its impact. But we should not overestimate the power of social media and its potential to decisively recast social outcomes. Two issues are at play here, one relating to the particularities of social media itself, the other concerning the necessity of deeper commitment to a cause than that which can be generated and sustained via social media.

To keep up the pressure takes time and energy. While university management is able to deploy the institution's resources to pursue its social media strategy – whether directing existing staff or contracting to external agencies – employees under attack and fighting for their jobs, whilst also continuing to do these jobs, are far more limited in what they can do. The PR machine of a university is typically built on the endless repetition and recycling of buzzwords, straplines and success stories. Archives can be plundered for images, old stories can be reactivated and misappropriated to justify or divert attention from current action. The ahistoricity of Twitter perfectly serves this machine. Resistance, on the other hand, requires that we write in what has been written out, it requires that we repeatedly remind others of what they are encouraged to oversee or forget. All of this is exhausting. To disrupt this repetitive and relentless PR machine requires both creativity and time. It might be true that social media has created a new frontier of workplace struggle, but this struggle remains asymmetrical.

Although the University of Leicester's senior management sought to neutralise our decentralised and uncoordinated Twitter campaign and although it monitored accounts and sought to subdue dissenting voices, we think that ultimately it was careless of the barrage of negative commentary on that platform and others, of the barbs, of the mockery, even of #BoycottLeicester and the global academic boycott which

A university's PR machine at work: spot the difference and repetition. Facebook posts from March 2017 and March 2021.

that hashtag referenced. Nishan Canagarajah, the president and vice-chancellor, on multiple occasions insisted that *this is normal*, where 'this' meant the disquiet and open dissent within his institution and the excoriation of it from without. He was mocked for the claim. At the time it seemed like more evidence he was 'out of his depth', as one academic quoted in the *Times Higher* suggested.[31] And in hindsight? Perhaps Dixon, Canagarajah, Burke and their advisors – management consultants and lawyers – expected that level of discursive dissent, perhaps they expected the institution's reputation to be trashed, perhaps the risk they took was calculated. Perhaps, according to their university restructuring playbook, everything *was* normal.

Accountability and reputation – stop making the university!

A university and its reputation are made by those that labour within it. The vice chancellor and other managers may play an enabling role, providing time, space and other facilities, but it's not managers – not even those senior managers who were once scholars – who have the ideas, conduct the research, forge the collaborations, instruct, care for and nurture the students. Still less do senior managers clean the classrooms, labs and offices, maintain the buildings, and so on – but regrettably this labour is invisible to many academics and researchers too. In the neoliberal university, managers' effect is more disabling than enabling, their efforts to measure scholarly activity in order to better manage it, more often than not, undermining the very conditions of that wealth-creating labour. A university's leaders also seek to claim for 'the university' – and themselves as purported personifications of the university – the achievements of those who make it. 'For many (though not all) contemporary VCs and self-styled Presidents, however, "the university, c'est moi". The properly constitutional and earned legitimacy of an institution ... has been translated into unconstitutional and anti-democratic authoritarianism.'[32]

This is the particular function of the university's marketing and communications department. The head of this department is typically a member of the university's senior leadership team or executive board and, at Leicester, its holder – Kerry Law – was promoted to the position of deputy vice-chancellor shortly after our dismissals. But individual scholars – those whose labour makes the university – do much of this marketing work. Every time we include our institutional affiliation in a biography we enhance our employer's reputation. Every time we organise a conference, workshop, or other event and mention the institution we work for, we again burnish that institution's repute. This is how we not only create wealth but also make the university and – in as much as the university is *not* ours – cede that wealth to the university. Throughout the redundancy dispute at Leicester, Vice-Chancellor Nishan Canagarajah sought – as we have emphasised – to insist that everything was 'normal'. He and his senior managers sought to maintain a cordon sanitaire around those facing redundancy and our allies, and to isolate us from the usual making of the university and its reputation. We made a concerted effort to break through this, asking colleagues not to cease their scholarly activity, but to cease making the University of Leicester.

Our efforts here had mixed results at best. On the one hand, many colleagues, both within and outside of the University of Leicester, did dissociate themselves from it and the actions of its management. Many allies presented papers to national and international audiences using a Teams/Zoom/Skype background affirming *No one is redundant* or carrying a similar message of solidarity. Many allies noted in biographical details that they opposed the executives' strategy. Many events due to be hosted by the university were cancelled. These included at least five major international conferences, two prestigious annual lectures and more than a dozen seminars and workshops. The editors of academic journals based at University of Leicester reported withdrawals of submissions and refusals to undertake reviews. Several external examiners, such as Catherine Clarke, mentioned above, resigned and a number of external collaborators withdrew their support from grant applications under development.

But several newly promoted professors, scheduled to deliver the customary professorial inaugural lecture – which also acts as a marketing opportunity for the university and, in these circumstances, an opportunity for managers to promote their *everything is normal* narrative – decided to proceed, as normal. This included two professors who worked in departments where many of their colleagues were facing redundancy. The organisers of a public-facing event, Literary Leicester, an annual literature festival hosted by the university, demurred to our suggestion that they (privately) brief their guest speakers, inviting them to make some remarks about the redundancies – which were, after all, happening in English, amongst other departments. The organisers justified their decision on the twin grounds that they 'couldn't risk doing anything to jeopardise' the festival's future and that they thought it 'not appropriate to use Literary Leicester as a platform to address [the UCU cause]'. This reluctance is a perfect example of the moral vacuum at the heart of the modern public university: it can put its imprimatur on a literature festival as it simultaneously sacks a large proportion of its scholars of literature.[33]

This episode with the literary festival is a perfect example of one of the separations that run through the modern university, in which the university's 'normal' business – which is not supposed to involve sacking people – is insulated from the redundancy process and its fallout. Such a separation (and asymmetry) also operates when it comes to individual managers. When a boss accomplishes something laudable, they are named, a smiling photograph is published and they take personal credit. When the same boss is involved in some more unsavoury activity, such as executing redundancies, even those contesting the redundancies conventionally decline to name them, instead identifying them only by their job title. Thus the 'disinvestment from research and scholarship in Critical Management Studies and political economy' was overseen by the pro-vice-chancellor and head of the College of Social Sciences, Arts and Humanities. Simultaneously, Henrietta O'Connor, Professor of Sociology, continues her scholarly life, giving talks at sociological conferences, maintaining her connections with the British Sociological Association, and so on.

We sought, very intentionally, throughout the redundancy process, as in this book, to refuse this separation – to make *scholars* accountable for their active participation or complicity in the redundancies. We did, in fact, have one success that is worth highlighting for it provides an example of what must happen more frequently. In July 2021, O'Connor and her longstanding co-author John Goodwin – deputy head of College and responsible for threatening at least one colleague and comrade for their dissenting tweets – were scheduled to present the closing keynote talk to an International Visual Sociology Association conference – clearly a prestigious scholarly undertaking. An ally in the School of Business contacted the conference organisers, alerting them to what was happening at the School and in the university. The organisers, in turn, contacted O'Connor and Goodwin, expressing concerns and requesting that O'Connor and Goodwin allay these. According to our sources, the would-be scholarly keynotes were quite indignant at being challenged in this way – at the suggestion they might be (made) accountable for their managerial actions – and withdrew from the conference.

It is too early to tell how quickly, or even whether, the university's reputation will recover – or that of the School of Business or other academic departments whose members were targeted. It is not even clear whether a 'reputation in ruins' – in our minds and those of our allies – translates into a reputation sufficiently damaged to materially affect the university's ability to recruit fee-paying students or attract other sources of income. It seems certain that the University of Leicester is, at the moment, an 'employer of choice' for very few scholars – but very few scholars have much choice of employer at the moment. Certainly, we failed to make managers accountable in any way sufficiently forceful to alter their actions and – as with the social media war – these same managers were clearly willing to wager the university's reputation in order to assert their own right to manage. In fact, as we'll see later in this chapter, when it came to the university's future, its management proved more willing to engage in high-stakes gambling than did those staff seeking to resist redundancies.

Strike and the drama of Queen MAB

Exactly one week after colleagues received their at-risk letters, Leicester UCU held a well-attended emergency general meeting, which passed a motion of no confidence in the university's vice-chancellor. Canagarajah had, we charged, 'abdicated his responsibility as a guardian of scholarship. He has betrayed our University's history and mission and is not fit to lead it.' Two days later, the branch communications officer appeared on BBC Radio Leicester to speak against the redundancies. In a pattern that continued throughout the campaign, Nishan Canagarajah declined his invitation to put across the executive's case. A week after that Leicester UCU declared a formal dispute with 'the University' – that is, with its executive board. As we noted above, our national union subjected the University of Leicester to a global academic boycott on 4 May 2021, taking this step at the wishes of our branch. The branch also moved quickly to seek legal authority for industrial action – both strike action and so-called action short of a strike or ASOS – usually considered the most militant form of trade union activity.

Turnout on the ballot was 56% – comfortably exceeding the legal 50% threshold – with 70% in favour of strike action, while 84% voted for of action short of a strike.[34] While a branch officer again appeared on local radio to explain the positive strike mandate, with Canagarajah again declining his invitation to argue the university executive's side, the university's marketing department did in fact amplify the news. In an incredible tweet, it quibbled over *Times Higher Education*'s reporting of the result. Like so many of the university's tweets, this one was also ratioed, eliciting numerous scornful, sarcastic and disgusted replies.

Branch members began industrial action short of a strike as soon as possible following the result, on May 4 – the same day the global academic boycott commenced.[35] ASOS had several specific

An incredible tweet: the university's marketeers help promote the strike ballot result. University of Leicester (@uniofleicester), 'We would like to clarify that 56% of @ leicesterucu's members took part in the vote — 69.7% of those that participated opted for industrial action', Twitter, 15 April 2021, https://bit.ly/SfM-208.

elements, all quite usual in universities, such as refusing to cover for absent or unavailable colleagues, or to reschedule lectures, classes, appointments, meetings and other tasks cancelled due to industrial action. We advised members not to undertake any work beyond that contracted, nor to volunteer any actions or ideas – that is, to make managers manage. Finally, and most importantly, we refused all marking and assessment activities. Apart from the marking and assessment boycott, which we'll discuss later, most of these actions comprised various forms of *working to contract* or *working to rule* – but this didn't stop the university's executive seeking to intimidate staff by describing them as 'partial performance' and threatening to deduct wages. Such aggressive moves have become all too common in British universities.

The branch also called three days of strike action, in the second week of June – a compromise position between those members who saw little value in all-out strike at this time of year, when there is little university business to be disrupted, and those who argued for three weeks of continuous strike action. In retrospect, the decision was, we think, a good one. Although its materially disruptive effects might have been marginal, the collective experience of being present together, sharing an antagonism against the university's leadership, was incredibly powerful – especially following 15 months of pandemic-induced isolation. For some newer members of Leicester UCU, it was their first time on strike, again an incredibly powerful affective moment.

The physical association enabled by the three strike days was especially important for those colleagues engaged in the marking and assessment boycott or MAB, which had begun a month earlier. It was an opportunity for them to share experiences and, importantly, to reaffirm their commitment to their action. The MAB was one of our most powerful weapons, though its potency only became apparent towards the end of the dispute. It's a simple tactic. Members refuse to set examinations and assignments. They refuse to mark or 'moderate' examinations and assignments. They refuse to attend examination boards and panels, the meetings in which students' overall marks for an academic year or their final degree classification are decided. If applied at the right time, a marking and assessment boycott can threaten the progression of students to the subsequent year of their studies or, for final-year students, their graduation. Our union's last major national victory – at time of writing – was won in 2006 following a marking boycott.

In the event, only a relatively small number of university employees engaged in the MAB. In some departments it was just two or three people, who consequently felt isolated and pressured. But, as we discovered later, even this small number of academics refusing to mark student assessments and exam scripts had considerable power to disrupt the university's business as usual. Managers' first priority was understandably the graduation of final-year students. They dealt with missing marks in one of three ways: by asking colleagues not observing the boycott to take on extra marking; by having managers themselves mark or moderate work; and by using algorithms to fill in gaps. Very few colleagues answered the call to take on additional marking activities, especially not to cover for those taking industrial action. Managers' attempts to personally grade unmarked student work was problematic in the extreme. Few school and department heads had the necessary specialist-subject knowledge and this resulted in students being awarded grades that were wildly inaccurate. University leaders also abandoned the normal practices of 'quality control': in many cases student work was marked by just one person, often not appropriately qualified, but there was no second- or moderating marker. And, of course, many external examiners had resigned or refused to take up posts because of the redundancies, so there were far fewer external checks on marking consistency than university regulations stipulated.

Unsurprisingly, the university leadership's use of algorithms to compute absent marks was also extremely controversial. The executive board, for instance, sought to disavow one email sent by managers that had informed staff that 'any gaps [in student marks] will be filled … algorithmically.'[36] The executive board claimed this was an 'unauthorised communication' and that 'the University does not condone the arbitrary use of algorithms to account for missing marks'.[37] We can only speculate on the inclusion of the adjective *arbitrary* in this statement. Ultimately, we do not know exactly how many final-year students had marks missing on their record, nor how managers filled in or smoothed over these gaps, thus enabling these students to graduate. We do not know how many graduating students appealed their degree classification, nor how many of these appeals were successful. We do not know how many graduating students suffered detriment but did not appeal their result. Though less of a concern to us, we do not know how many graduating students received an 'unfairly' generous award.

There are two things we do know, however. First, although university leaders – with great difficulty and some risk – were able to graduate all final-year students without too much delay, they was not able to progress other students onto the subsequent year of their studies. The marking and assessment boycott was extremely successful in preventing this. This success we only deduced – by a process of elimination – in mid-July, when the university's executive, after months of stalling, suddenly became very concerned with resolving the dispute. There followed a week in which we met with the deputy vice-chancellor, Edmund Burke, and other executive board members five times in as many days. By this point our power was too diminished and any sort of – for us – favourable resolution was impossible. Even our attempts to secure better financial settlements (beyond statutory redundancy payments) for those being dismissed were rebuffed. Despite this, we remain certain of the potential efficacy of a reasonably well-observed marking and assessment boycott, timed to disrupt progression and graduation.

Second, our experience with the marking and assessment boycott confirmed that university managers care little about students, their experience or 'academic standards'. As we have recounted, bosses were willing to allow students to graduate with awards calculated with many missing or 'low quality' marks, awards that may well have been widely 'inaccurate'. Moreover, this happened after many years – years that, not coincidentally, align with the years of increased managerialism described in later chapters – in which we have suffered the imposition of a proliferation of new rules, processes and procedures purportedly designed to guarantee 'quality' – not to mention executive-level posts. More generally it has resulted in additional work for academics and administrators alike and a loss of professional autonomy. University managers' willingness to ignore and override all of their policies when there is an industrial dispute to be won and a union to be defeated conclusively gives the lie to their narrative that they – and not us – are the guardians of academic standards and scholarly integrity. At a national level, we can easily make a similar charge against the Office for Students. Charged by the government with regulating quality and standards in English universities, to the best of our knowledge its officers took no interest in events unfolding at Leicester in 2021.

The fear of ruins: reflecting on defeat

Our defeat was not inevitable. Indeed, at least some of us were motivated by the conviction that we might not only be able to save our own jobs but force the departure of Dixon, Canagarjah and Burke and to democratise the university's governance – we return to this in the final chapter. So let us here seek to understand the reasons for our defeat and how our struggle might have turned out differently. Some aspects were particular to the specific circumstances of the dispute. We ourselves – the UCU branch or elements within it – also made a number of missteps.

First, our redundancies took place against the backdrop of COVID-19. The coronavirus precluded the chance encounters with workmates and the one-to-one and small-group conversations so crucial to political organising and maintaining solidarity. The COVID-19 pandemic was most certainly not a circumstance of our own choosing. The second circumstance also outside of our control – at least beyond our control by the time 2020 rolled into 2021 – was the identity of those targeted with redundancy. As we've insisted, we believe senior leaders specifically targeted active trade unionists and other individuals they perceived as too critical of their leadership. Several of us in the School of Business were officers of Leicester UCU: Gareth Brown, as we noted above, was co-secretary, a branch negotiator and a caseworker; David Harvie was communications officer, a branch negotiator and a caseworker; Simon Lilley was representative of professorial staff and a caseworker.

Third, the targeting of union officers – whether deliberate or happenstance – had several consequences. One was that we not only suffered our own redundancy battles, but also the stress of helping others fight theirs. Another was that we were acutely conscious of the risk that some branch members might feel that we were putting our own personal interests – of saving our own jobs – above those of the branch and/or that our personal 'interest' in the dispute was clouding our judgement. But maybe we were too harsh on ourselves. Other senior officers of the branch – including its chair, vice-chair and second co-secretary – were not personally at risk and were as involved in the defence of jobs and livelihoods as those officers who were being made redundant. And the branch's membership had voted overwhelmingly on several occasions in favour of a 'no redundancies' position – in this and previous disputes. This was *not* a whim of individual branch officers.

Fourth, as the number of staff still at risk of redundancy declined so too did staff anger at the executive. One hundred and forty-five colleagues were informed they were at risk in January 2021. By May, 'only' 26 individuals had received notices of dismissal – a result of some people being removed from scope or redeployed, but of many more accepting so-called voluntary redundancy from the university. Between May and August, when we ceased to be University of Leicester employees, a further eleven came to some other arrangement with bosses such that, in the end, 'only' fifteen people were dismissed. We understand that workers are more angered by the likelihood of 145 compulsory redundancies than by fifteen. And, of course, the lower the number still at risk, the less likely any other employee is to know one of these individuals, while those ex-employees leaving via the 'voluntary redundancy' route are prohibited from discussing the circumstances of their departure by non-disclosure agreements.

Finally, as active support from 'ordinary' members within the branch appeared to wane and as bosses' intransigence appeared to deepen, those of us at risk and our allies grew more desperate. In this sense, there might indeed be some truth to the concern that our personal involvement in the dispute clouded our judgement. In our frustration at bosses' machinations and despair at some colleagues being seemingly indifferent to our plight and to those bosses' machinations, we gave more vent to our anger. We would have done well to heed Proverbs 29:11: 'A fool vents all his feelings. But a wise man holds them back.' In a vicious cycle, more enraged utterances only served to further alienate those 'moderate' colleagues weary of the dispute and ready to 'move on', and to substantiate bosses' narrative that they were the reasonable actors whilst our behaviour was 'unprofessional'.

A tipping point perhaps occurred towards the end of May, when our own perceived self-interest diverged from some others in the branch. On May 24, our national union published a press release – one that had been drafted and approved by Leicester UCU's officers – titled *Prospective students should not apply to study at 'international outcast' University of Leicester, say staff.* The press release claimed, 'the job cuts are so destructive to teaching, learning and staff morale that students could not be guaranteed the education they deserve – and should instead consider applying elsewhere'. The message was reinforced by quotations from the branch communications officer (one of this book's authors) – 'So many good staff have been bullied out. Sadly, myself and colleagues in the University of Leicester UCU branch can no longer recommend the university as a place to study, let alone work' – and UCU's general secretary – 'we feel obliged to tell prospective students they should not apply to study at Leicester whilst this dispute is ongoing'. The call for prospective students to boycott University of Leicester, which found its way into a story about course closures in *The Guardian*, proved both explosive and divisive.[38]

A number of branch members including committed activists who had been fully engaged in fighting the redundancies, expressed their grave unease with the position. They argued that discouraging student applications would 'invite disaster', by jeopardising more departments and jobs; that therefore this 'doubling-down' strategy would only demoralise staff and undermine support for industrial action and other aspects of the global academic boycott; and that this strategy would 'open the door to charges that it is the union or its actions' that are damaging the reputation of the university. If committed activists thought this, then it is, of course, likely that many other 'quieter' colleagues took a similar view. Following a robust discussion on the branch activists' email list, we asked UCU's head office to remove the statement.

We – the authors of this book – believe that encouraging prospective students to avoid the University of Leicester was consistent with the global academic boycott and, in fact, one of the many replies to the university marketeer's 'disappointed' tweet of mid-May anticipated the position: 'My son almost went to Leicester Uni, had the grades. Very glad he didn't.'[39] More importantly, we believe the approach had the potential to move the hitherto immovable university executive. As with most universities, tuition fees constitute more than half of the University of Leicester's income: to us, seeking to undermine this income stream seems like a sensible industrial strategy. Indeed, this is the strategy that most workers adopt when in dispute with their employers. As one contributor to the branch discussion put it, 'If people aren't prepared to act to harm the university's finances then this action is over and we need to be honest about that.' It's also true, of course, that such a strategy carries risks – as it does for all workers who disrupt their employer's income stream.

The fallout from the press release and the subsequent discussion did much to reveal a fault line within Leicester UCU. Superficially, what was at issue was the limit of members' solidarity with colleagues being made redundant. It's more interesting to understand the division in terms of differing visions of what might be won from the dispute – saving jobs or a broader transformation of the university – and what was at stake, what was worth risking in order to achieve such a win. Those colleagues who accused us of advocating – even employing – a scorched-earth strategy were not entirely incorrect: our strategy, if embraced and adopted, *might* have destroyed the university. Our counter to this argument is that its most senior leaders were *already* destroying the university. As with their willingness to accept numerous resignations of external scholars associated with the institution and the near universal opprobrium, their willingness to discard mechanisms designed to ensure 'fairness' and 'quality' of student awards, their willingness to wager the university's estate in the financial adventuring we describe in Chapter 5, it was they – in our view – who were scorching the earth. In a sense, our focus was on what might be nurtured in this scorched earth, how something new might flourish. 'We [were] not in the least afraid of ruins.'[40]

Of course, it was materially rather easy for us – the authors of this book – to take this position. We were already at risk of redundancy and, by the time of this press release, had been handed notices of dismissal. By putting the university's future in jeopardy we were not assuming more personal risk – we were already losing our jobs, there was nothing else that could be taken from us. But even if we had not been in this situation we still think we would have argued that aggressively targeting student recruitment was an appropriate strategy and, indeed, many branch members not personally threatened with redundancy did argue just this. Whatever the strategy's merits, and however compatible with other aspects of the boycott, it was certainly a mistake to implement it without far wider discussion within the branch.

Finally, in this analysis of defeat, we should mention the more general difficulty of formulating crucial decisions – around the scope of the academic boycott, but also and especially around the strike and the marking and assessment boycott. We noted above that calling three days of strike action was a compromise position, one that we – the authors of this book – believed to be sensible. But this compromise was reached through motions to general meetings of the branch that were (in our opinion) imprudently worded. The result was a clear mandate against more strike action beyond those three days. While we are convinced the underlying decision to focus on the marking and assessment boycott was correct, it was unwise to so clearly rule out (additional) strike action so publicly – for union meetings are effectively open, as they should be, and therefore we can never expect our deliberations in such meetings to be secret from management. We thus sent a clear message to university management that 'all' they needed to break was the marking boycott.

In the end, though we made some errors, we think the reason for the defeat was more likely a more mundane accretion of factors: we didn't do quite enough, we didn't put quite enough material pressure on the university's executive and its governors (members of University Council), we failed to convince a sufficient number of allies to contribute to that application of pressure, we failed to convince a sufficient number of doubting colleagues to become and remain allies. However, this is of course certainly not the only industrial dispute in recent memory in which resistance has not ultimately resulted in a win for the workforce.

The redundancy dispute formally ended in mid-November, when branch members agreed to accept an offer from the executive board that there would be no compulsory redundancies as a result of 'Phase 2' of Shaping for Excellence (those at risk instead being encouraged to accept a 'voluntary severance settlement' or else accept redeployment within the university) and that it, the executive board, would 'rule out beginning any further restructuring leading to collective compulsory redundancies until January 2023' – a full 14 months hence. In exchange, the branch agreed to end its dispute and ask the national union to lift its global academic boycott of the University of Leicester.

To us it seemed a rather thin offer, for several reasons, but by this point of course we were no longer voting members of Leicester UCU and so our voices were not heard in the debate.

CHAPTER 3

LEADING TO MEDIOCRITY; OR, KNOWING YOUR PLACE IN ACADEMIA

We are the only ones with all the information to make the changes we need to make as a university.
– Nishan Canagarajah, President and Vice Chancellor, executive board Q&A session, February 2021

Like it or not, this is a competitive environment.
– James Devlin, dean of University of Leicester School of Business, collective redundancy consultation, 16 March 2021

The Chair [Gary Dixon] recorded his recognition of the stresses and strains placed upon members of the Executive Board by the current strategic change programme, exacerbated by the disrupting effects of the pandemic and the continued uncertainty brought about by successive lockdowns. The

> reaction to Shaping for Excellence consultations, in a small minority of cases, seemed to have progressed beyond fair and reasonable challenge to feature offensive and sometimes bullying behaviour. The position would be monitored closely against the expectations of the University's Dignity and Respect at Leicester Policy, and appropriate action would be taken where necessary. – University of Leicester Council minutes, 25 February 2021.[1]

Steven Jones opens his book *Universities Under Fire* by summarising the way in which the COVID-19 pandemic exposed the many deficiencies of the English higher education sector following four decades of marketisation. The picture, he suggests, is 'depressing'. The sector is 'confused about its purpose in society, compromised and fractured by marketisation and lacking in poise'. COVID, Jones continues, 'exposed the English higher education sector as fluent in the language of the market but mostly unable to articulate wider narratives around its underlying value to society.'[2] Whilst not sparing government policy and individual ministers from criticism, Jones excoriates university vice-chancellors and principals and their combine, Universities UK. He charges these so-called sector leaders with possession of an 'integrity deficit'. Thomas Docherty, another scholar of higher education, is similarly scalding. He accuses successive governments of the past four decades, in the UK and elsewhere, of treachery. They have 'systematically betrayed' the university, a betrayal that has been 'amply and enthusiastically supported... by a rising managerial class that has assumed leadership and control of the institution'.[3]

The diagnosis of marketisation is common in so-called Critical University Studies. Tied up with marketisation, and also a common trope in this critical literature, is the so-called managerial, or even authoritarian, turn in higher education.[4] Peter Fleming puts it succinctly: 'Under the aegis of market competition many universities (like most large corporations in the western world) now bear an uncanny resemblance to organisations inspired by [China's authoritarian president] Xi Jinping'.[5] In a recent discussion about the distinction between authoritativeness and authoritarianism as forms of management, two organisation scholars argue that the former is based on reason and debate and the later on power and coercion. Thus 'authoritarian management is one who rules rather than advises, commands rather than suggests, to make colleagues conform and obey'.[6]

In Chapter 5, we review the various reforms of university governance from the Thatcher era onwards, the direction of travel always being towards *more management.* Here we examine a more recent authoritarian turn of university management within that broader expansion of management and, specifically, the rise of a 'new managerialism' in higher education. This emphasises the import of the ideas, language and practices of the world of business into public service organisations, and the primacy of management above all other activities. New managerialism in higher education means a 'gradual shift away from academic collegiality in higher education institutions toward the power of managers (and perhaps also lay governors) to make decisions on behalf of and about academics.'[7] In other words, managerialism is concerned both with managers' 'right to manage' and the extension of this 'right'. There is a 'paradox' here. Why 'in institutions which teach about democracy, [is] so little of it … practised within their own walls'?[8]

We would be naïve to refer to a golden age of collegiality and shared governance – this never really existed – but the transformation of the sector is nonetheless striking. Whereas the rise of the managerial doctrine was 'supposed to make universities more efficient and productive, more lean and transparent, and above all, more modern', the 'spread of managerialism is also threatening the university's role as a centre of committed teaching, disinterested scholarship and critical research'.[9] In Liz Morrish's blunt assessment, it's 'driven us into a culture war'.[10]

What Benjamin Ginsberg describes as *the fall of the faculty* has both a quantitative and, more importantly, a qualitative dimension.[11] The quantitative dimension refers to the sheer expansion of non-academic staff in comparison to teaching and research staff. In the US, in 1975, 450,000 faculty and 270,000 administrators were employed by universities. By 2009, the number of faculty had risen by two-thirds to 729,000; the number of administrators on the payroll had more than tripled to 890,000. The situation is similar in the UK where, in 2015, academic staff were outnumbered by administrators in two-thirds of universities.[12] As Ginsberg notes, 'Universities are filled with armies of functionaries – the vice presidents, associate vice presidents, assistant vice presidents, provosts, associate provosts, vice provosts, assistant provosts, deans, deanlets, deanlings, each commanding staffers and assistants – who, more and more, direct the operations of every school.'[13]

The example of the University of Leicester is illustrative here. In 2021 academic, clinical and research staff made up just 40% of its total employment and, over the past decade there has been a proliferation of VC-lings.[14] Paul Boyle replaced Bob Burgess as vice-chancellor in 2014, with his own title being inflated to *President* and Vice-Chancellor. In 2018, as Boyle's disastrous leadership unravelled, the entirely new post of deputy vice-chancellor was created, to which Edmund Burke was appointed. Burke's responsibility, staff were informed, was the day-to-day management of the University. This left Boyle free from local mundanities and able to continue to globe-trot, whilst perhaps also seeking a dignified exit route once it was clear his term of office would not be renewed. In 2019, another new senior functionary position was created: the Chief of Staff, a member of the executive board with their responsibilities including 'providing executive and strategic support to the President and Vice-Chancellor'. Early in 2022, Boyle's successor Nishan Canagarajah promoted his chief marketing and communications officer Kerry Law to take up a newly inaugurated second deputy vice-chancellor position, alongside Burke.

This sort of proliferation of managerial roles has profound consequences for the leadership of universities. As David West argues, '[j]ust as modern academics are judged by their research outputs, modern managers are judged by the "reforms" or "restructuring" they bring about. These changes are the raw material of their résumé and the condition of their further promotion or dismissal. Unsurprisingly the modern manager tends to be intolerant of opposition'.[15] Thomas Docherty makes a similar point, claiming that '[t]he institutionalisation of "management" ... embeds the function of "change-management" at the centre of our practice... [S]enior management justifies its own existence and standing by very visibly "doing its job", primarily by instigating change, labelled as "reform"'.[16] This injunction on management to constantly reform doesn't justify the intransigence of the leaders in our case or in any other cases. However, it helps to explain the path dependency of managerial decisions. The second part of David West's observation, concerning university managers' 'intolerance of opposition' highlights another important issue. Whereas opposition to change can bring serious trouble, loyalty can pay off, becoming 'the unspoken condition of managerial favour and professional success.'[17]

The growth of managerial and administrative positions supports the dominance of managerial and administrative *values*. We locate our experience outlined in the previous chapter in this context of burgeoning bureaucracy and authoritarian management practice. We do so because our experience was not a one-off, or a failure of industrial organisation within a single workplace, but rather part of a movement for managers to exercise uncurtailed and uncriticised power. One colleague who was closely following the events at Leicester expressed his suspicion that other VCs might see Leicester as a 'test case' about the unlimited and unchallenged 'right to manage'. This 'right to manage' should be of concern to all who care about universities.

The 'Right to Manage' and the shape of excellence

The assertion and extension of managers' 'right to manage', their intransigence and patrimonialism all play their role in the execution of leadership at the University of Leicester and at other universities. Our case demonstrates how senior leadership made use of the commonly assumed distinction between management and leadership, a distinction that tends to glorify leadership in contrast to the more mundane and boring work of management. The use of the term 'leader' aggrandises and glorifies an individual. It is a 'celebratory label', 'predispos[ing] us to see elites in ways that are positive' and 'gloss[ing] over basic conflicts that lie at the heart of the employment relationship'.[18] In general, the notion of leadership promotes a discourse of benevolence and harmony, where a leader is working for the benefit of all. We observed this unitarist discourse at work when the executive board or the vice-chancellor sought to identify themselves with 'the University' – an identification Leicester UCU vigorously contested, as discussed previously. The discourse of leadership also provides 'justification and cover for the "tough decisions" in which the deterioration of workers' rights and conditions is simultaneously evidence of supposedly strong and visionary leadership'.[19] At the University of Leicester, Canagarajah and his team never tired of reminding employees that they were 'not doing this lightly' and that their decisions were 'tough' ones, which were, however, necessary for the University's survival 'for the next 100 years'. It is this hyperbolic and sometimes 'evangelical language'[20] which framed the Shaping for Excellence programme and which played a role in the formation of obedient and docile 'Citizens of Change'.

Before we turn to the mechanisms underpinning the creation of docile Citizens, let's take a closer look at the more everyday aspects of the process of authoritarian leadership. The forms of leadership and change management we experienced are representative of broader trends across the sector. They're best described in terms of 'command and control', where instrumentalism prevails over academic values and managers disregard professionalism and due process. We were subjected to a manifestation of the 'boss syndrome', a mindset 'where academics are viewed as hired labour who can be replaced at a moment's notice', a mindset which has unfortunately been internalised by much of the workforce too.[21] Consequences include the replacement of collective self-governance by the assertion of management prerogative, the exercise of unaccountable power, bullying, and the silencing of dissent. The instrumentalism manifests in the ways bosses seek to legitimate their decisions. Here we were confronted with the elusive language of 'excellence', a vacuous term that encapsulates the supposedly new imperatives of 'efficiency', 'effectiveness', 'relevance' and so on – themselves ill-defined terms – deployed by managers in place of rational argument.[22]

A full quarter-century before Canagarajah's attempted shaping of the University of Leicester, Bill Readings comprehensively debunked the concept of *excellence*, noting its 'singular advantage of being entirely meaningless, or to put it more precisely, non-referential. ... Today, all departments of the University can be urged to strive for excellence, since the general applicability of the notion is in direct relation to its emptiness.'[23] More ominously, 'Excellence draws only one boundary: the boundary that protects the unrestricted power of the bureaucracy. And if a particular department's kind of excellence fails to conform, then that department can be eliminated without apparent risk to the system.'[24]

The work that *excellence* does for the bureaucracy Readings describes here fits with our experience. The senior managers who executed our dismissals insisted on many occasions that the *quality* of our research – its *excellence* – was not in doubt. Rather, it had been decided – *they* had decided – that the *sort* of research we undertook was no longer required. That is, our excellence failed to conform. Here – as at countless other institutions – the ideology of *excellence* prevailed over values such as the search for truth, reason, intellectual curiosity and debate, academic freedom, critique, or the common good. These latter values have been systematically delegitimised by higher education's decision-makers. 'Our senior managers are no longer amenable to rational debate at all. Yet they are leading institutions whose very function has a good deal to do with the enhancing of honest and open reasoned argument. This is awkward.' Instead, university managers 'govern by whimsy [which] is to govern by brazen power: it is intrinsically authoritarian.'[25]

Of course, when one governs by whimsy, by 'brazen power', other norms of decent behaviour, professional conduct, following due process, showing respect, can be easily and callously discarded. This is exactly what happened in our case, to the point that incompetence, carelessness and incoherence all became inconsequential. Whilst we were constantly reminded to act in a professional way – that is, to comply in silence – management treated us with contempt. One middle manager – a 'concerned colleague' – who, during the course of the pandemic and the redundancy struggle shared screenshots of dozens of tweets from disaffected staff with her superiors, received one of the VC's 'citizens' awards' just a few months after our dismissals. 'Loyalty' certainly 'paid off' for this 'enforcer', 'rush[ing] to carry out the latest orders from their chiefs in an ecstasy of obedience'.[26]

We shall now turn to some of the other mundane mechanisms through which authoritarian leadership was executed and normalised at the University of Leicester, again representative of broader trends across the sector, starting with the control of information, space and time.

Managing information, regulating time and space

Controlling the flow of information is crucial to the authoritarian manager and there were many instances of this at Leicester. In our department, as in others shaped for excellence, bosses organised 'pre-change engagement' surveys and sessions in the autumn of 2020. During these sessions, senior managers delivered a series of truth claims, giving their audience – university staff – no real chance to critically engage with the assertions made or with the overall narrative. In the business school, at least, this narrative made clear that 'global competition' was now the name of the game, that research-led education and 'excellence' were to be conceived in terms of 'practical relevance for business' and 'executive education', and that the 'business community' was the main stakeholder. Managers refused to share survey results with staff, instead releasing their own 'summary', which presaged much of what was to come a few months later.[27] According to this, Critical Management Studies was a 'domineering force' in the School of Business, which threatened to impose 'a common mindset' standing in the way of 'genuine diversity'.

The 'business case' for our redundancy – the *Case for Change* – too, despite supposedly setting out the future strategy for the School, was shared only with staff directly at risk of redundancy. Like most documentation and communications we received, it was marked 'strictly confidential' and remained so throughout the whole process – so-called non-affected colleagues were left in the dark.

[redacted]

[redacted]

[redacted]

[redacted]

[redacted]

[redacted]

[redacted]

[redacted]

[redacted]

Controlling information (nothing to see here). Extracts from the results (we eventually received) from one of many Data Subject Access Requests submitted in 2021.

(Or would have been, had many threatened staff not contested managers' control of information by routinely sharing 'strictly confidential' documents and correspondence.) Finally, the sparse and restricted flow of information was characterised by constant delays on the part of managers and their Human Resources 'business partners'. They delayed sending copies of presentation slides, they delayed responding to queries, they delayed providing information about various 'review groups' charged with double-checking the validity of our at-risk status, to mention just a few examples. Such delays of course made it difficult to contest the management narrative, as well creating an enormous amount of additional stress for those of us at risk and our allies. All the while, as we were kept waiting for information necessary to play a full part in what was nominally a period of *consultation*, the clock kept ticking, approaching the set date on which we would receive managers' verdicts – redundancy, in almost all of our cases. This leads us to the second aspect of enacting authoritarian leadership, the regulation of time and space.

Time was not on our side. It was obvious from the outset that the university's senior managers wanted to drive through their Shaping for Excellence redundancies as rapidly as possible. They also sought to present this chase for change as a one-off exercise – regrettable, but necessary – that, if done thoroughly, would allow the University of Leicester to thrive for a further century, and would not need to be repeated. "I don't want to have to do this ever again", claimed Canagarajah. As in the case of the restructuring of 'Euro Business School' – a thinly disguised Warwick Business School, under the leadership of former foreign exchange trader and International Monetary Fund economist Mark Taylor – the change process at Leicester was rolled out with 'speed and violence'.[28] Managers exploited all loopholes and ambiguities in the university's Redundancy Ordinance. Whereas the ordinance defines non-negotiable deadlines for staff at risk of redundancy, it is much more ambiguous when it comes to the duties and actions of the employer. In particular, the word 'normally' – which appears frequently in the ordinance – was invoked talismanically by management to deflect any procedural challenge.

There were numerous instances of this. While the ordinance states that collective consultation will 'normally' begin seven months in advance of the first effective date of termination, in our case this was reduced to a period of six months. While the ordinance states that employees are obliged to lodge any appeal against their notice of redundancy within ten working days and that this appeal should 'normally' be heard within a further 15 working days, in our case, appeal hearings only took place more than 30 or even 40 days after we lodged our cases. Senior managers pleaded that the departure from 'normal' practices was justified given the difficulty of 'coordinating diaries', on account of annual leave or the many hearings to organise.

Managers' control of time was not restricted to the operationalisation of the formal ordinances. It was also apparent in their arrangement of meetings and 'consultations' with both at-risk and 'non-affected' staff. While all meetings, including redundancy consultations, were strictly limited to 50 minutes – an attempt to mitigate Zoom fatigue during the pandemic – bosses took up much of this time making their own PowerPoint presentations, severely restricting the time available to raise questions.[29] Any meaningful discussion about the business case was of course impossible. Managers always refused to extend meetings, often pleading that they had another to attend – the managerial life is a busy one and there is much more to be done than to answer the questions of staff who are at risk of redundancy – and requests for follow-up meetings were always denied. Instead we were instructed to put our questions in writing – questions that, as we explained above, were not answered in either a timely or complete manner.

Authoritarian leadership also attempts to regulate actions and behaviour through the control of organisational space. During the period of the redundancy struggle, University of Leicester bosses refused all requests for an all-staff meeting. Instead, the School of Business's dean, James Devlin, arranged so-called divisional meetings, which fortuitously kept largely separate the categories of 'affected' and 'non-affected' staff. Thus, managers' regulation of space hindered our attempts to organise a collective response to the threatened redundancies and their rationale and, more importantly, allowed bosses to disseminate different messages to different groups. Various staff email lists did, however, remain a 'space' open to us, a space that we made much use of to communicate our message to 'non-affected' colleagues, and frequently initiate salvos critical of managers' plans. But these channels were one-way, in the sense that managers remained largely silent, declining to publicly respond to our many communications. Managers did, however, monitor the space – just as they monitored our even more public social media posts – for they often sent individual responses to those colleagues who did contribute, clearly as an attempt to intimidate these individuals into acquiescence or at least silence. Thus, the all-staff lists were a very imperfect space for meaningful conversations.

Managerial blah and the 'regime of truth'

Another key instrument of authoritarian leadership is the manipulation of meaning via shifting truth claims and definitions, as well as the use of language as a tool for hyperbolic announcements and regular obfuscation, or 'managerial blah'.[30] For sociologist Yiannis Gabriel, managerial discourse uses language in such a way that it constitutes a 'systematic assault on meaning'.[31] Hyperbole and euphemisms conceal the bleak reality of market logic and management diktat. No rational explanations or arguments are present. Rather, such discourse communicates decisions, dictums, commands. In our case, this was evident in numerous documents produced and circulated by senior management. For example, the *Case for Change* opens by declaring that 'the business school sector in the UK is characterised by increasingly fierce competition'. Multiple invocations of 'it is clear…', 'it is not surprising…' and 'given the high degree of competition…' lead inevitably to the conclusion *we need change*. (Such an apparently straightforward three-word phrase. But each of those three words is problematic and ambiguous.) "Like it or not, this is a competitive environment", we were told. In the *future* – a word repeated no fewer than forty-nine times in the fifty-nine pages of the 'business case' – ULSB must be a 'sector leader'; it must be a 'champion of business research'; its research must be 'world class', must have 'excellent potential for impact and relevance', and must 'provide graduates with the skills and competencies required for future success as global leaders'.

This stuff is tedious and mind-numbing. Worse, however, is that it also serves to close down the space for critical interventions, for it constructs a harsh reality to which *there is no alternative*. It's a profoundly unscholarly narration of the world. In a student essay it would be rewarded with a failing mark and pocked with endless side notes requesting 'sources?' As with the 'ideology of modernisation', such language 'disables criticism'.[32] The invocation of anonymous, fetishised forces ('competitors', 'markets') along with the inferences of urgency ('the world of work is changing at a rapid pace') together justify 'decisive' managerial action and reinforce authoritarian leadership: in short, a playing out of the *shock doctrine*.[33] In sum, the language of the business case was a textbook example of managerial blah: 'stale, vapid, and self-validating and, of course, chock-full of nouns'.[34]

The discourse deployed against us also served to delegitimise the critical approach to management supposedly dominating the business school. It was claimed, for instance, that 'in some markets promoting our critical management approach could be damaging to our recruitment – many read this approach to management as overly politicised, this can be off putting to students'. Note here the use of weasel words ('*could* be' and '*can* be') and the reference to some apparently known but unspecified generic subjects ('some markets', 'many read'); the Dothrakian 'it is known', for aficionados of *Game of Thrones*. For a school and a university that boast of and aspire to *research excellence*, such lackadaisical argumentation is, echoing Docherty, awkward. Moreover, the School's leaders framed the critical approach to management as outdated, out of step with the 'needs of business' and the current or future 'world of work'. As with bosses' restructuring of 'Euro Business School', 'it was necessary to ensure that the past was not available as a valid position from which to criticise the present. In other words, the past needs to be articulated as a problem, as something that needs to be escaped from'.[35]

We must also pause to reflect on the phrases 'needs of business' and 'world of work'. They have become so familiar, so clichéd, that it is easy to let them pass without recognising that they are, in fact, knowledge claims: claims that the speaker knows the needs of business and the demands of the world of work (and, by implication, that the listener does not). We are on the terrain of Council Chair Gary Dixon who proudly asserts that his 'experience is pretty scarce, locally'. But with the exception of Dixon's very particular experience of a small start-up and Devlin's as a banker, there was on the management side no more first-hand experience of work outside of universities than there was on ours. The senior managers who deemed our contributions redundant are all career university bureaucrats. When we add in the testimony of former students who speak glowingly of the relevance to their present working lives of what they were taught at the University of Leicester School of Management, what we are left with is not an argument, but an assertion that managers, and not the people who have studied the subject for years and are recognised authorities on it, will decide what is to be taught and what is to be studied.

The control and obfuscation of meaning was also discernible in the very definitions of Critical Management Studies and political economy upon which our redundancies hinged. (Recall that at the centre of the *Case for Change* was a plan to 'disinvest from research and scholarship in critical management studies and political economy'.) For any redundancies resulting from this plan to be considered fair or, at least, objective, one would expect clear and operational definitions of these two research fields to have been formulated. But no such definitions were offered either in our first redundancy consultation, nor in the *Case for Change*. Given managers' control of time, described above, *what do you mean by critical management studies?* and *what do you mean by political economy?* were two of many questions we were unable to put to them.

We only received a definitional document a week later – following repeated requests. This document, a little over two pages long, revealed senior managers' utter lack of comprehension of these areas. They had constructed Critical Management Studies as a strawman opposed to so-called mainstream business education. Deliberately neglecting the diversity, transformations and inconsistencies of Critical Management Studies, managers' definitions were based on the misappropriation, decontextualising, and misquoting of sources. In a nutshell, they had made things up.

When we insisted on clarification regarding the way these (highly problematic) definitions had been applied to identify people at risk of redundancy, we were told that *a view was taken*, or that senior managers *felt that, on balance*, our work aligned with these definitions. Further probing revealed that the School's dean James Devlin and his deputy Daniel Ladley took no notes during their screening of business-school staff, an exercise which involved, or so they claimed, reviewing the publications over a period of seven years of around 70 scholars – at least 350 books, book chapters, and journal articles in total. This failure to keep notes, if true, is astonishing. When, during individual redundancy 'consultations', we pushed Devlin and Ladley to justify their judgements regarding one particular article or another, they would sometimes flag up a word or sentence from that text, taken out of context, that supposedly demonstrated 'guilt' – the publication's categorisation as either Critical Management Studies or political economy. At no point did either Devlin or Ladley demonstrate any substantial engagement with or understanding of our scholarship. (We give a few examples of managers' 'methodology' of reading in Chapter 6 on academic freedom and provide more in the book's Appendix.)

The examples of obfuscation and confusion were endless. Bosses tied themselves in discursive knots over the distinction between Critical Management Studies, a discrete research area, from which the School wanted to divest, and critical studies *about* management, a perfectly acceptable, even normal, approach to the study of management. The distinction was significant: on it hinged decisions about whether one was sacked or saved. Pressed to explain this distinction, head of College Henrietta O'Connor first introduced an understanding of CMS as 'anti-management': 'critical management is fundamentally opposed to management'. Later in the process, this was denied: '"Being opposed to management" was at no time part of the definitions', we were told. (This example also illustrates the ideological 'flexibility' of at least some managers; their malleability. Just six years before putting herself through these discursive contortions in the service of brute managerial force, Henrietta O'Connor had written, with her long-term collaborator and then deputy head of college: 'there is perhaps much that youth scholars could learn from critical management studies'.)[36]

Mystification was evident in the use of journal titles as indicators. Publishing in journals with titles such as *ephemera*, *Culture and Organization*, or *Organization* and *Critical Perspectives on Accounting* was cited as evidence of doing Critical Management Studies or political economy. In the case of *Critical Perspectives on Accounting* it was said that this journal 'as the name suggests offers "critical perspectives"'. This is obviously inconsistent with O'Connor's insistence that critical study – as opposed to CMS – was *not* being targeted. But by this point it should be apparent to the reader that inconsistency was one of the few consistent parts of the process. Publications in the other journals were deemed suspect because they were often targeted by CMS scholars. A clear case of guilt by association. After further pushing, we were finally told that 'publishing in journals with the word "critical" in the title was not used as part of the criteria for selection or as part of the basket of indicators', which occluded the reality that there was in fact a distinct list of journals classified as problematic.

Finally, we should note the magical meaning managers ascribed to the word *primarily*. Insisting that what mattered was the 'whole basket' of any particular scholar's research – and thus evading challenges to their characterisation of any single article or book – Devlin and Ladley on many occasions stated that they had *taken a view* – or *felt* – that such-and-such a person's research was 'primarily' in the area of Critical Management studies or political economy, whilst someone else's was 'primarily in areas aligned with School strategy'. However, these managers, along with O'Connor, also insisted, when pressed, that their use of 'primarily' was non-quantitative – and thus entirely resistant to any rebuttal grounded in quantitative evidence. One of the many ironies of the process was that, according to the *Case for Change*, our research was deemed redundant because it was misaligned with new strategic priorities, such as quantitative research.

We were here in Lewis Carroll's *Wonderland*:

> 'When I use a word,' Humpty Dumpty said in rather a scornful tone, 'it means just what I choose it to mean – neither more nor less.' 'The question is,' said Alice, 'whether you can make words mean so many different things.' 'The question is,' said Humpty Dumpty, 'which is to be master – that's all.'[39]

Or, more chillingly, in George Orwell's *1984*: whilst we did not end up in Room 101, Devlin's, Ladley's and O'Connor's insistence that we bow to their definition of 'primarily' is really not so different from the Party's control of language and meaning.[40]

Fostering obedience, creating docile citizens

It is astonishing that academics, especially ones that boast of their critical bent, let themselves be led in the authoritarian fashion we have just described. Why was there not more of an outcry from staff at such egregious attacks on traditional academic values of truth, reason, democracy or the public good, the resistance described in the previous two chapters notwithstanding? Our incredulity in the face of so many colleagues' compliance was not unique to Leicester. It's been expressed in various studies of the neoliberal university and its authoritarian management. Take staff acquiescence to the 'earth-shattering change programme' at 'Euro Business School', for instance:

> This workplace was a university populated by responsibly autonomous professionals, and … a particular group of these people were invested in these critical traditions [such as Marxism, interpretivism, Critical Management Studies, feminism and poststructuralism] as well as being members of the relevant trade union. [Therefore] one might have assumed that this was a place in which resistance was more, not less, likely.[41]

Senior managers' manipulation of language and their regulation of information, time and space might go some way to explaining staff quiescence. But there are further factors at play that might explain employees' disempowerment: intimidation, the pathologisation of dissent, and the use of unitarist discourse.

Under the universities' 'new managerialism', bosses have instigated a climate of incipient threat, a 'pervasive culture of control and intimidation'.[42] A toxic environment is created and maintained, where fear, threat, surveillance and bullying all became commonplace. Despite explicit claims to the contrary – 'we don't monitor colleagues', insisted Kerry Law, at that point chief marketing and engagement officer and now deputy vice-chancellor – senior managers and their more junior minions routinely monitored the social media accounts of both at-risk employees and our 'not-affected' allies. On several occasions, staff were subjected to sanctions, disciplinary action or its threat. We suggested above that managers' behaviour was, at times, Orwellian. In fact, staff who invoked Orwell or Kafka in tweets, Instagram or Facebook posts, or used words such as 'putsch' in their attempts to describe what was happening at the University of Leicester, were typically sanctioned. And as we mentioned in the previous chapter, university bosses hired an external agency to do the dirty work of surveilling staff. Armed with the university's 'Dignity and Respect' policy, senior leadership took 'appropriate action against' the, in their words, 'small number of staff in breach of the policy in their social media communications'. We imagine that such announcements had a chilling effect on others and it is certainly the case that union organisers were required to divert precious time to defending colleagues – often ourselves – who had been threatened in this way.

In terms of their scholarly activity, too, staff who were not 'directly affected' were subtly intimidated. The business school dean's supposedly reassuring insistence that staff who had not been selected for redundancy should not worry about their future research and should 'carry on freely doing the research they want' was qualified by the insidious threat that '[a]s would always be the case, over time it is hoped that all staff will reflect on their personal research agenda and how they might best contribute to the strategic priorities of the School through discussions with mentors, cluster leads and department heads'.

Pathologisation was a second way that senior managers sought to disempower dissenting staff. Protest was depoliticised and placed instead on the terrain of psychology, emotions and feelings. One way to undermine dissent is to infantilise it, to transform it to the (understandable) psychological reactions of 'whining' or hurt individuals – complainers – or to reduce it to an understandable form of 'self-interest'. The senior managers responsible for conceiving and executing the redundancies repeatedly sent condescending messages in which they expressed their appreciation that 'feelings were running high' and that these times were 'difficult' and 'unsettling' for those affected. All individual consultations started with the executors of our dismissals stressing that this was very much a 'listening exercise', following which 'all feedback' would be 'taken into account'. All individual consultations ended with the executors of our dismissals thanking us for our 'professional conduct' in these 'difficult', or 'incredibly emotional times'. Every email from the executors of our dismissals concluded with a reminder of the existence of various programmes supporting staff well-being, highlighting in particular, 'our confidential Employee Assistance Programme and staff counselling provider, Validium'.[43]

This constant messaging, which was rendered in modified form to 'not affected' employees, sought to reshape angry dissent into a set of emotions that could be more easily assuaged and appeased – therapy as convenient substitute for politics. The pathologising – and thus undermining – of emotional responses to structural violence is a tactic that readers who are marginalised by gender, race, or otherwise under patriarchy will no doubt be familiar with. Indeed, in a supposedly reassuring message following the issue of twenty-six notices of redundancy by dismissal across the University as a whole – a number, it was stressed, 'significantly fewer' than the 145 staff initially placed at risk – head of the College Henrietta O'Connor claimed that she did not 'underestimate the impact on those directly affected and colleagues in and beyond the affected areas is significant' and that 'the current industrial action shows the strength of feeling amongst some members of staff'. In this way O'Connor attempted to depict a material and collective response against her and her fellow managers' actions as merely a manifestation of 'strong feelings'. Of course, the equally important corollary here – which is left implied – is that less 'emotional' employees should have no reason to participate in the industrial action.

In general, we were both witnesses to and victims of the operationalisation of change and *change management* in the modern university. The very term implies that change is something that can and should be managed. As the first paragraph of the University of Leicester's 'Leading and Managing Change Principles' informs us:

> Change is an ever-present and essential part of life, and the University is a constantly evolving organisation. While this can make it a dynamic and vibrant place to

> work, change can present challenges for individuals and groups, and needs to be expertly managed if we are to realise the benefits of making changes at any scale.[44]

Change is conceived here as something which inevitably creates negative emotions (that need to be overcome with the help of counselling, 'resilience training', and so on) but is ultimately a good thing. In fact, at the University of Leicester under the leadership of Nishan Canagarajah, this uncritical valorisation of 'change' has been elevated to a key or guiding principle, at least in the University's branding. Whilst the university's dignified motto, *Ut Vitam Habeant* – 'so that they may have life' – has not formally been discarded, it has been superseded by the buzzword *change*. Students and staff alike are referred to as *Citizens of Change*, whilst the University's centenary celebrations (which, unfortunately for Canagarajah, began whilst his institution – our university – was still subject to a global academic boycott) were marked with the slogan *Celebrating 100 years of change*.

These principles explicitly refer to the so-called change curve, developed in the 1960s by psychiatrist Elisabeth Kübler-Ross to understand the grieving process. Despite their acknowledgement that it is 'much abused and misrepresented', the Principles' authors claim that it 'nevertheless proved valuable in understanding and helping people who are experiencing change.' By invoking this approach, bosses thereby frame resistance to change as a state of mind that can and should be overcome with the help of change management tools. Framing resistance in terms of negative emotions (shock, denial, anger) deliberately undermines the validity of any critique and denies the legitimacy of any alternative vision for the university. Everyone must *move on* – to the stages of acceptance and integration. Or, for those of us who were made redundant or resigned in solidarity and in disgust, we must move on to the stages of acceptance and *dis*integration. 'The implicit pathologisation of those who complain is never far from the surface. Healthy individuals conform, oppositional individuals are maladjusted.'[45]

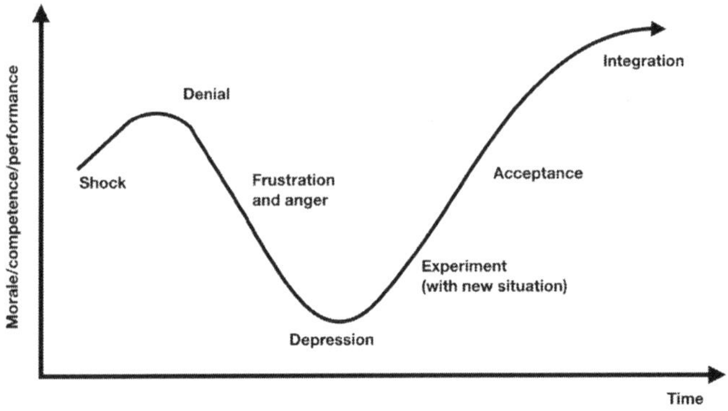

The Change Curve. *Source*: Elisabeth Kübler-Ross, *On Death and Dying* (New York: Macmillan, 1969)

The discourse of change management leads us to the third way in which authoritarian leaders foster obedience: the use of a *unitarist* discourse. We've mentioned *Citizens of Change* already. We apparently became such 'citizens' in February 2020 – a year before we were put at risk of redundancy – when staff and students were informed about the launch of the university's 'new identity'. That new identity, we learned, 'builds on the University of Leicester's heritage whilst looking to the future and supporting our mission, vision and new strategic plan. It is not just about how things look – it's about how we tell our story and our outstanding research and student experience.'[46] Imagined as Citizens of Change, we were simultaneously invited to 'initiate change towards creating a better world', whilst being deprived of the power and structural conditions to make any changes that would depart from the new direction determined unilaterally by the newly arrived vice-chancellor and his senior leadership team. *Citizens of Change* were conjured up as docile subjects who would embrace the new corporate line. Those who expressed dissent were depicted as resisting change. In this unitarist perspective, a community of tractable 'citizens' was invoked: conflict had been ironed out and dissent stigmatised.

The unitarist discourse and the expectation – injunction even – that all employees submit to one common interest was evident in the 'disappointment' (likely sincere) expressed by both the vice-chancellor and his deputy at our national union's decision to call a global academic boycott of the university. It was also evident – much more seriously for our cause – in the fury with which some of our colleagues, many of them also members of UCU, reacted to the suggestion that this boycott implied prospective students should not apply to the university.

The head of College played on this sense of shared commitment to students' interests in order to stigmatise Leicester UCU's refusal to mark and assess student work. Acknowledging that 'some UCU members had voted for industrial action', Henrietta O'Connor also insisted 'that everyone has the students' best interests at heart and we are all focused on ensuring that they continue to receive a high-quality experience'. What is particularly execrable about O'Connor's contention was that she – and her fellow members of the University's executive board – absolutely did not have students' best interests at heart. It was this reality – and our inability to predict and counter it – that contributed to the defeat of our struggle. As we recounted in the previous chapter, bosses' response to the marking and assessment boycott – algorithms and unqualified scab markers – meant a precipitous drop in the 'quality', 'reliability' and 'fairness' of University of Leicester degrees.

The key point is that the University's senior leadership team was quite prepared to sacrifice a reputation for scholarly integrity regarding student assessment to gain advantage over the union struggle with its employees. This is astonishing. For many years, university leaders – not only at Leicester – have insisted on the necessity of ever more convoluted and laborious 'quality assurance' mechanisms that codify every aspect of the student assessment process and which have added enormously to the workloads of both academics and our professional services colleagues, whilst removing professional autonomy. As was proven at the University of Leicester in 2021 – though long-suspected, again not only at Leicester – when push comes to shove these university leaders care little for quality, equity or fairness. Employers' handling of UCU's national marking and assessment boycott, ongoing as we finalised this book in summer 2023, further proves this point. The many protests of students against 'sham' graduations are a testament of the fundamental flaws of the marketised university.

Sole traders and authoritarian fragility

We should not assume that all staff had to be forced into docility or compliance. Some seemed to willingly collude with authoritarian management. Maybe it is not surprising that in the neoliberal university, many academics have embraced the 'rules of the game', transforming themselves into neoliberal subjects adept at managing their career as a series of enterprising projects and eager to compete with peers for rewards and recognition.[47] As accounting professor Michael Power, amongst others, has noted, many academics have turned into 'sole traders' using universities for their own career development. 'Rising individualism is hollowing out departments', Power warns.[48] One of the ironies of Nishan Canagarajah's imagined and imposed community of Citizens of Change is that it creates its own category of 'sole traders'. The instrumentalism that increasingly prevails in universities incentivises academics to jump from institution to institution, using them merely as stepping-stones for their own careers, making any form of attachment to the research culture of a university department, to colleagues, or even to the idea of academic freedom something that holds little sway over conduct.

Authoritarian leadership is not the sole doing of leaders and managers, however much they want to assert their power. Followers must assent, even if only by their silence in the face of injustice. Quiescence has to be widespread. We found that many of our erstwhile colleagues were willing to acquiesce to Canagarajah's *Shaping for Excellence* programme. In the name of their own survival, maybe of personal revenge, of careerism or simply for the sake of an easy life, many were complicit in the changes driven by management, content to 'dwell in the ruins' of academia, maybe even spotting an opportunity for personal advancement.[49]

However, authoritarianism's victory in the university is a fragile one. Our own resistance – along with that of countless others in other universities – is what produces its fragility. Our pressure forced authoritarian managers to expose their authoritarianism, to show their true colours. Having said that, our experience also highlights the limits of resistance. Dialogue and reasoned argument are certainly insufficient. 'We're told that dialogue is an egalitarian thing; we are equal in a dialogue. Dialogue actually is the weapon of the powerful.'[50] Authoritarian power cares little for reason. It can only be fought with what power understands: power. What this means is that academics and university workers more generally must build institutional alliances – across universities, with local community organisations and other trade unions, with other scholars. It's a common view that academics are poor builders of alliances, poor at expressing solidarity, poor comrades. This was E. P. Thompson's belief, articulated in his description of *Academicus Supercilious*:

> Academic Freedom is forever on their lips, and is forever disregarded in their actions. They are the last people to whom it can be safely entrusted, since the present moment is never the opportune moment to stand and fight. Show them the last ditch for the defence of liberty, and they will walk backwards into the sea, complaining that the ditch is very ill dug, that they cannot possibly be asked to defend it alongside such a ragged and seditious-looking set of fellows, and, in any case, it would surely be better to write a tactful remonstrance.[51]

We think this is too pessimistic. We prefer to look for the glimmers of hope. Although authoritarian leadership won at University of Leicester in 2021, we do not believe its victory there and then was permanent. We do not believe authoritarian leadership is sustainable. Indeed, at Leicester we believe it is reaching its limits: erosion of trust, reputational damage, the exodus of many decent people, many others learning to speak out and speak up. All these factors undermine the long-term survival and credibility of Canagarajah's university. Although we lost one struggle, that does not mean the struggle has ended. The idea of the university as a place where critical thinking might occur is always being lost: it requires continual defence, it must always be struggled for.

CHAPTER 4

CRITICAL THINKING AND/IN THE BUSINESS SCHOOL

> The problem with the business school is inextricably entangled with the problem of the university and its relation to the world, and this is an old problem.
> – Martin Parker[1]

> The university is a critical institution or it is nothing.
> – Stuart Hall[2]

> "In human society," Mr. Ringold taught us, "thinking's the greatest transgression of all." "Cri-ti-cal think-ing," Mr. Ringold said, using his knuckles to rap out each of the syllables on his desktop, – "there is the ultimate subversion." – Philip Roth, *I Married a Communist*[3]

We've looked at the specifics of our struggle and described the authoritarian leadership that prevails in many universities. We'll now move on to place this struggle in context. How could it have happened? How did things come to this? In this chapter, we first explain how business schools became so dominant, to the extent that one in every six students enrolled in a British university today is studying business, management or a related subject. Next, we explain how critical thinking became possible in the business or management school – an institution whose primary *raison d'être* is often seen as serving the needs of business and of capital. Finally, we look at the particular history of the department we created, defended and, eventually, were expelled from.

How did business schools get so big?

The massification of business school education has its roots in Thatcherism's attacks on higher education in general, and the arts, humanities and social sciences in particular, which took place in the 1980s. And ironically this massification is also implicated in the process through which some business schools became a home to critical thought. The underfunding and sometimes closure of other disciplines saw many academics trained therein seek refuge in the business and management schools that were expanding, as previously hospitable terrain was curtailed. Sociologists reinvented themselves as industrial relations scholars or organisational theorists. Historians became business historians. Psychologists, scholars of Human Resource Management. And political economists, unable to find employment in Economics departments beholden to neoclassical and neoliberal orthodoxy, found business schools more tolerant of their heterodox views.

The growth of the business school in the UK came with diminishing resources outside of fee income. With other sources of funding restricted and/or in retreat, fee income directly from students became an ever more important constituent of the increasingly business-like university financial model. Ideal courses in the portfolio mix become those onto which students can be recruited in their many hundreds with minimal overheads for module delivery (unlike well-regarded but expensive-to-run modules in the areas of human health). Business studies is thus big business for universities, providing subsidies for other more costly but prestigious schools and faculties.

Embroiled in these shifts since at least the late 1970s is what Stuart Hall described as 'the great moving right show', during which Margaret Thatcher became leader of the Conservative party in 1975 and then prime minister four years later.[4] Thatcher's spell as Secretary of State for Education (1970–74) left her with a hatred of the Department of Education and Science. She believed it to be 'self-righteously socialist', with its civil servants enjoying a relationship with the teachers' unions that was 'altogether too cosy'.[5] Worse still were the academics and intellectuals whom she castigated as the 'usual' source of wholly unwelcome 'revolutionary doctrines.'

> They have a terrible intellectual snobbery and their socialistic ideas come out of the top drawer. They think that they can destroy what exists and that only they know what those who come from the same human clay want… [I]n enlarging your responsibility, why should you not have your own property, just like the top drawer does? But some academics and intellectuals do not understand that and are putting out what I call poison. Some young people, who were thrilled to bits to get to university, had every decent value pounded out of them.[6]

In the early 80s Thatcher's government made savage cuts to the funding of tertiary education (of 18% between 1981 and 1984); a policy of 'slow strangulation—though in some areas it is not so slow'.[7] The cuts were administered by the University Grants Committee, a central body that had allocated university funds since 1919, and it adopted a 'selective strategy', targeting the social sciences for 'substantial reductions' in student enrolments.[8] Alongside this selective restriction was a wholesale contraction in the unit of resource per student for those for whom places remained.

Five years later, the University Grants Committee warned of further real-terms cuts in university grants and falls in student numbers in all areas apart from medicine, computer science, engineering, education, *and business studies*. In its wielding of the axe, the University Grants Committee was only reflecting government policy. The 1985 Green Paper, *The Development of Higher Education into the 1990s*, stressed the need for 'a distinct emphasis on technological and directly vocational courses at all levels' and stated that 'the proportion of arts places in higher education as a whole can be expected to shrink'. This Green Paper also cast doubt on the employability of arts graduates and, foreshadowing the introduction of the fees (and debt) model of student funding, suggested that 'a greater financial engagement of the part of students would cause them to take greater care over their choice of study'. Four decades on, little seems to have changed – think of prime minister (at the time of writing) Rishi Sunak's brash July 2023 promise to 'crack down on rip-off university courses', which 'don't lead to good jobs'.[9]

In the second half of the decade, the publication of a 1987 White Paper, *Higher Education: Meeting the Challenge*, preceded the Education Reform Act of 1988.[10] These first envisioned and then legislated for a far greater degree of centralisation and state control over Britain's universities. The word 'planning' appears numerous times, and the goal of this planning was quite explicit: to better align tertiary educational provision with apparent business need. In the words of the White Paper's Introduction:

> Meeting the needs of the economy is not the sole purpose of higher education; nor can higher education alone achieve what is needed. But this aim, with its implications for the scale and quality of higher education, must be vigorously pursued. … The Government and its central funding agencies will do all they can to encourage and reward approaches by higher education institutions which bring them closer to the world of business.

Under this new regime, the University Grants Committee was abolished, with monies instead disbursed by a new University Funding

Council. The former committee was comprised solely of academics. Of the 15 members of the new funding council (all appointed by the Secretary of State), between six and nine would be appointed on the basis of their 'experience of, and ... capacity in, industrial, commercial or financial matters or the practice of any profession'. Indeed, this funding council might not include anyone we would recognise as an active university scholar or teacher: the Act specifies that 'not less than six and not more than nine of the members shall be persons *appearing* to the Secretary of State ... to be currently engaged in the *provision* of higher education' (our emphasis). Over time, these legislative changes have facilitated the emergence of a new cadre of senior management office holders who head the now strangely misshapen UK university. Their interests are in projecting business-friendly strategic visions, bringing in money – still mainly via students – and seeking to navigate their positions as pseudo-CEOs of a sector constantly shifting with the whims of the unpredictable (but consistently overwhelmingly negative) diktats of government policy.

There is no doubt that the wholesale attack on the public roles and responsibilities of the university that accelerated with the raising of fees are a culmination of broader trends in government policy that are relatively independent of the hue of the governing party. The working group, chaired by former BP CEO Lord Browne, which proposed the rise in student fees to £9000, was created by the New Labour stalwart, Peter Mandelson. (This tripling of fees was implemented, however, by the Conservative David Willetts, who was later appointed Chancellor of University of Leicester, as we've already noted.) The privatisation of the current UK university which has accelerated over a decade of Conservative government was already underway apace during the New Labour years.

The intellectual space afforded by business and management schools

The emergence of organisational theory and critical thinking in UK business and management schools was generated in part by works like Gibson Burrell and Gareth Morgan's *Sociological Paradigms and Organisational Analysis*, published in 1979, and Harry Braverman's 1974 book *Labour and Monopoly Capital.*[11] Classic works of organisational theory and industrial relations such as these helped to carve out a critical field in business and management schools that has, in subsequent decades, increased in scope and range, encompassing feminism, ethnography, political economy, and post-colonial thought, amongst other areas of social and political analysis that often go under the broad rubric of organisational studies. Thus, the UK business and management school provided a space (at least initially) of relative security in which to undertake a wide variety of critical social thought, largely because of continuing high levels of student recruitment, which increasingly compared favourably to other social sciences and the humanities. For those academics 'putting out socialistic poison', the chance to do so to lecture theatres containing 200, 300, sometimes as many as 500 students, was an exhilarating opportunity.

'Multi-disciplinarity' is frequently lauded in universities and in contrast to the traditional department, a business school can, at least in some cases, be intellectually liberating. This is a result of the business school's origins in vocational training and its relatively recent history. The École Spéciale de Commerce et d'Industrie opened in Paris in the early nineteenth century, followed by several other business schools in (continental) Europe. The first American school was the Wharton School (University of Pennsylvania), established in 1881, but it is not until the 1960s that the business school took off in the UK, despite earlier and sporadic presence of provision in 'commerce'. The ostensible purpose of these new business schools and management education was to train managers, to further the ends of business (hence the much-overused marketing slogan of many a business school, including the University of Leicester's between 2016 and 2018 – *Leicester Means Business*). 'Business' here becomes a curiously empty place, where most of the conditions and consequences of capitalist action – discrimination, exploitation, violence, etc. – are absent.

However, with an increasingly crowded market, a lack of any agreed substantive canon, and a labour force largely trained elsewhere, space partially opened up for a limited critical project that questioned some of the shibboleths of business education. This is the space that Leicester, along with a few notable fellow travellers in the UK, sought to inhabit. To be clear, the critical space potentially afforded was always going to be narrow, given wider constraints. But as two former Leicester faculty note, 'because extreme externalisation, the pushing away of all cost and the hoarding of all profit, in scholarship or in business, always ends up revealing that what is pushed away is the only thing that can save those who externalise from the oblivion of being about nothing.'[12]

So, counterintuitive as it may seem, engaging with this struggle to illuminate and bring into focus what had been 'pushed away' and thereby 'revealed' – the conditions and consequences of capitalist action – became for some, at least for a time, an exciting and diverse intellectual project. Following from this, it should not surprise us that a major battle leading to the (further) subversion of academic principles would be fought, not in a humanities department, but a business school.

Strategic emptiness

University 'leaders' – the ever more arcane vice-chancellors, principals, rectors, giving way to presidents and the like – are fond of bold 'visions', mission statements and grand strategies. Let's take a particularly ludicrous example, one that is central to our story. In October 2020 Nishan Canagarajah launched his new strategy for the University of Leicester. Six months after this initial announcement and following extensive social media commentary pointing out that strategic change in the absence of a public strategy was something of a joke, university bosses finally delivered their punch line. Three 'strategic themes' were heralded: 'research-inspired education', 'world-changing research'

University bosses published their new Strategic Diagram in April 2021. Leicester UCU responded immediately and caustically. It also used the occasion to advance its own alternative vision. Leicester UCU (@leicesterucu), 'It doesn't. Nor was it worth the 12-month wait. A whopping 912 words of generic Buzzword University Leadership Lingo Selling Hubris Insipid Twaddle', Twitter, 14 April, https://bit.ly/SfM-4-06; and Leicester UCU (@leicesterucu), 'We have responded to @NCanagarajah's strategy for @ uniofleicester with one of our own', Twitter, 15 April, https://bit.ly/SfM-407

and 'our citizens'. These were handily summarised in what the university's marketeers described as a Strategic Diagram (their capitalisation).[13]

Unsurprisingly such an empty and bland articulation of 'strategy' was met with howls of derision. 'Never mind what they say, Nishan, I think it's lovely. Did you colour it in yourself?', was the memorable response of Peter Armstrong, the (then-)emeritus professor whom we encountered in Chapter 2.[14] Leicester UCU offered its own ripostes, one derisory, one more serious. Again, Bill Readings, whom we quoted in the last chapter, is prescient and apposite: 'The appeal to excellence marks the fact that there is no longer any idea of the University, or rather that the idea has now lost all content.'[15]

A university is constituted in two ways, which exist in tension. From the bottom up, there are individual scholars, students, administrative staff, other employees. These individuals create and maintain multiple relationships with others: writing partnerships, research clusters, discussion groups, course teams and so on. These relationships are typically most dense within departments, but they also exist across departmental and disciplinary boundaries, and scholars typically maintain relationships with others outside the institution who are working in the same or similar fields, through conferences, journals and, again, writing partnerships. Any individual scholar usually seeks validation and (self-)esteem through these relationships, and above all, respect from their peers. A scholar is likely to take pride in the work they themselves have done, as well as that produced by colleagues in their department or research group, students they taught and so on. Such excellence is, of course, subjective, and it might be found in any institution and in any department.

In contradistinction to its ancient origins and forms of governance, a contemporary vice-chancellor observes, and attempts to constitute, the university from the top down, using a range of representations and techniques, with 'excellence' being but one of these. But how can anyone compare the 'excellence' of the research done in a physics department, say, with that done by historians? How can the quality of the historians' research be compared with that of their peers in another institution? How can research excellence be compared with that in teaching? It's as topsy-turvy an idea as comparing yards of linen with a coat, or with so many quarters of corn or hours of labour-time.[16] But it is by making real these abstractions that the capitalist world is constituted, and likewise the modern university as constructed from above, in a strange hall of mirrors that accepts the validity of – and thus validates – the equivalence of different concrete manifestations of 'excellence', which are then selectively amplified.

In the past few decades – in fact since Thatcher's reforms of the 1980s – we have seen the emergence of myriad measures and metrics intended to commensurate 'excellence' in different disciplines and different aspects of a scholar's working life, with material consequences flowing from these processes of commensuration. The

Research Assessment Exercise (RAE, first conducted in 1986), the Research Excellence Framework (superseding the RAE in 2014), the Teaching Excellence Framework (launched in 2017): these and other emerging similar and interrelated mechanisms around 'impact' and 'knowledge exchange' are woven into rankings and league tables, created by bodies such as *Times Higher Education*, the *Guardian*, and the *Times*. These measures and metrics have been consciously invented, championed, imposed and administered by a fetid imbroglio of government ministers, civil servants, policy wonks, higher education 'experts' and consultants, vice-chancellors, and complicit senior academics. And ordinary scholars have, at the end of the day, submitted to this discipline by orienting themselves towards its reproduction for purposes of survival and/or promotion – or some combination of the two. It was in part through such changes that the University of Leicester School of Management was shaped and given life in the often angry attempt by critical academics to generate alternatives to the dominant trends in the British university. Perhaps paradoxically, by achieving relative success as registered by such measures we were able to buy the space in which to keep alive an alternative conception of what it means to study and research in the university. Of course, this was the 'wrong' kind of excellence, and with managers dictating what excellence is, the attack on critical thinking at the University of Leicester comes as no surprise. But ours is not a tale of one flower cut down but rather a broader tale about salting the land of criticality.

Critique and the 'anti-management' centre

Novelist James Kelman invites us to 'Imagine a university without philosophy', before adding parenthetically, 'The last sentence demands an exclamation mark but doesn't deserve one.'[17] In its 100-year history, Leicester University has never had a department of philosophy, nor does it offer any formal degree programmes in philosophy. In 2003, however, a small group of graduate students and faculty created a Centre for Philosophy and Political Economy (CPPE).[18] This centre went on to organise countless reading groups, a blog, several dozen conferences, symposia and workshops, and hosted numerous keynote talks, public lectures and other events delivered by international scholars.[19] The CPPE was located in the University of Leicester's Management Centre, which subsequently became the School of Management and, in 2016, following the unwanted (by both parties) merger with the Department of Economics, the School of Business.

Following a 2004 conference organised by the CPPE, political economist and scholar of the commons Massimo De Angelis, enthused to one of the present authors: "There's this management centre at Leicester university. It's more like an *anti*-management centre. We should both get jobs there!" The promise – or charge – of being anti-management is interwoven with the School of Management's history and, as we've seen already, was ultimately a charge levelled against us in our redundancy cases.

But things are more complicated than that. By 2021, Critical Management Studies – one of the two areas which University of Leicester bosses, including Henrietta O'Connor, had targeted for disinvestment – had long become institutionalised, with various annual international conferences (inaccessible due to high registration fees to all but those with institutional funding) and official streams and subgroupings within the mainstream management studies organisations, conferences, and journals. Many have argued that CMS was and is insufficiently critical. It is also the case that in one very important respect – the bottom line – the University of Leicester's School of Management, despite some of the critical rhetoric, was very much *for* management. Each and every year it generated large financial contributions above local costs, typically around £10 million, earned by charging market rates to overseas students for MBAs and other Masters degrees, which delivered handsomely to University central coffers. If (some) scholars were attacking management and business, well, this was a profitable business.

At the turn of the millennium the University of Leicester had no department of management or business. These subjects were taught, rather profitably, to international students usually via means of various distance-learning programmes run out of a Management Centre, itself a semi-independent spin-off from the Economics department. Things changed in 2003, when then-Vice-Chancellor Bob Burgess appointed Gibson Burrell as the Management Centre's new head, supporting Burrell's 'radical plans for "rediscovering a Utopian sprit" in management research and teaching', backed with the money necessary to recruit more academics and double the Centre's size. As Burrell explained to *Times Higher Education*:

> The context for management research in the UK has become more Americanised, and I am deeply disturbed by what appears to be a return to the intellectual conservatism of the mid-1970s, where it becomes more difficult to develop different research areas and adopt different methodologies. ... It is essential that as academics we are independent, standing outside a topic, and can address it without worrying too much whether the implications of our conclusions will be relevant to a particular client group. ... Business schools don't all have to look the same, and I want to prove it is possible to create something different. I see this as a once-in-a-lifetime opportunity to help build an alternative to the conventional management centre, which is driven by an American agenda where quantitative methods are seen as unquestionably superior to qualitative methods. ... My plans for Leicester are to create a more egalitarian community – an intellectually exciting place where the quality of work not the quantity is seen as essential. There would be no publishing for publishing's sake.[20]

In the first decade of the twenty-first century, the strategy of the Centre, which formally became the School of Management in 2007, was definitely not mimetic isomorphism. It did not and would not follow every other management or business school, mimicking structures, systems and strategy – a strategy of *seeking excellence by aiming for the average*. Instead, the Management Centre/School of Management differentiated itself by promoting *critical studies of management*. In a marketeer's terms, this was its unique selling point. In a series of statements of orientation and intent produced during this period, the Centre/School and its head worked out what *critical* and *management studies* could be. This, moreover, was reflected in the foundational courses students undertook when enrolled at Leicester. We understood – and still understand – critique to involve seven key facets:

First, there can be no critique without a grasp of power, its distribution, exercise and reproduction, and of the politicisation of the social world. To ask questions about power and how it can be challenged is itself a political act.

Second, critique means being iconoclastic, challenging the dominant icons and prevailing imagery of the day – the figure of the organisational 'leader', for instance. No icon is above critique. No symbol is beyond being unmasked.

Third, critique involves interrogating the foundations upon which knowledge claims are erected, upon which 'common sense' rests. This requires a quest for real depth or epistemological complexity.

Fourth, critique encourages close scrutiny of the role and behaviour of ruling elites, with the aim of bringing onto the public agenda items the powerful might prefer to remain unexamined. This includes treating any agendas laid out by the 'Establishment' with deep suspicion.

Fifth, critique encompasses some vision, call it Utopian if you will, of a better, more human future. We criticise the world because we believe it could be different, better. In fact, creative critique is only possible if one has – maybe only at the back of the mind, maybe only hazily defined – an image of some Utopia.

Sixth, critique is driven by a sense of intellectualism. It's driven by the conviction that ideas can have a revelatory effect, that ideas can provoke a liberatory experience in those who are confronted with them. And thus, critique is also driven, in part, by the desire to teach, to spread such potentially revelatory and liberatory ideas, to proselytise. It believes in education, where education means *educere* – to lead out by the illumination of new ideas.

Finally and above all, critique is *oppositional* – and this is the concept that ties together the other six strands. Critique involves continual challenge to the powerful, the orthodox, the iconic, the Panglossian: in short, to 'Royal Science'.[21] And of course, this means that 'critical management studies' itself must also to be critiqued and opposed. The critique of its critique must be welcomed and celebrated as a part of permanent opposition.

What about *management studies*? The word *management* can be understood in various ways, some complementary, others incompatible. It can mean the group – or class – of individuals who represent capital vis-à-vis labour, and whose interests are thus implacably opposed to those of labour or the working class. Hence the 'managerial class'. The word can also mean – a definition that overlaps with the previous one – that group or cadre of people who stand in the organisational world between the owners of capital or the state, on the one hand, and lower-level employees, on the other. 'Management' can refer to the actions of either of the two previous groups of individuals. Finally – and this is the incompatible definition – it can mean the activity that all sentient human beings perform in their day to day lives.

While the word *studies* seems more straightforward, it's not an innocent term, for it places us, its practitioners, as research-orientated, publishing scholars above anything else. For whom do we write? There are (at least) four possible socio-economic groupings that constitute our intended or potential audience, namely: (i) CEOs and other board members or their equivalent; (ii) middle managers; (iii) the subordinate employee; and, of course, (iv) other academics, as well as students and wider, more 'public' audiences. Much of so-called strategic management seeks explicitly or implicitly to gain the ear of those who inhabit the most senior levels of the organisational and business worlds. Thus what is key is the relevance of what's said for the widespread process of 'strategising'. But the research is typically done with and on senior executive levels of the corporation, or its equivalent in the public or voluntary sectors. This seems to reflect a view that, like medics, our status comes from what or with whom we usually interact. Our 'raw material' designates our status. Thus, just as the brain surgeon and the pedicurist gain cultural capital to differing degrees on the basis of which particular piece of human flesh they incise, strategic management only seeks, wholeheartedly, to learn about what the corporately powerful think and do. This, of course, can be exceptionally valuable as an aid to our understanding of organisational life but the issue is whether we write *for* and in the interest of these elite groups – or not.

For us, management studies is largely about *management* in many of its guises – both as practice and the ways in which the various groups mentioned above relate to their hierarchical superiors and subordinates. For us, management theory is concentrated around the knowledge/management dyad. But the precise links between the two poles of this dyad must be thought through too. Is management theory about knowledge *for* management, knowledge *by* management, or knowledge *of* management? The first of these leads to responsiveness to demands for approaches which are deemed relevant and interesting by employers and by MBA audiences and their sponsors. In this case, the task we face becomes one of producing material that is thought to be fit for consumption and immediate digestion by managerial audiences.

Unlike many business and management school academics, we reject this role – it's not the basis upon which we seek validation. While in some contexts it might be desirable to produce knowledge for managers, many of whom face daily workplace stresses in their roles, our desire to provide this sort of knowledge is of a secondary nature. Knowledge possessed by managers – gained through their daily lives – is of some interest, but we don't see such experiential learning as a superior form of understanding. Rather it is a form of knowledge in which we had an 'anthropological' interest. In short, we wanted to understand management not as our client group but as our theoretical object – we were undertaking studies *of* management, not studies *for* management.

More generally our interest was in *organisation* and *organising* – management being just one, hierarchical, mode of this. Thus scholars investigated and often were active in a wide range of so-called alternative organisational forms – cooperatives, experiments in utopian living, social movements, anarcho-syndicalism, alternative economies, community groups and the like. This interest, both scholarly and participatory, in alternative organising was, in fact, written into the Management Centre's mission statement, which also included commitments to post-coloniality, heterodox methods and the importance to both intellectualism and the human spirit of enjoyment and excitement, comradeship and conviviality.

Of course, bold statements of intent are seldom fully reflected in the entirety of what is delivered in their name and certainly the Centre/School was sometimes found wanting when judged against its grandiose aspirations. But the reader does not need to trust our judgement when it comes to the distinctive ethos of our mutual creation. We'll quote (at some length) from geographers Katherine Gibson and Julie Graham, who visited in 2005:

> A startling thing happened just as we were preparing to write the introduction to this new edition of *The End of Capitalism (As We Knew It)*. We had traveled to England to give the opening lecture for a workshop called "Contesting Capitalism: Practices and Strategies," hosted by the Collective for Alternative Organisation Studies (CAOS) at the University of Leicester Management Centre. On the day before the workshop, we walked into the Centre to meet our hosts and were welcomed into an entirely friendly intellectual and political environment – one in which thinking about and experimenting with alternatives to conventional capitalism were the order of the day (and the plan for the decade or

decades to come). The next day was even more astonishing. We encountered sixty to seventy workshop participants, including local activists and social scientists from the United Kingdom and Europe, and soon realized that while Leicester might be institutionally advanced, it is in no way isolated: individuals and groups are pursuing research on all manner of alternatives, from cooperatives to local currencies to community credit institutions to commons restoration. Moreover, their studies are being conducted in a spirit of openness to possibility, rather than in the more familiar negative spirit in which co-optation, failure, and falling short are expected and confirmed. Alternatives, whatever that disputed term might be taken to mean, are no longer simply jottings in the margins of a central text about global neoliberalisation; they are to be considered in their own right, with their own specific and contingent problems and successes, achievements and shortcomings, disappointments and hopeful surprises.[22]

Knowledge against management and the expunging of critical research

Critical approaches remained the mainstay of the School of Management at least until its merger with the Department of Economics in 2016 and the rebranding as the School of Business. While it lasted, the School of Management offered students a 'liberal arts' management education, emphasising the importance to business leaders of skills such as rhetoric and an appreciation of history, philosophy, and management's 'dark side'.[23] This approach later became known as 'the Leicester model' and in one assessment of 'the competitive (dis)advantages of European business schools', it was singled out for approval three times.[24] In the past few years, particularly since the financial crisis of 2009 and growing alarm around the climate catastrophe, other business schools around the world started to catch up and newspapers like the *Financial Times* have cottoned on. In a special report on 'responsible business education', for instance, the dean of Berkeley's Haas School (no. 12 in the *FT*'s world rankings, for those who are wondering) is clear about the trend: 'I think there has been a really profound shift in teaching at business schools, from learning how to be rich to going out to make the world a better place. Students who [previously] might have studied public policy want to come to us to make a difference.'[25]

The years in which the School of Management (as it was then) proclaimed itself interested in Critical Management Studies was also the first time it was subjected to the National Student Survey. In 2005, 2006 and 2007, when students were fully aware of the School's statement of intent and of its commitment to critical work on the management of all organisations – including itself – the School was rated 1st, 5th and 6th of all business and management units across the UK. In *Guardian* league tables of 2010 and 2011 it ranked 2nd and 6th, respectively, for business and management. Students did not reject 'political economy': courses on cooperatives, climate change, surveillance and financial impropriety, to name but a few, were all well attended and received strong feedback.[26] It delivered this performance alongside very substantial financial surpluses that kept the rest of the institution afloat. (These handsome surpluses did not prevent some of the university's senior managers complaining that it would be more successful in recruiting students if it was less 'anti-business'.)

The early years of the twenty-first century, years which saw the Management Centre's birth, were the years of New Labour, of the beginning of the decades-long 'war on terror', of globalisation and the 'end of history'.[27] They were also years in which the global justice movement reached its zenith, years in which Thatcher's *There Is No Alternative* (enthusiastically echoed by her successor Tony Blair), was vocally rebuked by *Another World Is Possible* and the Zapatistas' *One No, Many Yeses*. The University of Leicester Management Centre was one of those *Yeses*. By the end of the century's second decade, the prevailing ideological climate had become very different: jingoistic, populist authoritarianism in the ascendant and universities were portrayed by politicians and new media alike as part of the problem. Attacks on 'woke' academics in the tabloid press coalesce neatly with the rejection of the idea that universities should ever serve as sites of diverse and critical intellectual engagement. One might expect, one would certainly hope, that a university would seek to protect its members – its staff and its students – from these forces, to provide a sanctuary in which scholarship can be continued free of outside interference. This has not been the case.

We can trace the Leicester redundancies of 2021 – especially our own, from the School of Business – to the shifting of the ideological climate and, specifically, to our *response* to the increasingly tightening space. In short, as we saw in Chapter 1, we began to use Critical Management Studies and political economy as intellectual tools to question the university itself – *our* university, *our* employer. Beyond the three forms that the management/knowledge dyad might take – knowledge for management, knowledge by management and knowledge of management – there is a fourth possibility: knowledge *against* management (or knowledge of management against management). Here the intended or potential audience is the subordinate employee or, more generally, the social subject in struggle against 'the present state of things'. The School of Management always included many scholars who understood their scholarship in this way, directing their research towards areas that could support various campaigns, movements and struggles. Beginning in around 2014, with the appointment of Paul Boyle as vice-chancellor, the management of the University of Leicester increasingly became the object – the target even – of such research.

The difference between Boyle and his predecessor Bob Burgess was striking. Burgess was old-school, genuinely interested in ideas for their own sake and, as we've explained, sympathetic to our 'social scientific' approach to studying management. Boyle's jib was cut from very different cloth. Boyle saw himself as a 'moderniser'. When he arrived at the University of Leicester, he decided that it needed a business school: 'leading' universities had business schools, therefore Leicester should have one too – an instance of mimetic isomorphism, of course. Boyle soon appointed Zoe Radnor, a proselytiser for lean management, as dean (the new title replaced 'head') of the School of Management, to make the new business school a reality.

From this point onwards, university leaders not so subtly and increasingly consistently sought to minimise work that drew on political economy and that was critical of management. The visibility of such work in communications to students and prospective students was downplayed. Radnor appointed faculty who were either indifferent to heterodox approaches to the study of business and management or actively opposed. She also 'divisionalised' the School, an apparently 'rational' response to its growing size, though another instance of mimetic isomorphism, since 'all' business and management schools have a department of accounting and finance, one of marketing, another of management and so on. Divisionalisation functioned to divide up and atomise – for many, any sense that we were part of a collective project evaporated. Of course, Radnor also executed the merger between the School of Management and the University's Department of Economics, in order to create the School of Business, of which she was dean. Few in either department or school desired this merger and the Economics department's head resigned as an expression of his own opposition. Finally, Radnor and Boyle conceived plans to move the(ir) new business school to a new location a mile away from the main campus. Again, there was robust opposition, with faculty objecting both to the off-siting of our scholarship, which we believed belonged at the heart of the university, and to the inadequacy of the new facilities, which offered neither sufficient teaching space nor sufficient office space.

Presiding over an autocratic regime, Radnor did her best to destroy the respected cultures of both constituent departments. The imaginative (such as the strapline *Management is too important not to debate*) was replaced by the bland (first *Leicester means business* and then *distinctive and relevant*).[28] Radnor left Leicester in June

Management: no longer too important not to debate.

Photo: the authors

2018 to become a vice-president at City, University of London: in her two-and-a-half years as dean almost fifty academic staff and more than thirty professional services (administrative) staff resigned from the School of Business.

When James Devlin arrived in mid-2019 – following a year-long period of relative calm under an interim dean – he and his deputy Daniel Ladley concluded the process of divisionalisation. What's noteworthy here is they corralled into a single department (that of management and organisation) almost all of the scholars subsequently targeted with redundancy. This included David Harvie, an associate professor of finance and political economy (and an economist by professional training), and Geoff Lightfoot, an associate professor of accounting and entrepreneurship. It is curious why Harvie and Lightfoot were not assigned to the Department of Economics, Finance and Accounting. Neither of us questioned our moves, but when this was happening in spring 2020, neither of us could have predicted the consequences on our livelihoods of intra-departmental membership. We do know that six months following Devlin's and Ladley's allotment of faculty to various divisions and department, they conducted a screening exercise, which resulted in Harvie and Lightfoot being put at risk of redundancy and subsequently dismissed. We also know that Ladley and Devlin explicitly excluded all members of the Department of Economics, Finance and Accounting from their screening process and no member of that department was put at risk. What we do not know is what they knew in spring 2020.

Several faculty did in fact challenge their allotment to new divisions or departments. These were individuals whom Devlin and Ladley had proposed move to the Department of Marketing, Innovations, Strategy and Operations; they, the individuals, preferred to remain within Management and Organisation. None of these faculty members were threatened with redundancy. We can thus speculate that our bosses' plan A was the wholesale closure of the Division of Management and Organisation. But given the continued presence in this division of staff they wished to retain, they concocted plan B, the 'disinvestment from research and scholarship in Critical Management Studies and political economy'.

By 2021, the University of Leicester had fallen to 110th in the *Guardian* league table for provision of business, management and marketing (out of 123 providers). (It subsequently climbed to 78th for 2022, on data collected prior to the redundancies, and dropped to 87th in 2023). Thus, the evidence from students does not support the Leicester bosses' contention that Critical Management Studies is irrelevant, and that political economy no longer offers a valuable framework for understanding the world, including the 'world of business'. The absolute contrary would seem to be the case. It seems clear to us that University of Leicester's senior management disliked (and dislikes) any critique of management. And this senior management team particularly disliked (and dislikes) any criticism of *its own* management.

We began to voice such criticisms from the middle of the decade. It's from this time, too, that (old) School of Management faculty, already highly unionised, became more involved in the local union in far larger numbers, taking on officer roles within the branch, as well as deploying management-research expertise in support of its various campaigns. One such area where we used our scholarly or professional skills to inform union activity was the University of Leicester's governance structures and its finances. We turn to this in the next chapter, replicating, extending and generalising analysis we initially conducted in the service of mobilising university employees against their employer. Such Critical Management Studies- and (critical) political economy-informed hostility to University of Leicester's managers gave them good reason to seek our dismissal.

CHAPTER 5

MAGIC BEANS: ON FINANCE AND CORPORATE GOVERNANCE

> My experience is pretty scarce, locally.
> – Gary Dixon, Chair of University of Leicester Council[1]

> The page of an accounts book is there for your use, like a love poem.
> – Thomas Cromwell, as imagined by Hilary Mantel[2]

To understand the contemporary university, we must understand the (unchosen) circumstances of those who make it, including those who make their livelihoods within it. Those circumstances include the university's governance structures and its finances or, more accurately, the financial logics that increasingly seem to determine the university's activities. The two issues are entwined – which is why we treat them together in this chapter. The various governance reforms we discuss have facilitated finance's greater dominance, whilst financial logics demand more 'efficient', more 'business-like' structures of governance. There is much to be uncovered.

We begin by summarising the history of university governance, from the reforms of various Thatcher governments onwards. There has been a systematic expulsion from universities' governing bodies of scholarly expertise, that is, of university workers. As these governing bodies have come to be dominated by those with 'scarcer' experiences – by which Gary Dixon simply means experience in business – the nature of decision-making has changed too. Without the more heterogenous and multidimensional knowledges and ethics of a community of scholars – even a relatively elite and homogenous one in socio-economic terms – the more universalising logic of metrics has assumed ever greater significance. Money, of course, is the universalising metric par excellence. Beneath the braggadocio of the chair of the University of Leicester Council lies banality. His 'experience' is not at all 'scarce'. In fact, when finance and its logics are allowed to dominate, a process that accelerated under Gary Dixon, we suffer a reversion to the mean. Almost every sense of the word *mean*, including mediocre, is applicable here. It's in the university's annual financial statements that we see the recurrent use of the phrases 'sector norm' and 'sector average'. The privileging of such financial metrics to drive strategy reveals university leaders' meanness of vision. The resultant treatment of the university community – in particular staff and students – reveals their malevolence. Much of the chapter focuses on the University of Leicester, but its history and lessons are of much wider relevance. Senior figures in many other institutions are similarly seeking to hollow out university governance – if they haven't already – and are embracing financial logics as a means of guiding decisions. What happened at Leicester is *normal*.

The forgetting of universities' charitable status

Legally, universities in the UK are charities, but charities of a particular type. Most English universities are so-called exempt charities and are regulated by the Office for Students, and, before that the Higher Education Funding Council for England (HEFCE), rather than the Charity Commission.[3] Universities' charitable status dates back four centuries to Elizabethan times; it was restated in the Charities Act of 2006, which, according to legal scholar Mary Synge, 'offered a brave, if inadequate, reminder that universities are charities and subject to charity law'. As Synge remarks, in the many recent accounts detailing 'multiple concerns regarding the university sector, including top-down management and poor accountability, excessive executive pay and unmanaged conflicts of interest, falling educational standards and grade inflation, ... the charitable status of universities, and the significance of that status, is strikingly absent'.[4]

Synge explains what's at stake, regarding the duties and responsibilities of those entrusted with administering a charity, which 'include a duty to act in accordance with the charity's constitution, exercising powers only for proper purposes and with appropriate care and skill':

> This duty to act in the best interests of the charity is paramount, but may be little understood. In the context of advancing education, a 'functional purpose' – as opposed to an investment purpose of generating income and/or capital growth – is appropriate; this means in the best interests of fulfilling those purposes for the benefit of society generally. The strategic goals, set by a university's governing body, of maximising growth in income or student numbers, for example, might well be in the best interests of the institution's finances, but that is not the same thing at all.[5]

Unfortunately, the promise of the 2006 Act – and the subsequent Charities Act 2011 – has not been realised. There are multiple problems. The Office for Students (OfS) does not scrutinise universities with the same rigour – regarding financial impropriety, financial controls, conflicts of interests and disclosures of interlocking directorships, for example – that charities are subjected to by the Charity Commission.

There's a general absence of transparency and the problem has worsened since the OfS replaced the HEFCE in 2018. The OfS, for instance, has removed the obligation on universities to 'report serious incidents', including 'unverifiable donations over £25,000, abuse of students, disqualification of trustees and alleged or real links to terrorism'. A university is not even obliged to make easily accessible its constitution, trustees' details, corporate governance arrangements, or information about its charitable status and objectives. In sum, 'weak enforcement mechanisms render charities [in particular, exempt universities] especially susceptible to abuse'.[6]

This forgetting of universities' charitable status has occurred over the decades during which universities have become more like businesses. Over this period scholars have diagnosed and described, bemoaned and decried the 'entrepreneurial university' and the 'managerial university', 'academic capitalism' and 'the decline of donnish dominion' as well as the 'proletarianisation' of academics and academic labour. Perhaps, as Martin Parker has suggested, the university as a whole is becoming more like a business school.[7]

Shaping for efficiency

A university's supreme governing body is its Board, Council (as with University of Leicester) or, in Scotland, Court. It is 'responsible', to quote from the University of Leicester governance page, 'for taking all final decisions on matters of fundamental concern to the University, including our academic mission and strategic direction'. Council appoints the vice-chancellor or principal, the de facto chief executive who, along with an executive board and/or senior leadership team, makes day-to-day and executive decisions, whilst remaining accountable to Council. Alongside Council are typically two other bodies – which often nominate members of Council: Senate, which is made up mostly of academics, and Court, an external 'stakeholder' body.

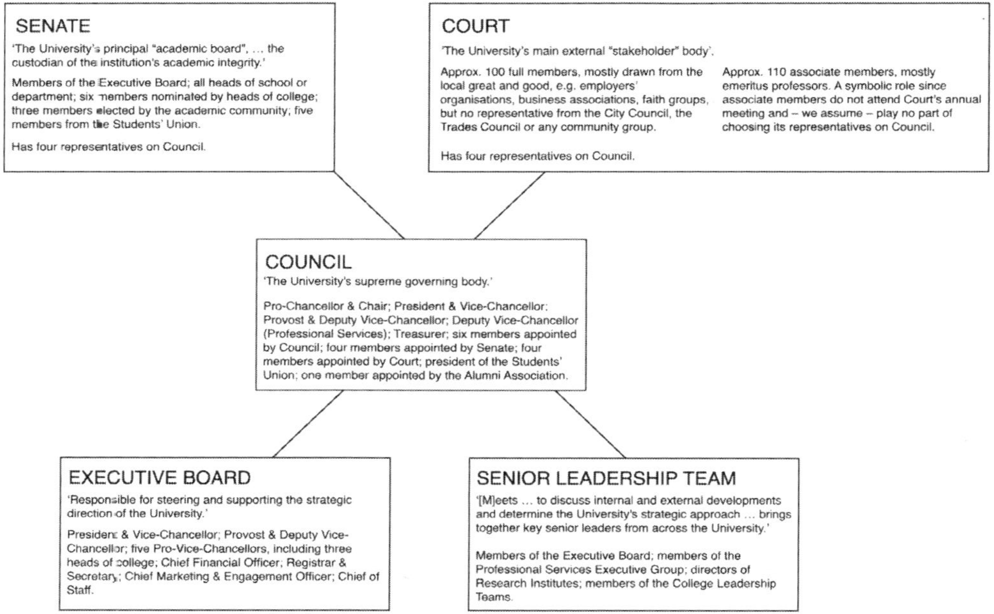

Governing the University of Leicester

In 1984 the University Grants Committee (UGC) recommended that 'every university should examine its machinery of government, to ensure that its decision-making processes are effective'.[8] The same year, the Committee of Vice-Chancellors and Principals, whose chair happened to be Leicester University's VC Maurice Shock, established a Steering Committee for Efficiency Studies in Universities. This twelve-man[9] Steering Committee was itself chaired by Alex Jarratt, chairman of publishing conglomerate Reed International PLC and Chancellor of Birmingham University. The other members were three vice-chancellors; the Master of a Cambridge college; the Principal of London Business School; a university registrar; Professor Sir Peter Swinnerton-Dyer, the Cambridge mathematician who chaired the University Grants Committee; the Chairman of Cadburys Schweppes PLC; the finance directors Plessey PLC and the Ford Motor Company; and the prime minister's Adviser on Efficiency. Besides the absence of any women, nor was there any staff or trade union representation.

Published in 1985, the Jarratt Report, was based on case studies of six universities and contains no criticisms of universities' various 'outputs'. The authors are glowing in their praise, noting that universities 'make outstanding contributions to our national life', benefit from a low 'wastage rate' and 'play the leading role in maintaining and advancing scholarship in the humanities and the social sciences, where their achievements are high by international standards'. '[A]ny policy that diminished the role and status of the universities would damage many aspects of our educational, cultural and industrial life.' Despite this (in their own words) 'a constant theme in this Report' was a perceived 'need for change throughout the university system'. The committee's members never once stopped to reflect whether UK universities' 'outstanding contributions' might be possible *because* of the 'inefficiencies' they believed they had identified. Their task (as they judged it) was 'to examine whether management structures and systems were effective in ensuring that decisions are fully informed, that optimum value is obtained from the use of resources, that policy objectives are clear, and that accountabilities are clear and monitored'. But perhaps the low 'wastage rate' indicated that something close to 'optimum value' was *already* being 'obtained from the use of resources'.

Features which, 'complicate[d] the managerial and administrative process' included: the 'immense range and variety of activity undertaken within each university'; 'divided loyalties' which see academics seeing 'their academic discipline as more important than the long-term well-being of the university which houses them'; the 'tradition of self-government' that can be used 'to delay or block difficult but necessary decisions'; the 'tenure issue', which 'has inhibited change and even the discussion of change'; lack of regular formal appraisal of academic staff; insufficiently powerful and assertive Councils, which has 'increased the potential for Senates to resist change and to exercise a natural conservatism'; and heterogeneity amongst universities and their governance structures, including a 'wide range of management styles and modes of operating [of VCs]… In some cases the Vice-Chancellor sees his [*sic*] role quite clearly as providing leadership and exercising executive authority; in others he sees his role primarily as that of a chairman seeking consensus'.

Unsurprising conclusions followed from the diagnosis. Universities should be recognised 'first and foremost [as] corporate enterprises to which subsidiary units and individual academics are responsible and accountable'. Vice-chancellors should adopt 'a clear role as the executive leader… [with] the necessary authority to carry [this role] out'. University Councils should 'assert their responsibilities in governing their institutions'. 'Reliable and consistent performance indicators' should be developed. The Jarratt Report also includes a cryptic remark on academic freedom, which we take up in the next chapter: 'So far as the universities are concerned, we share their conviction that academic excellence is crucially dependent on academic freedom. But they should be on their guard against confusing freedom with licence.' Two years after the publication of the Jarrett Report, the UGC reported that many of its recommendations were being implemented 'across the board'.[10]

In the 1990s, both the Committee on Standards in Public Life, chaired by Baron Nolan, and the National Committee of Inquiry into Higher Education, chaired by Ronald Dearing, considered university governance. The Nolan Committee's first report, published in 1995, established Seven Principles of Public Life: selflessness, integrity, objectivity, accountability, openness, honesty and leadership. In its second report, published a year later, the Committee stated that it had found 'no evidence' of 'substantial misconduct' in universities. We leave it to the reader to judge the conduct of the University of Leicester's leaders against the seven Nolan Principles.

Dearing's review of higher education was the most comprehensive since that chaired by Lionel Robbins in the early 1960s. Slightly more diverse than the Steering Committee for Efficiency Studies in Universities, four of the Dearing Committee's members were women, including a former general secretary of the printers' union SOGAT (Society of Graphical and Allied Trades) and the headteacher of a state school. The committee also included a students' union officer. Apart from this trio, membership was dominated by senior university leaders and chairmen, chief executives and directors of large private companies. Their report, published in 1996, is important – infamous – for many reasons. One of its ninety-three recommendations, for instance, was that 'graduates in employment should make a greater contribution to the costs of higher education in the future', thus paving the way for the current (almost bankrupt) fees-and-debt funding model: 'If our vision of a learning society is to be realised, students will have … to make a greater investment in their own futures'. Another was that government funding should be shifted 'away from block grant towards a system in which funding follows the student', thus introducing greater competition into the system. In terms of resources and governance, Dearing echoes Jarratt – and foreshadows the *We can't be complacent* rhetoric of Tony Blair a decade later. The report first acknowledges that 'arrangements now in place are working well', before moving on to set out 'ways in which the arrangements could – and need to – be improved'.

> Looking ahead to the next 20 years, a sustained effort to improve the effective and efficient use of resources by institutions is required ... Institutions need to satisfy government, students and other funders that they are making a contribution to the total costs of higher education by continually seeking better value from their resources. This is a requirement in almost all aspects of national life and is part of the new compact with higher education.

Besides magicking into existence a 'new compact with higher education', the Dearing Report here is long on generalities but short on both evidence and concrete suggestions.[11] It falls back on assessments, by the National Audit Office and other unnamed interlocutors from outside the sector, that although 'institutions have achieved improvements in value for money, ... scope for further improvement remains' and that they 'need to apply a wide range of management skills and experience if they are to survive and prosper, particularly at a time of tight financial constraints'. It suggests that 'institutions might be able to move to a different [lower] cost curve were they able and willing to adopt more radical models for some of their work'. It recommends 'a more corporate approach' in terms of management style and that departmental heads (amongst others) 'are helped to develop management expertise and skills to help them contribute to securing value for money'. It stresses the necessity of realising potential gains in 'institutional effectiveness and efficiency' from Communications and Information Technology. In other words: more management, 'better' tech, work smarter (though not, presumably in this idealistic rendering, harder).

Ensuring that universities 'meet their obligations to their wider constituencies' seems to be rather low on Dearing's list of priorities, though it is mentioned. Institutions 'therefore need to have in place a mechanism by which external constituencies can contribute their opinion and advice in a systematic and transparent way.' So-called Courts are flagged as an effective means of achieving this. In terms of universities' charitable status, whereas Jarratt in 1985 had dealt with the issue by declaring 'a need to separate operations which are incompatible with the legal status of the university as an educational charity', 12 years later, Dearing only acknowledges the issue in a single, factually incorrect sentence.[12]

In summary then, following Jarratt and Dearing, we've seen top-down management bolted onto structures that, in many institutions, have survived for a century or more.

We noted Jarratt's fretting over 'the potential for Senates to resist change and to exercise a natural conservatism'. At many universities – including Leicester – in recent decades this 'potential' has been much diminished by the removal from Senate of elected staff members and trade union-nominees, while heads of department are now almost exclusively appointed by vice-chancellors (or their proxies), as opposed to 'taking turns' or being elected by faculty. In other words, few vice-chancellors find their behaviour much impeded by their university's Senate. Voices more likely to be critical of the vice-chancellor and their right to manage have also been purged from many universities' stakeholder bodies. At Leicester, for instance, all professor emeritus members of Court were informed (by the chair of Council) in 2015 that henceforth they would only be 'associate members', an honorary role, since they would no longer be entitled to attend meetings nor play any part in the appointment of Council members. Remaining on this body were mostly representatives of the great and the good, individuals drawn from business associations, employers' organisations, faith groups and so on – but no one from the city or county councils, the trades council or any community group.

To try to understand the university's priorities – at least those of its vice-chancellor, executive board and Council – we now turn to its accounts. It turns out they reveal much about university leaders' activities and their choices.[13]

Pop goes the weasel...

This 'streamlining' or 'modernisation' of both Senate and its Court is just one instance of the way that events at the University of Leicester, especially following Bob Burgess's retirement in 2014, are perhaps indicative of what was intended for the sector all along. Jarratt and Dearing both recommended stronger and 'more effective' governance structures, with greater clarity regarding the vice-chancellor's role as chief executive. When Paul Boyle replaced Burgess as vice-chancellor he took on a new title, as we recounted in Chapter 1: as *President* and Vice-Chancellor. The rationale offered for this was that it provided a clearer signal to external audiences that he was indeed the man in charge. But to internal audiences, in particular to university employees, Boyle's role was rather less clear – and the same is true of Boyle's successor, Nishan Canagarajah.

Where Burgess was hands-on and appeared genuinely interested in scholarship, Boyle was a bean counter, mostly concerned with metrics, financial and otherwise. Moreover, he was a bean counter who delegated the concrete activity of counting and managing those beans to others. For much of his five years in charge, Boyle simply wasn't there, a style of leadership that Canagarajah has kept up: avoiding representatives of trade unions; avoiding student representatives; rarely engaging with the university's committees; only meeting with departmental-level staff in the most mediated and managed situations. To manage the University of Leicester on a day-to-day basis – activities that include negotiating with trade unions – the University Council in 2018 created, as we saw in Chapter 3, an entirely new post, that of deputy vice-chancellor, with an associated salary of around £200,000. In this new governance and management regime, it is not clear exactly what the role is of the president and vice-chancellor. It seems to include much globe-trotting, drumming up business for the university and attempting to broker international 'partnerships'. (Only a handful of VCs spent more than Boyle on hotel accommodation and air fares – almost all in business or first class, of course.)[14] The point here is that, for university employees and for their trade union representatives, there has been and continues to be little clarity regarding lines of authority. Who is in charge? Who is making the decisions? The vice-chancellor? The deputy vice-chancellor? Or, as we increasingly came to wonder, the chair of Council?

We've noted that the requirements for *greater efficiency* and *better value for money* are themes that pervade both Jarratt and Dearing, whilst many of both reports' recommendations boil down to some variant of *more management*. There is plenty of evidence of this – and more – in the University of Leicester financial statements – not to mention the lived experience of employees.

In 1999, the year of Burgess's arrival as VC, the University of Leicester's income was £123 million – about £223 million in 2023 prices. Its expenditure was a little higher, resulting in a small financial deficit of around 1%. The University employed around 2900 people and its staff costs made up roughly 59% of its total expenditure. When Burgess retired, a decade and a half later, the university's income had grown by almost four-fifths and its expenditure by two-thirds. This gap between receipts and spending opened up in 2006/07 – before then, the two had tracked each other closely – and from this year, the university began making annual operating surpluses, which ranged from £6 million to, in 2014/15, £17 million – 5.5% of income.[15] Staff numbers also grew – by almost a third by 2017/18 – though they have subsequently contracted by around a tenth in the subsequent four years, a result of three restructuring programmes involving mass redundancies, both compulsory and 'voluntary' (the most recent of which saw our own expulsion from the university). The growth in student numbers has been greater. This is surely what Jarratt and Dearing would recognise as greater efficiency and better value for money, especially when we consider the stagnation of university salaries over the past two decades – except for those at the top.[16] The business minds that dominated Jarratt's and Dearing's committees would approve of the surpluses that universities like Leicester strive for – and often achieve. They would surely applaud Leicester bosses' 2021/22 achievement of pushing staff costs as a proportion of income down to 53.6% – below the 'sector average' of 55% – a target that had previously proved elusive.

This 'sector average' target is bizarre for multiple reasons. First, the financial statements, where it makes repeated appearances, provide no explanation regarding the calculation of such a 'sector average'. It's a context-free number, which ignores institutions' heterogeneity. Second, there is no attempt to justify *why* this sector average is an appropriate target – in 2016, Leicester UCU described this management method as *trying to achieve excellence by aiming for the average*. Third, the most important factor in education is the human one: it's strange that university bosses don't boast about *how much* they spend on their staff.

What's perhaps most astonishing about university staff numbers are the categories of staff in which growth and contraction has occurred. At University of Leicester the number of academics and researchers has grown by one-sixth over the past two decades and remains stable at around 40% of the total. But the number of staff categorised as 'administration, library, computer and other related' is now two and a half times greater. Its proportion of the total has more than doubled, from 12% to 26%, with spending on 'administration and central services' also doubling as a proportion of total expenditure, such that it now consumes around a fifth of all resources.[17] Such centralisation greatly facilitates the trend towards authoritarian leadership. This is the *more management* prescribed by Jarratt and Dearing.

We need to pause here to unpack these data. Many professional services staff (those categorised as 'administration, library, computer and other related') perform roles essential for the running of a university. We need IT specialists, time-tablers, counsellors, librarians and others who communicate with students on the 'frontline'. These people make possible the jobs of those who teach and do research. But it is also obvious to everyone who works in a university that the job of an academic or researcher has not become easier over the past two decades: as the number of administrators has risen, so has the administrative burden on scholars. It is not possible from the data we have here to untangle the chains of causation, but our guess is that many of these new university administration jobs are 'bullshit jobs'.[18] In fact, an increasing share of a typical academic's job is also bullshit: form-filling and box-ticking; complying with the reporting strictures of the Teaching Excellence Framework, the Research Excellence Framework, of 'quality assurance'; paperworking the various and proliferating accreditations, charters and awards. There is a mutual imposition of work here: administrators are ordered to administer and manage these multiplying tasks, including eliciting the necessary information from academics.

But as David Graeber, who coined the term, stresses, a bullshit job is rarely the fault of the person whose misfortune it is to perform it. Indeed, anecdotally, many employees themselves describe many aspects of their jobs as bullshit. Many of the new university administrators are themselves highly qualified and what is most tragic and wasteful is that many are themselves aspiring scholars and academics. They are interested in ideas, they read books and, when they can, publish articles and attend conferences. Offered the chance of redeployment, such that they directly support students' learning, we are confident many would leap at it. Others would be keen to retrain in much-needed roles as pedagogical specialists or counsellors.

It is not so hard for us to imagine a 'just transition' of the university, in which many more of its existing employees are drawn into the scholarly community, which at the same time allows students to receive the more focused, pedagogical attention and care that they currently lack. In the summer of 2020, Leicester UCU suggested the above as part of a set of 'alternative paths' through the COVID-19 pandemic – an opportunity, in fact, to remake the University of Leicester in its second century. The university's senior management first ignored our proposals and then scorned them as 'unrealistic'. But with national figures telling us that 88% of university employees feel pessimistic about the future of higher education, with alarmingly high proportions of both staff and students suffering from stress and/or mental distress, it's not an exaggeration to say the entire sector is in crisis.[19] As with so many crises we face as citizens of the world, it seems increasingly apparent to us that radical solutions are the only realistic ones.

Widgets not workers; buildings before brains

If university bosses are not investing in 'human capital', and, indeed, are determined to push down staff costs, where are they choosing to channel resources? The answer is buildings and other forms of fixed capital. 'Investment in [the university's] campus to ensure there are state-of-the-art facilities for our staff and students is essential for [the university's] future success.'[20] Machines, of course, don't talk back to managers, they don't go slow and they don't go on strike. We'll discuss buildings – and the associated financial implications – in the next sections. Here we'll make a few remarks about investment in equipment, including IT equipment, and on licensing of systems – the 'better tech' prescribed by Dearing.

It is not so easy to disentangle spending on systems from spending on the IT equipment that it's often bundled in with. But so-called *ed-tech* is big business. We know of no university that does not have some form of 'virtual learning environment', provided by a company such as Blackboard Inc., and many universities are investing in the hardware and software necessary for the audio and visual recording of lectures, courtesy of another privately owned corporation, Panopto. A third set of systems revolves around so-called attendance management: at Leicester, this required student ID card readers and associated software in every teaching space.

There are several matters of concern here. First, it's extremely hard to come by information either on the revenues and profitability of companies such as Blackboard and Panopto, or on the amount that any particular institution pays them. Their names do not appear in financial accounts and FOI requests seeking such information are repelled on the grounds that it is 'commercially sensitive'. Second, such systems are typically introduced by senior managers, without any consultation with teaching or other staff, often against the clear wishes of teachers, who may have multiple grounds of objection. Third, the pedagogical value of many of these technologies is often limited, if not actually negative. Panopto-captured lectures are often of poor quality (unless heavily edited – a task that a typical lecturer has neither time nor training to do), for instance, and may discourage both student attendance at the live event and the active participation of some students who do attend.[21] For its part, Blackboard is widely derided as 'clunky', 'user-unfriendly', and 'not-fit-for-purpose' by the unfortunate teachers compelled to use it. If these facilities are 'state-of-the-art', then this 'art' is in a terrible state.

Finally, these systems and technologies may actually serve nefarious ends. Many lecturers fear that recorded lectures or materials uploaded to Blackboard may be reviewed by managers as part of performance-management processes. These lectures and materials might also be used as a means of undermining the impact of striking teachers or used more generally to replace existing classroom provision. These changes entail an opening up of the labour process to managerial inspection and intervention and, at best, an etiolation of the relationship between academic staff and the means of production of another significant part of the academic product.

For its part, electronic attendance management systems – highly visible at University of Leicester, with signage exhorting students to 'Touch GREEN to be SEEN' – do the work of policing the UK's border, with universities having obligations to the Home Office's Visas and Immigration department, forcing lecturers, seminar tutors and professional service colleagues (often themselves migrants) to perform the role of border agents. This technological apparatus in fact comes with its 'own *un*seen, a whole ecology of (in)visibility that can show something only by hiding a considerable part of its mechanisms'. For '[w]hat we don't see are the emails sent to "international students" ... in which they are informed, with "kind regards", of having been withdrawn for non-attendance. And what even the recipients can't immediately see, as those emails carefully leave this aspect implicit, is that termination of their studies implies the suspension of their visa and... their possible deportation.'[22]

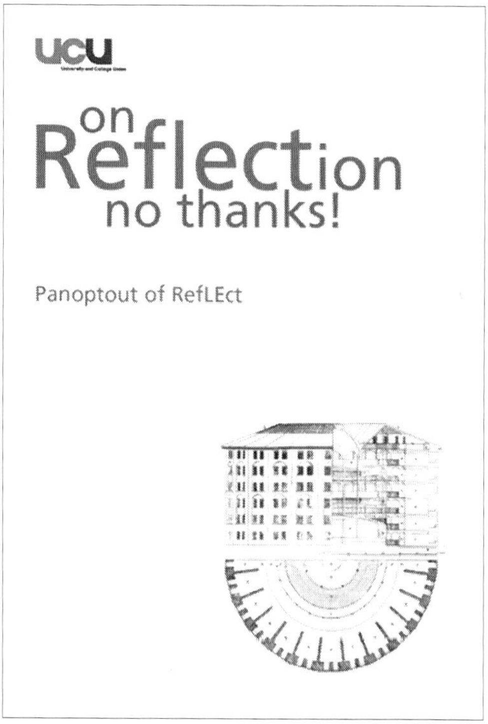

Leicester UCU contested the way university managers sought to impose compulsory 'lecture capture' in late 2016. Bosses called their system Reflect. It used software sold by Seattle-based ed-tech company Panopto. We don't know what either the initial or the ongoing costs of the system are.

'Touch GREEN to be SEEN': We don't know how much bosses paid for the university's attendance management system, but we do know that such systems serve state interests in managing the UK's border, not pedagogy. This image was produced by Leicester UCU to accompany the article it published critiquing the system, 'The green and the unseen'.

State of the Art? This small seminar room has two projectors and four 'smart' screens. It's one of several similarly equipped rooms in the university's Ken Edwards Building – former home of the School of Management and our old stamping ground – and dozens across campus. When the decision was taken to 'modernise' in this manner, no one we know was consulted on what they thought they most needed in terms of pedagogical support, nor about the associated costs and, more importantly, opportunity costs, of the technology which was adopted. We have never seen any of the smart screens being used independently of the main projectors and none of us was offered any training in their use. *Photo: Deborah Toner*

In a nutshell, this architecture of hardware, software and systems does little to enhance the university as a space of open enquiry and learning. Instead, its purpose is predominantly governmental, contributing to the algorithmic management of both students and staff, especially the increasing numbers of precarious staff. The scale of this questionable expenditure, however, is completely dwarfed by spending on new buildings.

Building ghostly forms – or, the spectres of university finance

During Bob Burgess's 15 years as University of Leicester VC he was nicknamed 'Bob the Builder', a not entirely complimentary sobriquet. When Paul Boyle took office in 2014 he told the *Leicester Mercury* that 'he was inheriting a "strong estate" where much work had already been done to ensure it was highly attractive to students. ... on the whole, it's in great shape."'[23] This didn't prevent Boyle from initiating, in 2016, his own capital-spending programme, with projects totalling £428 million. One of the first of these projects – relatively small in value, but significant in terms of its symbolism – was the half-million-pound refurbishment of the admin building's reception and 'executive corridor', parts of the university rarely if ever visited by students.[24] University of Leicester bosses aren't alone in their capital dreams. Total capital spending for the sector has averaged £4.6 billion a year for the five years to July 2022 and, during that period, twenty-four institutions have spent more than Leicester.

Capital spending is not so easy to trace, appearing in the financial statements in derivative and, increasingly, in ghostly form. But it's certainly growing. In Bob the Builder's final five years (2010/11–2014/15) around £168 million was spent acquiring fixed assets, predominantly buildings. In the most recent five years (2017/18–2021/22) the figure is £236 million.[25] This is a real-terms increase of more than one-fifth.

While the manifestation of capital expenditure on a university's balance sheet is not straightforward, the effects of decisions to undertake it are more long lasting. Infrastructure spending is financed either from grants, accumulated surpluses or, increasingly, from borrowing. It thus appears both as interest payments and as imputed depreciation costs. New builds, for instance, are assumed to depreciate over 50 years: thus, a building whose upfront cost is £50 million will appear every year for 50 years in the statement of income and expenditure as a £1 million addition to the depreciation total. Looking at these figures for the University of Leicester, there are only two years in the past fifteen where this depreciation total hasn't risen. For the most recent year, 2021/22, imputed depreciation costs were £28.2 million, more than 7% of total expenditure and 15% of the amount spent on staff. In 2006/07 these figures were £6.7 million, 6% and 3.6% respectively.

To stress, these spending commitments are baked in for the next half-century and the University of Leicester is not alone here, with many other institutions also expanding their estates aggressively. Across the sector, depreciation figures are around one-fifth higher in real terms now than they were five years ago. What's happening here (we think) is that vice-chancellors have taken advantage of eroded wages, and indeed have themselves helped to suppress those wages, in order to pursue ambitious infrastructure projects. But those very infrastructure projects result in new items – imputed depreciation sums – in universities' financial accounts that then appear to show that money is too tight to grant university workers salary rises that even match inflation. In other words, in this vicious circle, eroded pay and further eroded pay is the cause and the result. But not all universities have behaved in the same way, certainly not at the same time. In 2015/16, for instance, Leicester was mid-table in terms of capital expenditure. Four years later, only fifteen institutions (out of more than 150) spent more. What we've observed is a systemic hollowing-out of governance structures that has enabled a few individuals, including those with 'pretty scarce experience, locally', to shift the institution onto a new, high-risk, and highly indebted trajectory.

At some point in 2016, the University of Leicester effectively breached what are known as 'loan covenants' with two of its three principal creditors.[26] (The covenants attached to a loan exist for a very good reason, namely, to ensure that the borrower remains in a position to maintain the payments to the lender. To that extent, they are protection for both debtor and creditor.) University leaders sought and were granted a temporary exemption from these covenants, on the grounds of 'exceptional restructuring costs'. (We mentioned this restructuring in Chapter 1: it involved around 200 compulsory redundancies.) What happened next is instructive. A naïve observer might think that the best thing to do in such a situation, having effectively breached loan covenants but enjoying a one-year period of grace in terms of the consequences, might be to quickly get one's borrowing under control. Specifically, to take steps to ensure the university's financial and broader institutional conduct once more conformed to the constraints stipulated by the loan agreements. One might have thought that a leadership team focused on ensuring it delivered its responsibilities with the utmost probity would be concerned about that. However, this is not what transpired.

Instead, the university's senior leadership team decided that the best way forward would be to swell overall long-term borrowing, initially by £52 million, an increase of around 71%. The entirety of this increased debt is accounted for by three so-called private placements with two US insurance funds, Lincoln National Life and Pacific Life. Private placements require no prospectus and are very hard to subject to any scrutiny, since their terms are… well, private.[27] Unsurprisingly, the university's interest payment commitments also leapt at this point, from roughly £3 million each year up until 2017/18, to around £4.5 million per annum thereafter. Part of this new debt was incurred to fund some of the £428 million capital investment programme mentioned above, which involved spending on a new home for the School of Business, the redevelopment of the students' union building, and a new Space Park. None of these projects were unproblematic.

Even more troubling was one particular new joint venture, a 50-year partnership, which seems to involve the university bearing the lion's share of the potential risk, whilst private investors garner the lion's share of potential benefits. The details of the agreement are both arcane – since it involves 'clever' financial engineering – and obscure – since they are mostly contained in 'reserved' minutes and other documents not publicly available. But we can piece together at least its main elements from cryptic lines in the university's financial statements and minutes that have been published, from the details of similar deals that have been made public, and from the public statements of partners who believe they have more to celebrate than university bosses. The new venture, dated 2019, involves: an investment company, Equitix Ltd; a constructor, Engie; a financial services provider, BNY [Bank of New York] Mellon Corporate Trustee Services Ltd; a Bermuda-headquartered insurance operation, Assured Guaranty (Europe) plc (AGE); two new University of Leicester-affiliated shell companies, UOL Investments Ltd and UOL FC Ltd (both incorporated in 2018); and another new legal entity, a so-called special purpose vehicle, Freemen's Common Village LLP.

We should first explain the magic of securitisation, a term and practice that entered into public consciousness following the financial crisis of 2008, since the so-called subprime mortgages that were the initial locus of that crisis had been 'securitised'. Securitisation is a particular form of financial engineering, a way in which an entity, a corporation or indeed a university, may raise capital. It involves selling to investors part of the anticipated income from an asset and using the money thus received to purchase or build the asset in the first place. An income stream treated in this fashion is said to have been securitised. Naturally, the investors will require some collateral to insure themselves against any shortfall in the hoped-for income stream. Normally this will include the asset for which they are providing the funds, but, in the case of buildings, it may also include the land on which they are built. Part of securitisation's 'magic' is that the special purpose vehicle created in any particular instance – in this case Freemen's Commons Village LLP – is off-balance sheet, meaning neither the details nor the underlying debt obligations appear in the financial accounts.

Opened in 2022, Freemen's Common Village constitutes accommodation for 1,164 students, plus associated communal areas and cafés, some teaching space, and a multistorey carpark. The university's share of the entity itself is 10% but it has also provided what we can only interpret as a guarantee on that entity's liabilities to other investors, which took the form of £16.5 million held in an escrow account.[28] In other words, 90% of this new 'Village' is owned by financial investors, who receive dividends from student rents, presumably leasing fees, carparking charges and so on. (We can only speculate, of course, given the private nature of the deal.)[29] But to ameliorate the risk of investors' potential losses, the university has stumped up that £16.5 million.

There is an even more alarming aspect to the deal. The function of BNY Mellon Corporate Trustee Services Ltd is that of 'security trustee'.[30] This means that Freemen's Common Village LLP will be subject to certain 'enforcement events' if it allows certain 'events of default' to occur. Precisely what these events are, we do not know, because they are specified in a senior finance document which we cannot access. What we do know, however, is that both defaults and enforcement are financial in nature and will culminate in the handover of property – several folios of land of Freemen's Common – to the trustees if lesser remedies are not forthcoming. In

Whose security? Livelihoods and University of Leicester assets are at risk as a result of the Freemen's Common development, which includes accommodation for students, teaching space and a multistorey carpark. *Photo: Deborah Toner*

other words, part of the University of Leicester's estate has become collateral for the financial obligations of Freemen's Common Village LLP to the trustees.

Other actors have been keener than the University of Leicester to publicise the financial aspects of the venture. One such source is the insurer Assured Guaranty (Europe) plc (AGE): 'As a result of the guarantee from AGE, the bonds [on the Freeman's Common development] are rated AA by S&P Global Ratings. The underlying project is rated BBB–.'[31] In the nomenclature of the S&P ratings agency, BBB– ('triple B minus') is the lowest, the most risky, of 'investment grade' ratings, just one ranking above so-called junk bonds. Yet, by some financial alchemy, this 'lower-medium risk' project has been transformed into a 'high grade' investment for Assured Guaranty's clients – and a double A rating is just two ranks below the highest possible AAA, associated with the sovereign debt of countries such as Switzerland and the United States. This can mean only one thing: somebody, somewhere is absorbing the real risks attendant on the project before any investment opportunity is presented to potential investors.

Again, there is an absence of documentation in the public domain – the bonds, like the debt that enabled the university to participate in the set up that issued them, are all private placements. Therefore, our ability to understand the specifics of the deal is limited and again we must speculate. But our best guess is that it is the University of Leicester that has absorbed that risk gap – it appears to be the only party to the deal that has any capacity to generate the real underlying financial flows necessary to pay the financial obligations attendant upon it. The risk may have been trammelled by the university paying the premiums of insurance upon it and/or it may be through other contractual guarantees.

Bonds to the value of £124 million have been issued through the Freemen's Common Village special purpose vehicle. They're repayable over 40 years at an undisclosed, but index-linked rate of interest and, importantly, are 'asset-wrapped' – where the assets in question are Freemen's Common itself, the land, and any buildings thereon. In the event of default on the part of the borrower – Freemen's Common Village LLP – these will be forfeited to the bondholders via the 'security trustee' – BNY Mellon Corporate Trustee Services Ltd. We don't know the precise conditions under which the Freemen's Common estate will be forfeited. However, we do know that the special purpose vehicle will be required to set student rents at a level which will service the bonds and pay for the maintenance of the accommodation at a level competitive with the local market. The university, for its part, will need to deliver sufficient numbers of its students to maintain a specified occupancy level.

The implications of this have been starkly revealed over the two years of the COVID-19 pandemic. At various points university leaders 'lured' students back to campuses with the promise of shared-air teaching. In the words of one commentator, 'That promise can be safely broken only once rental contracts are signed and income streams flowing. What university managers have done this time is so clearly unethical that few are prepared to justify it by the usual appeals to economic necessity.'[32] University of Leicester students were amongst those so 'tricked' and in their case the trickery was even less ethical given both that the city of Leicester was in lockdown for a full year from April 2020, with local restrictions in place even when national ones were eased, and the parlous state of at least some of the university's accommodation, with occupants complaining of mould-infested flats and refusing to pay rent.[33]

In some ways, the Freemen's Common bond is a piece of clever financial engineering. Its 'cleverness' lies in the fact that the £124 million is not, technically speaking, a loan taken out by the University of Leicester. It does not, therefore, need to appear as a liability on its balance-sheet and does not interfere with pre-existing loan covenants. It is, as the financial statements for 2018/19 are at pains to point out, 'off balance-sheet'. It remains the case, however, that the only income with which Freemen's Common Village LLP will be able to service its £124 million debt will come from its student residences, shops, and teaching facilities. Whilst university leaders can truthfully claim that the assets placed at hazard in order to access this finance, namely the Freemen's Common estate, are those of the special purpose vehicle (SPV) rather than itself, this is only the case because a charge on them has been provided by the university to the SPV as a preliminary to the issue of bonds.

Life in the breach

Leicester is not the only university whose decision-makers have availed themselves of such financial technology. As far as we can tell, Assured Guaranty has also 'wrapped' bonds for six other institutions: the universities of Edinburgh (in 2013), London (2016), Essex (2017 and 2021), Sussex (2017), York (2019), and Kingston (2020).[34] We're particularly concerned by two aspects of these forays. First, of course, is the increased exposure to risk of 'the university'. As we have seen, we believe that part of the University of Leicester's estate has been put up as collateral and thus the university risks forfeiting this, in the event that the investment does not perform as promised. To ward off such forfeiture, however, university leaders will seek to shift costs and risks onto students, through 'trickery', as with the COVID-19 situation, and through increased rents. It will shift these costs to staff as with the sorts of redundancy programmes that saw us lose our jobs, and the ongoing threat of redundancy will remain a threat, one which might have the 'happy' side-effect for university management of 'disciplining' the workforce.

These issues are sector-wide. In the two years from 2018/19 to 2020/21 the UK's universities between them increased their income by 5%, almost £2.2 billion, while shrinking expenditure by 6.5%, more than £2.9 billion. Almost all of these 'cost savings' were due to an 11% reduction in staff costs. 'Restructuring costs' for the three years – 2018/19, 2019/20 and 2020/21 – totalled almost £400 million, suggesting that Nishan Canagarajah was not the only vice-chancellor to find in the COVID-19 months the 'perfect moment' to execute redundancies. Large as these restructuring costs are, they are dwarfed by interest and other finance costs: these averaged £875 million a year for these three years.[35]

The second concern is governance. Who is taking these decisions and on whose behalf? Who is responsible for providing checks and balances? Before exploring these questions, we will pause again to note two other troubling moments that occurred in late 2020 and early 2021. Recall that the University of Leicester effectively breached its covenants with two of its three principal lenders in 2016/17. In October 2020, we learned that the university once more had 'problems' with three of its five lenders.[36] Again we must resort to speculation. But in certain circumstances, when a company or institution is in danger of breaching, or has already breached, a covenant, some US placement lenders – such as Lincoln National Life and Pacific Life, both creditors of the University of Leicester – are likely to demand 'a seat at the table' – a role in the governance of the institution. We do not know if this was a possibility at Leicester, but we cannot rule it out.

Universities must normally publish their financial statements in mid-January, where these relate to accounts ending in July of the previous year. In 2021, the Office for Students relaxed the publication deadline a little, on account of the pandemic. The University of Leicester took full advantage of this extension – perfectly legal, of course – and, in the end, it was one of the last universities to publish its accounts for 2019/20, doing so only on the first day of March 2021. Why the delay? Of course, COVID-19 may have played its part. But we suspect, and yet again, we can only speculate, that the university's auditors, who must approve the accounts, were reluctant to do so. Their reluctance stemmed from doubts regarding whether the University of Leicester could be honestly described as a *going concern*, and indeed we find references to this in the unreserved minutes of a special meeting of University Council held on February 25.[37] The special meeting opened with the Chair, Gary Dixon, recording 'his recognition of the stresses and strains placed upon members of the Executive Board by the current strategic change programme'. It then dealt exclusively with the audit process, which had not been 'particularly smooth' and related financial issues, such as potential breaches of loan covenants, the establishment of further lines of short-term ('revolving') credit, and the *going concern* matter, a term that appears nine times in the minutes' four pages.[38] We also learn from these Council minutes that 'the external audit process had also highlighted some procedural issues and shortcomings inside the university which would need to be rectified in time for the next year's audit' and that a number of the university's 'specific operational areas … had been classified as High or Medium risk'. One of these was the Student Experience Recovery Plan, but no further details are forthcoming from the information available to us.

Going concern is an accounting term for a business or institution that has sufficient resources to meet its financial obligations when they fall due. An organisation's auditor cannot legally approve that organisation's accounts if it is not satisfied that it is a going concern – that it can meet its financial obligations. Of course, we must try to disentangle short-term stresses triggered by COVID-19 from the university's longer-term financial situation. Many universities, particularly the lowly ranked ones, struggled during the pandemic. The University of Leicester perhaps struggled more than many – it was one of only three to avail itself of the Bank of England's Covid Corporate Financing Facility, for instance.[39] But the university's vice-chancellor also insisted that the executive board's 'proposed changes underpin our long-term strategy for the University and are not determined by this year's financial position, which remains challenging'. When we strip out the presumably short-term 'emergency' borrowing, the longer-term direction of the University's financial 'strategy' seems clear.

At some point in 2016 the University of Leicester was in breach of some of the terms of roughly £76 million of long-term borrowing. University decision-makers' response to this breach was to unaccountably extend the borrowing. Six years later, the University's long-term liabilities totalled something like a quarter of a billion pounds, half of this buried in financial engineering and legal arcanery that obscure its nature. As part of this process, the university has sold off its rights to significant streams of the income that might have enabled the servicing of its ballooning debt and other liabilities. To understand how this came to pass, we have to return once more to the question of governance. One would imagine an institution with charitable status, such as a university, with a clear role contributing to public life, must have mechanisms in place to guard against inappropriate decision making.[40] And surely if oversight had not functioned as well as it might on occasion, those role holders responsible would be swiftly moved on. Let us have a look at some roles, responsibilities and timelines to see.

Again, the details are rather obscure, but three individuals and two committees of Council are key to the story.

The first individual is Gary Dixon, who became chair of Council, the university's 'supreme governing body', in August 2019, after serving as the university's treasurer. The role of its chair 'is separated from the role of the university's Chief Executive and Accountable Officer, the President and Vice-Chancellor.' When the Freemen's Common Village LLP was born on 2 August 2019, however, the University of Leicester had no permanent president and vice-chancellor – this being part of the interregnum between the reigns of Boyle and Canagarajah. Instead, Edmund Burke, deputy VC under both Boyle and Canagarajah, was acting vice-chancellor, a role he held from April until November of 2019. Burke is the second key individual. The third is Martyn Riddleston who, since 2011, held the most senior finance role in the university's salaried staff hierarchy, first as director of finance and then, upon the role's creation in April 2019, as chief financial officer.[41]

One role of the treasurer is to chair the University's Finance Committee, which 'monitors the University's overall financial health, advises on overall financial strategy, and provides oversight of key campus and capital projects and programmes.' This committee also 'advise[s] on borrowing policy, and to consider and approve proposals for borrowing and capital financing structures and related external funding arrangements, and the details of their terms, reporting as necessary to the Council.' The Finance Committee is kept in check by the Audit Committee, which 'provides oversight of the university's risk management, control and governance arrangements'. It is crucial here for effective corporate governance that the two committees be kept strictly independent. As the 2018/19 financial statements make clear: 'No member of the Audit Committee may also be a member of the Finance Committee, unless Council makes a formal decision to allow one Audit Committee member to sit on both.''This did not occur in 2018–19'.[42]

We do not know the precise make up of either of these committees since no minutes of their business are made available to university staff, students, or other stakeholders.[43] But we can glean from the terms of reference, membership, and constitution for 2019/20 that the deputy vice-chancellor (Burke) serves on the Finance Committee and the chief financial officer (Riddleston) is 'normally in attendance'. Both the deputy vice-chancellor and chief financial officer are also 'normally in attendance' at the Audit Committee.

In summary then, Martyn Riddleston (director of finance, then chief financial officer and later chief operating officer), Edmund Burke (deputy vice-chancellor), and Gary Dixon (chair of Council) all either chaired, sat on or 'normally attended' the two key committees – Finance and Audit – that are formally and constitutionally responsible for providing oversight of the university's financial dealings. These committees should have subjected the three private placement loans with two US insurers and the University of Leicester's involvement in the Freemen's Common Village LLP to the closest of scrutiny. As we explained above, it is these three loans that have increased the university's long term-debt by about two thirds and it is the LLP that has, in practical terms, nearly doubled again the university's long term financial liabilities.

That the university is struggling to meet the conditions imposed by its various creditors was recently confirmed by yet another breach of covenant reported in its 2021/22 accounts.[44] Unless rectified within a specified period of grace, a breach of covenant entitles the lender to immediate repayment in full – an obvious disaster given the tens of millions of pounds involved. On previous occasions, the university had managed to renegotiate the terms of its loans so that they still appeared as long-term debt in its accounts. This time, however, the breach occurred too late in the financial year for this to be accomplished. As a result, the 2021/22 accounts show an alarming increase of £42.3 million in short-term debt, the amounts that must be repaid within one year.[45] By way of reassurance that the breach of covenant was 'a technical issue associated with the COVID pandemic', a note to the accounts includes a helpful recalculation of short-term debt as it would have been, had the breach not occurred. It is not surprising that the university is paying handsomely for this finessing of its financial situation. Its external auditors' remuneration in 2021/22 was £155k, plus a further £32k for 'non-audit services'.[46] The extent to which the university's other creditors have been reassured by these exculpations remains to be seen, but for us, they are a stark reminder of the potentially disastrous consequences when loan covenants are breached.

Given the lack of appropriate transparency regarding the deliberations of the committees that oversee these processes and decisions, specifically the absence of any accessible minutes, we cannot judge how any of these individual office holders and decision makers exercised their respective roles or what concerns they may have considered in the process of doing so. What we can say is the decisions to increase the University of Leicester's indebtedness and to reduce its financial resilience were made more possible by a 2017 decision of the Senate and of the Council when both approved a presumably new Risk Management Policy and Risk Appetite Statement confirming a 'willingness to accept and encourage an increased degree of risk in pursuit of the University's mission and objectives, whilst minimising exposure to compliance, brand and reputation, and overall financial risks'.[47] Council discussed these two documents a year later and noted that the Risk Appetite

Statement 'would be circulated more widely within the University to promote increased awareness of risk appetite, and the possibility of describing more specifically the appetite for certain risks was also being explored'.[48] Yet, extensive searching yields no trace of this statement itself. It was certainly not 'circulated more widely within the University'.

The conclusion is inescapable. The University of Leicester – like, we suspect, many universities – is being steered in a new, seemingly more hazardous direction. But the majority of its employees, along with other stakeholders, have been left completely unaware, and unable to make themselves aware, of this new course. Yet it is employees – and students – who are made to bear the risks, with employees losing their livelihoods when leaders find it necessary to make 'difficult decisions'. It is employees who are thrown overboard when this hazardous direction leads to treacherous waters – as it almost inevitably does. But as we have shown, there are ways in which scholarly investigation can reveal something of the landscape of debt and borrowing in universities. The sort of stuff that might appear in journals such as *Critical Studies in Accounting*. Silencing such voices is what we turn to in our next chapter.

CHAPTER 6

NO QUESTIONING OF RECEIVED WISDOM: THE ATTACK ON ACADEMIC FREEDOM

[A]cademic staff have freedom within the law to question and test received wisdom, and to put forward new ideas and controversial or unpopular opinions, without placing themselves in jeopardy of losing their jobs or privileges they may have at their institutions.
– Education Reform Act 1988[1]

The University will maintain the right of staff to exercise their academic freedom … subject to the rights of the University to manage its activity efficiently and economically.
– University of Leicester Ordinance on Academic Freedom[2]

The protection of critical thinking has always involved a confrontation with power. … Critical thinking … is both the cause and effect of academic freedom.
– Joan Wallach Scott[3]

In the United Kingdom the notion of academic freedom – and its ostensible protections – arises from a major defeat for scholars within the university system. The relevant clause in the Education Reform Act of 1988, quoted in the second epigraph above, was the result of an amendment proposed in the House of Lords by Roy Jenkins, then chancellor of Oxford University. Jenkins and his fellow peers were 'ambushing' a bill – their amendment was opposed by the government – that ended academic tenure, at least for future appointments. (In fact, the clause legislating the removal of academic tenure was itself slipped into a bill concerned mostly with matters other than higher education.) Until this time, an academic could only be separated from their position as a result of 'gross moral turpitude' or 'gross incompetence'. Henceforth, what we tend to refer to as 'permanent' contracts are, as the case of Leicester confirmed for us, better understood as 'open-ended' ones. It is perhaps possible to assign a financial sum to the value of tenure: we know at least one then-lecturer (now retired) who, following the 1988 Act, refused promotion to a more senior post (worth tens of thousands of pounds over the course of a career), since accepting a new contract would also necessitate waiving their right of tenure.

The wording of Jenkins's amendment has been repeated in later legislation, such as the Higher Education and Research Act of 2017, and in the statutes and ordinances of many UK universities, including, as it happens, the University of Leicester's – though, as can be seen above, this ordinance includes an important qualifier. The statement presents the only clear legal defence of academic freedom for academics as individual researchers within English law, although more robust protection potentially resides in the European Convention on Human Rights – its Article 10 includes additional freedoms 'to disseminate information' and 'to conduct research and distribute knowledge and truth without restriction'.[4]

Nowhere in either the 1988 or 2017 Acts, nor anywhere else, are university 'teaching personnel' granted the right to criticise their own employer, as recommended by UNESCO in 1997.

Thus, a more general *employment* right – the right not to lose one's employment – has been lost and replaced by a far more curtailed 'right' concerning the voicing of 'controversial' and 'unpopular' opinions, and to question 'received wisdom'. One might assume this covers a freedom to do research that questions received wisdom in given disciplines without losing your job. But as we have seen from our own cases that does not protect you from redundancy if your work 'profoundly questions' mainstream managerial practices, and if senior managers have decided this questioning is the 'wrong' research direction for the business school.

Academic freedom in context

In the United States, academic freedom can also be understood as emerging from a retreat. According to Randy Martin, the establishment in the early twentieth century of the American Association of University Professors (AAUP) 'was itself the response to an exercise of conventional employer rights, that of hiring and firing workers.' 'At a time of militant labor organizing and revolutionary political activity, academic freedom for university professors would position itself in an autonomous realm of professional moral authority outside the politics of labor and government.'[5] In this account, academics in the US sought to insulate themselves from the proletarian condition of material insecurity by 'forgoing the status of employee as a basis for limiting the powers of employers' – that is, by insisting on their detachment from the working class and any partisan interests of that class. Instead, 'tenure was constructed to avoid this parallel by invoking a higher authority than the market along the lines of the secularisation of religious calling'.[6]

This highlights the extent to which academic freedom as a concept is accompanied by class connotations. What's involved is a form of liberal elitism in which academics claim protection through the 'higher ideals' of the university as a particular kind of public institution of learning and questioning. While this liberal-elitist conception has been voiced in the UK and we can hear its echoes in the Jenkins amendment, it's become more marginal in recent decades. Marginal enough to be seriously curtailed and increasingly trampled on by the privatisation and financialisation of UK universities, and through the deliberate and systematic removal of any remnants of academic self-governance – as the Leicester case reveals and as we've explored in previous chapters.

The transcendent connotation of academic freedom arises from a broader liberal tradition and presents the university scholar as autonomous of any wider societal antagonisms and struggles. The position would always be an uneasy one to maintain – and so it proved. In the US, the AAUP formalised its 1915 principles in 1940, the same year the Alien Registration Act (the Smith Act) made it a criminal offence to advocate the violent overthrow of the government or to be a member of any group or society devoted to such advocacy. Whilst this Act was used to prosecute leaders of both the (Trotskyist) Socialist Workers Party and the (Soviet-aligned) Communist Party of the USA, for academics, '[c]riticism of government or business must remain an idea, and even then one that is organisationally circumscribed'. The faculty handbook of New York University, which was based on the AAUP's 1940 statement, even had 'a separate clause to define what tenure cannot protect – sedition'.

> What counts as a seditious act or utterance is left to those who, as we shall see, will take it up as an accusation. Academic freedom is above all a regulatory principle for dealing with conflicts among spheres it takes to be both empirically and conceptually separable, even as the specific controversies that occasion its application speak to the ways in which the domains of authority covered by profession, labour, and government are, in actuality, deeply intertwined.[7]

One significant legal case was that of Paul Sweezy, the Marxist political economist famous for his analysis of 'monopoly capital' and co-founder of the long-running journal *Monthly Review*. After giving a lecture on 'socialism' to students at the University of New Hampshire in 1954, Sweezy was investigated by that state's attorney general under the New Hampshire Subversive Activities Act of 1951. Refusing to answer questions he believed 'infringed upon an area protected by the First Amendment', Sweezy was taken before New Hampshire's supreme court and, persisting in his refusal, adjudged in contempt of court and jailed. Although released on bail, it wasn't until three years later that Sweezy was cleared by the Supreme Court of the United States. As the Chief Justice put it:

> The essentiality of freedom in the community of American universities is almost self-evident. No one should underestimate the vital role in a democracy that is played by those who guide and train our youth. To impose any strait jacket upon the intellectual leaders in our colleges and universities would imperil the future of our nation.[8]

The principles of academic freedom and of free speech, with which it is often confused, are shot through with tensions and ambiguities. Since power is always present, and always a factor, academic freedom and free speech always constitute objects and sites of struggle. It is, in fact, the contestation around these twin principles that make both visible. Academic freedom and free speech are thrown into relief and must be defined only when threatened. As South African literary scholar John Higgins writes, 'reference to [academic freedom] is usually motivated by its absence. … [It] rarely if ever names, refers to or describes an existing state of things; rather it is always a normative ideal, called up precisely at moments when it is lacking or appears to be under threat.'[9]

In the late 1960s, universities were roiled by intense student movements, one effect of which was to destabilise disciplinary boundaries, opening up questions of who could speak and about what. In the 1980s and 90s some of these conflicts became known as the Culture Wars, a term which has undoubtedly acquired greater prominence in the contemporary period. In the UK, in 2008, Rizwaan Sabir, a graduate student at the University of Nottingham, downloaded an al-Qaida training manual from a US government website as part of his Masters research into terrorist tactics. He sent the 1,500-page document to a university administrator acquaintance Hicham Yezza, who had agreed to print it. When another administrator discovered the document, university officials alerted police, who arrested Sabir and Yezza under the Terrorism Act, detaining both men for six days. Upon his release, however, Yezza was immediately rearrested on immigration charges and only narrowly avoided deportation to Algeria.

The University of Nottingham was heavily criticised for the 'disproportionate nature of [its] response to the possession of legitimate research materials.' One such critic was one of its own lecturers, Rod Thornton, who documented his criticisms in a paper for the British International Studies Association. University of Nottingham officials' response was to suspend him and he subsequently left the institution.[10] When we learned of Sabir and Yezza's treatment, some of the authors of this book wrote to the University of Nottingham, protesting its failure to fulfil its duty of care towards its students and staff. We warned that, given this failure, we would struggle to recommend the institution to our own students progressing to higher-level study. We received no reply, but some weeks later, our own head of school summoned us to a meeting to discuss our letter. Nothing untoward came of this, but clearly University of Nottingham bosses had contacted their University of Leicester counterparts, requesting that they apply some mild intimidation.

What was being challenged here was not only our right to express our *opinion* – that University of Nottingham leaders had behaved badly – but also our right to form and express a *professional judgement*. It is common for students to request advice from their lecturers which universities might they apply to in order to progress their studies, which scholars to approach, and so on. This is a recognised part of the job. But, in this instance, the veiled implication – the intended threat – was that we should take care before proffering negative advice about an institution. We return to the distinction between the right to express an opinion ('freedom of speech') and the formation and expression of professional judgement ('academic freedom') later in the chapter.

In 2016, Liz Morrish was a lecturer at neighbouring Nottingham Trent University. In that year she published, first on her blog *Academic Irregularities* and then in *Times Higher Education*, an article entitled 'The kindness of strangers', which described her conversation with a group of students about managerialism, metrics and staff stress in universities (*all* universities, not only her own). Morrish was, in fact, covering the class of a colleague, who was absent due to a stress-related illness, and, moreover, this conversation took place on Universities Mental Health Day. A few days later, Morrish was summoned to a meeting with a senior manager (a pro-vice-chancellor) and Human Resources, who alleged breach of confidentiality, 'serious carelessness and negligence in the performance of duties', and bringing the university into disrepute. She was forced to ask the *Times Higher* to remove her article and delete it from her own blog. She was forbidden from writing more on the topic of stress and mental health in universities, and from discussing her case with anyone other than a union rep. Following a 12-week disciplinary process – which saw university administrators create a new charge of 'frightening the students' – Morrish was left with two counts of gross misconduct. She immediately resigned.[11]

This isn't a comprehensive survey of the 'state' of academic freedom, of course, and we haven't mentioned any cases outside of the UK or the US. It's worth noting, however, that in one comparative study of academic freedom in Europe, the UK is rated as affording 'low' protection on all measures, the sole state in this position.[12] In another assessment, the UK is described as the 'sick man of Europe' when it comes to academic freedom.[13] (These studies were published in 2007 and 2012, respectively. The UK would now be joined by countries such as Hungary and Turkey.) Finally, legal scholar Mark Davies states that 'despite [a] long history, academic freedom in the UK has few legal underpinnings', noting that the Jenkins amendment 'has been subject to very little judicial scrutiny'. Davies is able to provide only two examples. The first concerned a graduate student and part-time lecturer at South Bank University dismissed for whistle-blowing a senior colleague whom he accused of grade-fixing. In the second, *Volkswagen vs. Garcia*, the motor manufacturer sought to prevent a team of academic cryptography experts from publishing a paper that documented vulnerabilities in its car-immobilisation systems. According to Davies, the judge 'acknowledged "the enormous significance of freedom of expression and academic freedom", but went on to find in favour of the claimants' arguments that the publication in an academic paper of an algorithm which could facilitate car theft should be restricted.'[14]

As we will go on to explore, the University of Leicester's policies and procedures concerning academic freedom (unsurprisingly) offered us no succour, and at first blush, English law has provided little more.

Free speech versus academic freedom

Let's return to the distinction between free speech and academic freedom. In February 2021, less than a month after we were put at risk of redundancy, the government published new proposed legislation on *Higher education: free speech and academic freedom.*[15] Attempting to distinguish between free speech and academic freedom, the bill insists that both must be protected. However, in the contextualising discussion of the proposals, the two principles are frequently elided, while supposed threats to free speech are given far greater weight. The word 'censorship' or its cognates appear thirteen times and the paper refers to 'cancel culture' and a 'chilling effect' – a phrase used eight times – 'on staff and students, domestic and international, who may feel unable to express their cultural, religious or political views without fear of repercussion'. One of the proposals is 'to legislate for a Free Speech and Academic Freedom Champion with a remit to champion free speech, investigate infringements of free speech in higher education and recommend redress'; another is to impose a duty upon higher education providers to 'actively promote' freedom of speech.

Meanwhile, what protections for academic freedom the policy paper does appear to presage for individual scholars are diluted by its invocation of the principle of institutional autonomy. Thus, universities are also 'free within the law to conduct their day-to-day management in an effective and competent way [... including determining] the criteria for the selection, appointment and dismissal of academic staff and apply[ing] those criteria in particular cases'. We are back to the terrain of the University of Leicester's ordinance: the academic freedom of staff is to be guaranteed, but only provided it doesn't interfere with the managerial prerogative to hire and fire.

Reaction to the proposed bill was scathing. Jo Grady, UCU's general secretary, pointed out that 'the biggest threats to academic freedom and free speech come not from staff and students, or from so-called "cancel culture", but from ministers' own attempts to police what can and cannot be said on campus, and a failure to get to grips with the endemic job insecurity and managerialist approaches which mean academics are less able to speak truth to power.' National Union of Students vice-president Hillary Gyebi-Ababio agreed that, 'There is no evidence of a freedom of expression crisis on campus, and students' unions are constantly taking positive steps to help facilitate the thousands of events that take place each year.' Even the employers' body, Universities UK – which rarely sees eye to eye with either staff or students' unions – did not demur from this response. Their statement noted that: 'There are already significant legal duties placed on universities to uphold freedom of speech and universities are required to have a code of practice on free speech and to update this regularly.'[16]

Before we unpack the distinction between free speech, on the one hand, and academic freedom, on the other, it is worth recalling a few of the many jaw-dropping moments that public discourse has produced in recent years. These have largely been a product of misunderstandings – sometimes deliberate – of the meanings of, and conflation of, the two principles. Seeding and amplifying such confusion has proved a reliable tactic for the reactionary Right, a way to discombobulate and decompose their political antagonists, in a post-truth era in which we have all 'had enough of experts'. Joan Wallach Scott is writing in the context of the United States, but her argument is as relevant to the UK: 'These days free speech is the mantra of the Right, their weapon in the new culture war. Their invocation of free speech has collapsed an important distinction between the First Amendment right of free speech that we all enjoy and the principle of academic freedom that refers to teachers and the knowledge they produce and convey.'[17]

But academic freedom is not a free-for-all. For scholars such as Joan Wallach Scott, the principle is entangled with the concept of discipline and disciplinarity. She argues that academic freedom 'is not about unfettered freedom of speech'. The scholar instead 'voluntarily subjects [their] own speech to the rules of some sort of "truth procedure"': 'free inquiry in academia is predicated on voluntarily assumed forms of unfreedom that are unique to the academy'. In this account, the agents who enjoy freedom from 'interference from external powers (states, administrators, trustees, philanthropists, business interests, lobbyists, politicians, political activists)' are '*credentialed* scholars' [our emphasis].[18] While 'the ideal of academic freedom is crucial to our conception of the university' – 'the legitimating concept of the entire enterprise', in fact – it is,

> 'inherently problematic' because it is traversed by contradiction: free inquiry is essential to its definition, but it is inquiry patrolled and legitimated by disciplinary authority – a disciplinary authority that, in turn, warrants autonomy, the freedom of scholars from external pressure. The university provides knowledge essential to the operations of democracy, but knowledge production is not a democratic process because it rests on the expertise of researchers and teachers.[19]

Academic freedom thus imposes responsibilities on university scholars at the same time as it confers rights. These responsibilities extend to the classroom: professors and lecturers 'are constrained by the need to teach their subject matter; their job as educators limits their rights of free speech'. Thus an individual academic might privately believe that the moon is made of green cheese. But their responsibilities as an educator preclude them articulating such opinions in the classroom – or accepting them as valid if expressed by a student. 'Free speech makes no distinction about quality; academic freedom does.'[20]

But *discipline* has a double meaning, of course. The word refers to both a field or realm of study, and also enforcement and control. In fact, the two meanings are intricately connected. Power and politics are still present when we think of a scholarly realm. Who sets the rules of the 'truth procedure' the scholar 'voluntarily subjects' themselves to? Who awards the necessary credentials – and according to which criteria? Who polices any given discipline's borders (or boundaries) – and who appoints them and what is their legitimacy? These matters are particularly fraught given the common understanding of academic freedom that it makes possible the 'question[ing] and test[ing of] received wisdom' – the challenging of orthodoxy. There is a clear and obvious tension here. Joan Wallach Scott explains:

> Academic freedom protects those whose thinking challenges orthodoxy; at the same time, the legitimacy of the challenge – the proof that the critic is not a madman or a crank – is secured by membership in a disciplinary community based upon shared commitment to certain methods, standards, and beliefs. While that commitment doesn't force agreement at every level of practice, it does resist assaults on its fundamental premises … and in this way functions as orthodoxy. The critic of orthodoxy thus, ironically, must find legitimation in the very discipline whose orthodoxy he or she challenges.[21]

The question of disciplinarity is also central to our story. The executors of our redundancies – James Devlin, Daniel Ladley and Henrietta O'Connor – did not accuse us of poor scholarship or of being ill-disciplined. Quite the opposite, in fact: they stressed on several occasions that the *quality* of our scholarship was not being questioned. Rather, their case against us (and the business case for our redundancy) hinged on their ability to categorise our scholarship as falling within particular disciplinary boundaries. These were 'critical management studies' and 'political economy', which, according to the business school's new strategy, were no longer to be 'supported'. To make this case, Devlin and Ladley, abetted by O'Connor, were the ones guilty of poor scholarship, of cherry-picking examples in order, first, to define the disciplines of Critical Management Studies and political economy and, second, to adjudge our research as conforming to those definitions. In this way we found that subject disciplinarity can apparently be determined and imposed by managers in a deliberate and barely evidenced exercise of power and control, which, of course, provided the basis for collective compulsory redundancies. As we will see, academic freedom, as supposedly enshrined in both the United Kingdom's laws and the University of Leicester's ordinances, seemed to offer no protection against this. In fact, the Leicester case highlights the way in which the freedom of scholars 'to question and test received wisdom, and to put forward new ideas and controversial or unpopular opinions' stands counterposed to the freedom of university managers to structure the institution in a way they consider to be 'efficient' and 'economical'.

The University of Leicester and the subjugation of academic freedom

In Chapter 4, we referred to Margaret Thatcher's assault on universities. Sociology departments were particular victims of her government's cuts, being especially prone, in Thatcher's view, to the 'socialistic' thinking that was 'poisoning' young people's minds. Clearly this was an attack on academic freedom. In the face of this onslaught many sociologists, as we remarked, reinvented themselves as industrial sociologists or organisation theorists and found employment in management and business schools instead. Although the mechanism was different, there were similar consequences for critical thinkers trained in economics, which through the 1980s and 90s went through its 'new revolution'.[22] Responding to the breakdown of the post-war Keynesian deal,[23] which also sparked a crisis in economics, and the triumph of neoliberalism, the new orthodoxy congealed around so-called New Classical Economics. At its core were aggressive methodological individualism, rational expectations theory, an emphasis on formalism, and the almost fetishistic use of esoteric mathematical and statistical techniques. As those aggrandising this new orthodoxy consolidated their dominance of 'fortress economics' – seizing control of the 'top' journals, for instance – economists and political economists cleaving to alternative approaches were edged out. This included institutional economists, economic historians (who needs history, when economic laws are universal?) and those interested in developing the critique of political economy. Like their sociologist peers, many such (political) economists found management and business schools more willing to employ them. This was certainly the case for some of us: those of us who are (political) economists by training found the University of Leicester Management Centre (and later School of Management) not only more willing to employ us, but more than that, a scholarly community more intellectually vibrant than most Economics departments.

There is a cruel twist here. As we've recounted, in 2016 the School of Management underwent a forced merger with the university's Economics department to become the School of Business. In 2021 the definition of political economy that was used to justify our dismissals explicitly 'exclude[d] the orthodox rational choice [rational expectations] tradition as being a separate aspect of [political economy]'. In fact, there is a further twist. Several members of the School of Business's Economics, Finance and

Accounting department conduct research in traditions of political economy that firmly reject the methodological assumption of rational expectations: Austrian economics, for instance, or work that seeks to understand banking crises through elite capture. That these erstwhile colleagues were never placed at risk of redundancy (and, in fact, some of them actively sought to mobilise support for our sacking) and that rational-choice approaches were protected clearly suggests that it was *approaches* to research – a mode of inquiry – that was being targeted, not any particular object of inquiry. It makes clear that our targeting was ideological and political, rather than purely disciplinary. But, of course, adopting a different approach, applying a new lens, is one of the main ways in which received wisdom is tested and questioned.

We will provide some examples here. As noted in Chapter 3, Devlin and Ladley, the School's dean and deputy dean, who were responsible for drawing up the original list of targets, claimed not to have taken any notes during their screening of faculty. But the research publications of those of us targeted for redundancy were reassessed (we were told) by a 'Review Group', chaired by Henrietta O'Connor, head of the College of Social Sciences, Arts and Humanities. This Group included four other members: Devlin and Ladley, along with Richard Thomas, the College's dean of research and a professor of archaeology, and Philip Baker, the university's pro-vice-chancellor for research and enterprise, a medical researcher and no-longer-practising obstetrician. They shared its conclusions with us in March 2021 in the form of confidential letters of typically nine or ten pages, which included an 'individual outcome' appendix cataloguing each individual scholar's research outputs, and the Group's assessment of each output. This is the only place, that we have seen, at least, where any judgement of our research was recorded. (We reproduce many of these extracts in the book's Appendix.)

O'Connor and her associates wasted no more than a few words on each book, chapter or article they 'reviewed'. (A student would be highly aggrieved to receive such paltry feedback on any of their essays.) Categorising judgements were made on the scantest of evidence, a single sentence from its opening paragraph, for instance, or an isolated phrase. There is slippage between scholarship that is deemed to be in the areas of Critical Management Studies or political economy, and scholarship that is deemed to be 'not aligned with [the School's] future strategic direction', scholarship that 'does little to contribute to debates connected to mainstream business and management understanding or to contribute to future School strategic priorities'. We see that 'sociological perspectives' are also deemed redundant – a particularly rich irony coming from a professor of sociology and recent trustee of the British Sociological Association. In the assessment of a paper that was not in fact condemned, possibly because most of its co-authors were faculty who had not been targeted (though all soon joined the exodus), the Anthropocene was purported to be a 'contested concept' – it's remarkable that using or referring to a scientifically recognised geological era, even one that *is* contested by some scholars, could be considered problematic.

Articles were damned because of where they were published: *Critical Perspectives on Accounting* was adjudged verboten because its title includes the words 'critical perspectives'; *ephemera: theory and politics in organization* and *Organization* because these two journals are 'identified as closely associated with [Critical Management Studies] perspectives' or 'targeted primarily by those writing from a CMS perspective'. O'Connor, Devlin and Ladley sought scholarly substantiation for these claims regarding *ephemera* and *Organization* and their 'associations'. But they failed to provide the bibliographic information customary in any scholarly endeavour and necessary to enable sceptical readers to easily check their claims – and it turns out that they got these claims wrong, mixing up who'd said what and where, and who was quoting whom. One marvels that three senior university professors, entrusted with selecting colleagues for redundancy, can be so easily confounded.

Again, we should emphasise that at no point was the 'quality' of our research doubted – on several occasions bosses insisted that this was not a reason for our redundancy. In fact, whilst Leicester managers were justifying our redundancy on the basis of our publications, elsewhere in the university ecosystem other senior academics were judging the 'quality' of these publications as part of the UK's periodic and highly problematic Research Excellence Framework – itself a cause of much academic unfreedom. It is likely that the 'scores' of those of who were made redundant boosted the overall result for the School of Business, with journals such as *Organization* and *Critical Perspectives on Accounting* – both disdained by University of Leicester bosses – being rated 'internationally excellent'. In the very year in which he was dismissed, Gibson Burrell, one of the authors of this book, was honoured with a Lifetime Achievement Award by the British Academy of Management, which recognised his 'enormous contribution to the field', identifying him as 'an outstanding, globally renowned scholar'.

One striking feature of the process was the exercise of raw managerial power – an issue we already discussed in Chapter 3. We made many attempts to question *how* the terms *critical management studies* and *political economy* were operationalised. Were all our articles and books read, for instance? Were keywords used? How was a paper critical of Critical Management Studies distinguished from one more uncritically in the CMS tradition, and subsequently judged? What about someone who had published, say, ten articles that were adjudged to be either Critical Management Studies or political, but twenty that were in other areas? Such probing elicited from Devlin and Ladley responses typically along the lines of, 'we *felt* it was critical management studies' or 'we *took a view* that this person was *primarily* working in the area of political economy'. Managerial feeling did a lot of work in our dismissals, while the meaning of *primarily* was strictly 'non-quantitative'.

O'Connor's attempt to distinguish between adopting a *critical perspective*, which is a necessary part of good social science, and espousing hostility to management, which was how she characterised Critical Management Studies, was both hopelessly convoluted and hopelessly false. But she was correct in her recognition that we were often critical of, even hostile towards, aspects of management practice. And, as a manager herself – a manager in an antagonistic class relationship with us, the workers being made redundant – it is perfectly understandable that she, along with other members of the university's executive (and Council chair, Gary Dixon) would seek to neutralise this criticism. Here we approach what we believe was the real reason for our dismissals. UNESCO's 1997 recommendation concerning academic freedom states that 'Higher-education teaching personnel should have the right and opportunity, without discrimination of any kind, according to their abilities, to take part in the governing bodies and to criticize the functioning of higher education institutions, including their own.' Academics in the UK have no such rights – and there is nothing in the Higher Education (Freedom Speech) Act 2023 to suggest that we will be granted such rights any time soon.

Appealing academic freedom, testing academic freedom

The University of Leicester has an Ordinance on Academic Freedom – we quoted from it in one of this chapter's epigraphs. Many of us threatened with redundancy first appealed to the university's Staffing Policy Committee, invoking the Ordinance and claiming that our 'selection for compulsory redundancy on these grounds [i.e., research area or approach] constitute[d] undue interference, or suppression, of [our] professional responsibility and right to research, publish and communicate on what [we] see fit, subject to nationally and internationally recognized professional principles of intellectual rigour, scientific inquiry and research ethics.'[24]

What happened next provides a(nother) perfect instance of authoritarian management in action, including the regulation of time, control (restriction) of information, and the talismanic invocation of 'normally' (see Chapter 3). No such information about the Staffing Policy Committee – its membership, its remit, its lines of accountability – exists on the university's external website nor its intranet. In fact, we were only able to deduce the Committee's existence from the Ordinance on Academic Freedom, which accords it a central role in safeguarding academic freedom. But according to the Redundancy Ordinance Procedure, in instances where a scholar at risk of redundancy alleges breach of their academic freedom, the chair of the Staffing Policy Committee must convene a three-person panel to judge the case, with at least one member of this panel 'normally' a lay member of the university. At the time of our redundancy the Staffing Policy Committee did not actually exist. Nevertheless, its chair turned out to be the omnipresent Edmund Burke, the deputy vice-chancellor. Burke not only convened the panels, he also chaired each of them, and the individuals he invited to join him were, in every case, senior academic members of staff – no lay members were involved.

Burke dismissed our objections that, as deputy vice-chancellor and thus a central architect of the University's 'Shaping for Excellence' plan and associated redundancies, he had a conflict of interest. The panels took around two months to hear our cases – an unreasonable period, in the context of a three-month redundancy consultation process. In none of our cases were formal minutes of investigation recorded – we do not even have a record of the date(s) on which the panels met. Finally, despite panel compositions varying, we each received almost identical boilerplate responses to our complaints. The reason for our being placed at risk of redundancy was 'not due to an issue of academic freedom'. Rather it was a result of 'a strategic proposal to refocus research activity within [University of Leicester School of Business] … [that we were] placed at risk of redundancy because of an initial assessment that [our] research activity is not aligned with ULSB's proposed future strategic direction.' The panels emphasised that 'the right of academic staff "to carry out research work without any undue interference, or any suppression" is subject to "the rights of the University to manage its activity efficiently and economically".'

As we finish writing this book in mid-2023 it remains to be seen whether or not the University of Leicester's attack on academic freedom will be tested in court. Legal advice we received in 2021, while contesting our redundancies, was somewhat equivocal but appeared to support university bosses' stance. Specifically, we sought an opinion on whether the University of Leicester administration could be challenged by means of a judicial review, a legal proceeding which involves a judge assessing the lawfulness of a decision or action made by a public body. The opinion was fairly confident that a court would agree the University of Leicester is a public body. However, it doubted whether the particular decision – to make scholars redundant – was 'of a public nature'. Acknowledging that the University of Leicester 'has a number of public duties', as detailed in its Royal Charter, the author opined,

> I do not believe that [the University of Leicester] was performing one of those functions when it took the decision to disinvest in certain areas of research and to implement a restructure designed to increase research in areas currently underrepresented in the [University of Leicester School of Business] and perceived to be key to the future success of the School. Rather, I believe, the redundancy represents the exercise of an executive or management power. … With this in mind the relevant decision is incidental to the University's public functions and so regretfully would not be amenable to judicial review.

The opinion noted that the university's Redundancy Ordinance Policy contains provision for cases where redundancy is due to an issue of academic freedom. But because bosses had not invoked this but instead provided another reason – that we had conducted research in areas no longer aligned to the future strategic direction of the School of Business – our academic freedom could not, in fact, have been breached. Just as the deputy vice-chancellor was to adjudge whether he had any conflict of interest, the law, according to this opinion, appears to allow the employer to adjudge whether the reason for redundancy is academic freedom – or a legitimate management/executive decision. In other words, an employer that has the foresight to simply claim that a decision to make scholars providing research of a certain type or in a certain area is 'strategic' is protected against claims of breach of academic freedom.

Three weeks after we were put at risk of redundancy, Gavin Williamson, then-Secretary of State for Education, wrote to the outgoing and incoming chairs of the Office for Students (OfS), reminding them of the government's specific priorities, including its 2019 manifesto pledge 'to strengthen academic freedom and free speech in universities'. Williamson rebuked the OfS for its failure to take 'regulatory action … in relation to potential breaches of the registration conditions relating to freedom of speech and academic freedom, despite a significant number of concerning incidents reported since the full suite of its regulatory powers came into force.' Signalling his intention 'to publish a policy paper on free speech and academic freedom in the near future' – the bill we have already mentioned – Williamson also insisted that the OfS should 'clearly support individual academics whose academic freedom is being diminished'.[25] One 'incident' regarding academic freedom reported to the Office for Students – several times, in fact – was, of course, ours. The OfS acknowledged receipt in May 2021, promising to investigate 'the issues that you raise in your notification'. We heard nothing more. Nor did Williamson, despite his fine words, or then-Minister for Universities, Michelle Donelan, display any interest in events unfolding at the University of Leicester.

Indeed, we struggled to garner much support from the mainstream, even from those media outlets that have claimed to stand for free speech and academic freedom. *The Guardian* and *Times Higher Education* ran dedicated stories on what was happening at University of Leicester. The *Financial Times* expended 66 words on events at Leicester in a single story on universities' 'financial strains.'[26] Another article in the *FT*, on the teaching of 'real-world economics', devoted 150 words to the 'cuts to critical thinkers' at University of Leicester.[27] There was a reasonable amount of coverage by local media: BBC Radio Leicester, the *Leicester Mercury* and ITV Central's Peter Bearne took a keen interest and reported several times. *Private Eye* also penned a piece. But almost all of the already scant reporting treated the story as a 'straightforward' – all too familiar, not particularly newsworthy – instance of bosses wishing, rightly or wrongly, to restructure and workers attempting, again rightly or wrongly, to resist this restructuring. Not a single news outlet – not even *Times Higher Education*, whose raison d'être is reporting on universities, with a focus on the UK – mentioned academic freedom in relation to the University of Leicester story. The only person with a national platform to take an interest was the journalist and *Guardian* columnist Owen Jones, who invited one of our number onto the episode of his show dedicated to 'The Conservatives' war on free speech'.[28]

Managerial power and the imposition of discipline

The redundancies at Leicester reveal the stark tension at the heart of the public university. On the one side, representing one set of values, stands public purpose and the asking of difficult questions in the interests of responding to the many challenges humanity urgently faces. Global heating and ecological collapse, inequality, resurgent xenophobia, ageing populations and the care crisis are obvious examples. On the other side, representing a competing, even an antagonistic set of values, stand senior managers and administrators who personify the university-as-business, the product of four decades of neoliberal reform that we explored in Chapter 4. In the light of the prevalent forms of authoritarian university leadership that we discussed in Chapter 3, Thomas Docherty's observation is apposite: 'University management and leadership now arrogates to itself the kinds of control over academic freedom that are more appropriate to an institution designed for the propagation of a doctrine'.[29]

Our story is a part of a broader problematic trend that Docherty identifies in which 'research itself is no longer based in the free exercise of thought and speech; rather it is "governed", and governed primarily by financial, monetary and economic incentives'.[30] As we saw in the previous chapter, the Leicester case is compounded by a story of greater financialisation and the financial aspect of our former employer's affairs casts a long shadow. In fact, we might speculate that the imperatives of off-balance sheet, securitised real-estate deals supersede any claim scholars might have to challenge orthodoxy and test received wisdom. Yet these financial imperatives cannot be publicly and openly discussed since, in a further twist induced by those very financial imperatives, our managers persistently insisted that the case for redundancies was strategic and not financial – and thus they had no additional financial information that needed to be shared with us.

We can speculate further that university managers' problem – which became our problem when we were put at risk of redundancy – was not that we challenged orthodoxy, that we questioned and tested received wisdom, or that we put forward new ideas and controversial or unpopular opinions in any general sense. It was not even that we were critical of, or hostile towards, management in general. The problem, for us and for University of Leicester's senior management, was that some of us questioned the new orthodoxy of how the neoliberal, corporate university is governed and, in particular, we questioned the way that the University of Leicester was being governed and *its* management. Moreover, our questioning and criticism of University of Leicester management was informed criticism, scholarly even, drawing upon our academic expertise, as specialists in accounting, finance, organisation theory, political economy, and so on. At the same time, we mobilised our expertise as scholars of social movements, trade unions, culture and communications, and organisation theory to actively challenge this management, whether through formal or informal university networks and structures, through our branch of the University and College Union, or by means of more ad hoc, social movement-inspired interventions. As well as challenging particular actions or decisions of the vice-chancellor and other University of Leicester leaders, some of us most active in the union became more vocal and more proactive in questioning their authority and legitimacy *tout court* and demanding a greater role in university governance for ordinary university employees. (Involvement in governance is one aspect of academic freedom according to most comprehensive definitions.)

In fact, during the dispute, two pseudonymous colleagues used their professional expertise to analyse the data on who had been put at risk and who had not. Their conclusion was unambiguous:

> Statistical modelling shows no evidence to support the claim that redundancies in the School of Business are about disinvesting from political economy and Critical Management Studies. By far the most statistically significant factor is union activism. An underperforming Economics, Finance & Accounting professor who researches in political economy has a 5% chance of redundancy if they stay out of the union. However, if they decide to become a UCU officer, the chance of redundancy rises to over 80%.[31]

It would be glib and quite incorrect to claim that what happened at the University of Leicester in 2021 demonstrates that academic freedom no longer exists in the UK. What we have sought to demonstrate rather is that the freedom or right to question and test received wisdom – what we now call academic freedom – has long been contested. In fact, this freedom or right is, and has been, contested everywhere that scholarship – study and thinking – takes place. (The same is true of all rights and freedoms. No right is 'universal' and legal declarations to such effect are just one part, albeit an important part, of the contestations over rights and freedoms.) It is worth remembering that, egregious as the attack on our academic freedom was, we lost only our jobs. We did not lose our heads. We were not charged with treason or heresy. The more general point here is that power has always sought to control the production of knowledge and to contain the questioning of 'received wisdom'.

Joan Wallach Scott has suggested that academic freedom 'rested on the assumption that knowledge and power were separable', an assumption she questioned, as have we.[32] Almost four decades ago, members of the Steering Committee for Efficiency Studies in Universities declared their 'conviction that academic excellence is crucially dependent on academic freedom', before immediately warning 'universities' – that is, university *bosses* – to 'be on their guard against confusing [academic] freedom with licence'.[33] Our offence, and the reason we were targeted for redundancy, was that we took licence and, by late 2020, University of Leicester bosses were on their guard. The more particular point then is that, in the UK, the freedom of academics (or *some* academics – see the coda) 'to question and test received wisdom', as enshrined in legislation from 1988 onwards, only materialised as a counterpoint to the bolstering of university managers' right to manage, part of the Thatcherite 'reform' agenda and the 'great moving right show'. The two 'equal' rights exist, in the UK, as elsewhere, in a tense and often antagonistic relationship. 'Between equal rights', as Marx reminds us, 'force decides'.[34]

Coda – casualisation and academic freedom

In 2020/21, there were 225,000 academic staff employed in UK universities. One third of these were employed on fixed-term contracts – anything between three months and four years. Many universities pay a sizeable proportion of their academic staff on an hourly basis and, in 2019/20, 29 higher education institutions employed at least five academic staff on zero-hours contracts. The incidence of casualisation is somewhat gendered – 32% of men on fixed-term contracts, and 35% of women – and clearly racialised – 40% of Black academics, 43% of Asian academics, but 'only' 30% of white academic staff.[35]

We were informed we were at risk of redundancy on 18 January 2021 and dismissed on 10 August 2021. During those seven months, it's likely that 20–30,000 academic staff, both teachers and researchers, reached the end of their fixed-term contract period – an expected and normalised event throughout the sector. As we recounted in Chapter 1, during the early months of the COVID pandemic, University of Leicester bosses terminated the contracts of numerous hourly paid teaching staff. A number of those on fixed-term contracts that came to an end during the pandemic also found no extension to their employment being offered.

We believe our academic freedom was suppressed and we believe that, much more generally it is under threat in various ways, on various fronts, both in the UK and globally. One of these fronts is that of employment conditions and casualisation. It is difficult to conceive of academic freedom as anything other than a chimera when the termination date of one's contract and thus one's income is constantly on the near horizon. Apposite here is the question posed by South African literature scholar John Higgins: 'What does the right to academic freedom mean in a society where the material foundations for its practice are lacking or unevenly distributed because of material inequalities?'[36] Again, precarity does not only afflict scholars in the UK (and South Africa). After citing UNESCO's insistence that 'Tenure constitutes one of the major procedural safeguards of academic freedom', Kathleen Lynch and Mariya Ivancheva conclude, 'In all types of countries, having tenure (even on limited terms) has become the privilege of a minority; there is a class-related generational injustice in this process, as older (generally) and established academics retain security while new entrants face a work life of increasing precariousness'.[37]

Events at University of Leicester were just a part of a much wider degradation of academic freedom. Every day in British universities, there are micro-attacks against academic freedom, a slow violence that is enacted every time a fixed-term contract comes to an end – ending not only an individual's income, but also their library access and their email account. This violence manifests itself every minute this scholar is forced to spend job-seeking rather than developing their ideas, every night that is broken not by the worrying of a seemingly intractable intellectual problem, but the worrying of how to pay the rent and put food on the table.

The identity of staff working conditions and student learning conditions. The proliferation of casualised contracts in universities has undermined academic freedom in UK universities. Postcard produced and distributed by Leicester UCU, March 2018.

CHAPTER 7

COULD THE UNIVERSITY BE OURS?

> The university is ours! – Common slogan

> One can only sneak into the university and steal what one can.
> – Fred Moten and Stefano Harney[1]

> We need a new vision for higher education – and Leicester is perhaps one place that will emerge.
> – Jo Grady, UCU general secretary[2]

On 1 April 2021, Leicester UCU published a thread of five tweets:[3]

> We welcome last night's decision of Nishan Canagarajah, Edmund Burke and Gary Dixon to resign from their respective roles as President & Vice-Chancellor, deputy Vice-Chancellor, and Chair of Council of University of Leicester. // We look forwards to working with other campus unions – Unite, Unison and Leicester [Students'] Union – our national union UCU,

> and remaining members of executive board and Council to establish interim governance structures. // All redundancies will, of course, be immediately cancelled and we will seek urgent meetings with the Office for Students, with creditors, and with stakeholders. // Moving into University of Leicester's second century, we hope we can pioneer a new model of university governance, that is collective, collegiate, diverse & inclusive of all members of our communities. Universities must serve the needs of society, not bow to the logic of finance. // We understand that this is likely to be a distressing period for Nishan, Edmund and Gary. We would like [to] remind them of support available from our staff counselling provider Validium and that redeployment opportunities may exist at Swansea University.

The set of tweets was not so much a *fool* or a *hoax*, but rather it was built on what we might describe as an *alternative fact*.[4] It articulated an alternative vision for the University of Leicester – a vision that resonated with a large number of our colleagues, a vision that many of us believed to be within our grasp. A little over two months into our redundancy battle, some of us believed that it might be possible not only to save our own jobs, but also to force the resignations of the institution's most senior leaders and to set the university on a different path.[5]

Universities are a cauldron of conflicting views and clashing values (rarely explicitly acknowledged or recognised) of what the university is – or should be – and how we should relate to it. To what extent are we *in* it, to what extent are we *against* it, to what extent are we *beyond* it? For that matter, who exactly are *we*? More prosaically, universities are riven with class and class conflict – from above, from below and from the side. Sometimes this is very obvious, other times it is much more subtle (one of the authors of this book, Gibson Burrell, was once asked by the registrar to moderate his Geordie accent when reading out graduates' names at Warwick University). As we suggested in our Introduction, class is *happening* in universities. Almost every major struggle we can think of manifests itself in some way on campuses in Britain. The so-called hostile environment (which includes the government's racist Prevent programme, which requires university staff to report students they suspect of terror-related activities, as defined by the state), as well as debt, free speech, the rights and dignity of trans and other people marginalised by gender, Britain's colonial legacy, climate justice. There are plenty of other examples.

Are we professionals, proletarians or something else? A keyword is *professionalism*. Throughout our redundancy process, bosses insisted that they would behave in a 'professional manner' and exhorted us – those whom they were in the process of dismissing – to behave likewise. Such 'professionalism' was supposed to span our conduct in meetings, our communications and our social-media utterances. In this context, professionalism was understood to mean behaving calmly and 'rationally', not making 'personal' attacks, not – for instance – accusing a manager of lying (especially when they had, in fact, just issued a lie). But in other contexts of university life, employee professionalism is not invited or welcomed by bosses: a scholar's 'professional judgement' vis-à-vis the university's 'values' or research priorities or curriculum content, for example. A university is not a sausage factory or a car factory.[6] But if it were, then it is – or bosses would like it to be – a factory akin to the Nissan factory that opened in Sunderland in 1986, described with alarm as one where 'managers and workers alike wear white coats and share the same canteen, … a company where there have never been strikes, where trade unions are not forbidden but are redundant because workers enjoy good conditions and identify with the aims of the company.'[7] Thus we end up with a university in which strategic decisions are taken by the vice-chancellor and their coterie, while 'ordinary' members of staff are expected to 'professionally' align themselves to this strategy to ensure its success.

Against bosses' directives and expectations, many academics invoke their own professionalism as a form of resistance.[8] But the professional impulse is also what drives some academics to reject collective action, pleading that their care for students precludes them from striking or participating in other industrial action for fear of harming those students. (For instance, one group of University of Leicester academics, who were in other ways our allies, abandoned the marking and assessment boycott due to their concerns regarding fairness and equity.) The question of our status – are we professionals, proletarians or professionals becoming proletarianised? – opens onto the question of whose university it is. Bosses seek to present themselves as the guardians of the university and its values (whatever these are). Thus, their communications always invoke 'the University', a reification of great utility, by which they mean *themselves* – and they usually juxtapose 'the University' to unions or some other subset of (implicitly recalcitrant) employees. To counter that, *we are the university* – meaning that *they* are merely bosses or the executive – is one useful riposte to this. But with ownership comes responsibilities. If we are the university then what of the strategy of undermining the university's reputation? Are we not, in this case, undermining our own reputations and, thus, ourselves?

Is the university a sausage factory? Postcard produced and distributed by Leicester UCU, March 2018.

Here we arrive at two truths that are too frequently forgotten.

First, class struggles – or value struggles – are a struggle.[9] The best or 'correct' course of action is rarely obvious and always involves risk. In university ballots for industrial action, votes in favour of action short of a strike (ASOS) always outnumber those in favour of strike action – typically by 10–15 percentage points. We suspect that this is because many university workers believe ASOS to be somehow easier – less risky perhaps – than striking. But all action, if it is to have any chance of success, necessarily involves a wager. Every worker who has ever walked out on strike has, whether consciously or not, accepted this wager. If the strike is too effective in undermining profitability then it jeopardises the institution's future and the jobs of many or all. In the case of a university this means the recruitment of students and, in the case of our struggle against redundancy, it was the targeting of student recruitment that proved to be too risky a wager for many colleagues and (former) allies.

Second, our struggle is against ourselves – and that is where we focus the larger part of our attention. We are divided. If we were not, then defeating the bosses would be easy. But, as we learnt to our great pain and cost, there are always those who will side with management, those who will keep making the university, even as we call on them to stop. A big part of the challenge – the struggle – for militants is to seek to persuade those colleagues – and persuasion must always start by listening. It is also to make more apparent the tensions between the university worker as professional vis-à-vis the university worker as proletarian, the university as ours which we must occupy and recover vis-à-vis the university as an institution from which we first steal and then flee. And from there to make those tensions productive as opposed to stifling.

We are not the university

One persistent mantra of many UCU activists and organisers, at least since the national disputes of 2018, has been *We are the University!* We repeatedly made this claim at University of Leicester, contesting bosses' identification of themselves, along with their agenda and values, with 'the university'. UCU activists and organisers have similarly insisted, *The university is ours!*

It is clear, from events at Leicester and at so many other universities in recent years, that the university is *not* ours. It may be the case that we *make* the university, but we are not the university, and the university is not us. The trajectory over the past four decades has been away from faculty governance of universities and towards greater managerialism, as vice-chancellors and their business-minded allies have insisted on and exercised their *right to manage*. In recent years this has frequently and increasingly manifested as authoritarian leadership and, when it came to academic freedom, bosses insisted that this principle is 'subject to the rights of the University to manage its activity efficiently and economically'. Ultimately, our struggles to prevent our own dismissals were unsuccessful.

So why did we lose? Why did we lose our jobs? How should we conclude – and with what tone? Perhaps we should be optimistic, presenting our fate as being due to a whole constellation of unusual and specific conditions that colleagues in the UK and abroad are unlikely to face. If it was a set of elements that are quite outside the normal operation of university politics then it should be easier for others to successfully resist. Perhaps we should be pragmatic, suggesting ways of neutralising the forces that were arrayed against us. If we were encircled at individual, group, departmental, school, university, national and international level, surely there would be means of breaking out in a managed way where our opponents were weakest. What are those ways and in what order should we attempt egress from the circle? Perhaps we should be pessimistic, telling all interested readers that despite our efforts and developing collectivisation there is little you can do in the face of senior managers whose politics are very different from our own. Perhaps we should say there is no future for properly critical work in the business school of the contemporary university. Or even that there is no future for properly critical work anywhere in the contemporary university.

Another issue we must consider is the personality of those involved against us, revisiting our discussion in the book's Introduction. Should we say things at the personal level about named individuals when clearly most senior managers are blown this way and that, by forces other than internal, psychological ones? Should we regard them as malign, or disturbed, or weak, or as careerist, or just limited in what they could do against the machine? Are they mere personifications of the university-as-capital, the university as an instantiation of capital? But who or what is 'the machine', the university-as-capital? Clearly there was a constant torrent of communications amongst the managers and administrators who executed our redundancies. But because 'the university' refused us sight of these internal conversations – recall the mass of black boxes that shrouded the late-arriving results of our data subject access requests – it's tempting to over-emphasise the machinic nature of the process. The university itself becomes a black box – the 'outputs' of which were a set of dismissal notices and many more 'voluntary severance settlements', each with its accompanying 'non-disclosure agreement'. Given this systemic appearance of the whole, were we justified in naming those more senior individuals who played a role in making us redundant? Thus, is this a narrative of an organisation or one of some organisational members? More importantly, is it a narrative of *us* and *them* in a provincial university or a tale of wider university politics in the first quarter of the twenty-first century?

In searching for answers to these questions, we conceptualise the struggle we faced (and continue to face) according to four constellating forces: society, institution (both the university, and *universities*), group, and individual. Our aim is to situate the general and the specific side by side to help us navigate issues such as academic freedom, accountability, and care in UK higher education.

Throughout *society* the neoliberal agenda has been embraced, including at structural level in universities. The concept of globalisation, which accompanies neoliberalism has underpinned university bosses' assumptions that students from all over the world wanted to come to the UK to learn how the Anglo-American ideology worked. That's what business schools were, or are, for. Since the neoliberal agenda became hegemonic in the 1980s, the idea that *there is no alternative* has gained acceptance and leftist narratives have struggled to retain mainstream relevance. This 'great moving right show' has also involved an attack on the legitimacy of trade unionism and collectivism more generally.

One particular casualty has been the notion that education might be enlightening and that learning might have a value in its own right. We suffer the tireless and tiresome promotion of so-called STEM subjects (science, technology, engineering and maths) and the simultaneous delegitimisation of the arts, humanities, and social sciences in general. For a particularly crass example, see a poster published in 2020 by 'HM Government' that showed a photo of a ballet dancer alongside text reading 'Fatima's next job could be in cyber. She just doesn't know it yet' – the implication being that the arts don't pay, and that artists need to retrain in STEM subjects.[11] Neoliberal capitalists, including many politicians and university senior managers, suggest that arts and humanities are non-essential subjects for they cannot (so the argument goes) be used in the service of productivism and productivity. Hence, the vow of current UK prime minister (at the time of writing) Rishi Sunak to 'crack down' on 'rip-off university courses', which we mentioned in Chapter 4. Sunak's target was courses that do not lead to a 'good return' on university fee investments (fees introduced by politicians) in arts sectors that offer low pay (in part owing to defunding initiatives introduced by politicians).[12] As a result, scholar-practitioners in arts and humanities fields must constantly justify their position to those who seek only to aid the economy rather than question the polity. Within the UK (and elsewhere), politicians, administrators, theoreticians and cultural commentators who believe that the public will accept, even embrace, an anti-intellectual agenda have been emboldened. Despite much bombast about the defence of academic freedom (and freedom of speech) no-one in government paid any attention to events at the University of Leicester.

Several related issues are relevant at the level of the *institution*. The Russell Group of 24 self-styled 'leading' universities has been afforded a central position in representing all British universities. This body now exerts undue influence across the entire sector. Paradoxically, it's in the Russell Group that anti-intellectualism first took root, since bosses there viewed 'their' staff not even as a 'human resource', certainly not as a source of wealth, but rather as an obstruction, a problem getting in the way of the 'smooth' running of the university, and as a cost to be minimised.

Business schools are almost everywhere treated as cash cows by university managers. They are often seen – both by managers and unfortunately many scholars in other departments – as devoid of intellectual gravitas, their *raison d'être* simply to generate a surplus that might be used to subsidise the activities of, for example, geologists or chemists. Any threats to this pan-university supporting function – such as when business school scholars question the business school itself – are obviously extremely problematic for institutional leaders.

Moreover, we faced a senior management team that appeared to have little in the way of strategy for dealing with the crisis in the university's financing except to borrow more in ways which appeared to us as counter-productive. As part of its strategy of mimetic isomorphism, University of Leicester management sought to drive down to the 'sector norm' the ratio of salary costs to total costs – a tactic that seems to have played out in similar ways at other UK universities. At the time of our redundancies, there were, in fact, doubts regarding the University of Leicester's status as a *going concern*, suggesting its financial situation was somewhat challenging. Although bosses denied it, insisting that *Shaping for Excellence* and its associated redundancies were not financially motivated, we think it likely that (potential) creditors' demands were very much in the mix.

Finally at this level, just as the status of academic, research, and teaching staff (if not senior administrators) has declined, so too has the influence of trade unions. One reason for unions' declining influence is that they are frequently, like many institutions, riven by political and ideological differences. Our union, the University and College Union, is no exception; our recourse to seek material solidarity from it – at branch, regional and national levels – was often disappointing.

In terms of *group organisation*, the key decision makers in the collectives arrayed against us were protected by their collective status and as such were hard to identify. The senior management team was, for example, supported by the University of Leicester Council, its supreme governing body (which tends to the right politically). It might appear obvious that if you are written to by a named individual, whose signature appears at the end of the communication, then that individual has taken the decision. This is not always the case – the signatory might in fact hate what they are (apparently) executing and authorising but they nevertheless appear as the actor. We have little evidence that any of those who executed and who signed and sealed our fates objected to their task, but we were not able to work out the exact mechanics of who was doing what to whom in the group we faced.[13]

On our side, we as a group were not coherent in all we thought, said, or did. Sixteen of us (in the business school) were put at risk of redundancy in January 2021. But some of our number accepted so-called voluntary redundancy, some were successful in their appeals, and some left of their own accord. While we practised collectivism in our meetings and a variety of coordinated actions, readers should not think moving in the same direction is easy: it is not. For instance, we were not sufficiently perceptive to realise that we had alienated a number of our own business-school colleagues through past actions and inactions. We assumed that we would have the support of a department reasonably full of sympathetic colleagues, fellow 'critical thinkers', and even friends. But that was not always the case. Some colleagues refused to back us, either because of past affronts (whether perceived or 'real') or because of their fear of management (again, whether illusory or justified).

At the individual level we have several things to say. There is a temptation to write about senior members of the university *qua* individuals in hostile ways. These, after all, are the personifications of our redundancies and therefore the most obvious recipients of our criticisms.

A number of *individuals* played key roles. The then-dean of the School of Business, James Devlin, and his deputy (now successor) Daniel Ladley were tasked with enacting our dismissals. Both are economists in a disciplinary sense; neither know much of their 'targets', which were deemed to be 'Critical Management Studies' and political economy. It appeared at times that they perceived this to be a 'paradigm war' in which economics was placed against sociology in a bid to reduce the status of the latter in the School – or even to expunge it. We do not know when they took the decision to seek out those who embraced a critical approach to organisation studies and political economy, or those who played central roles in the university's UCU branch. We do not know if it was their initiative or whether they were instructed to move against us. One possibility we think likely is that more senior figures provided Devlin and Ladley with a 'list of names', leaving the latter to determine the means to reach the end goal of dismissals. We do not know whether Devlin and Ladley wished to undertake this activity.

Henrietta O'Connor, a pro-vice-chancellor and head of the College of Social Sciences, Arts and Humanities, also played a leading role in executing our redundancies. Her signature appeared on many communications we received, including our dismissal notices, and she was one of the five members of the 'Review Group' which approved Devlin's and Ladley's original judgement of our scholarship. She was possibly an architect too – we don't know.

Her deputy John Goodwin played a supporting role, threatening on at least one occasion other colleagues in the College of Social Sciences, Arts and Humanities who had allegedly breached the university's Dignity and Respect policy in their criticisms of university management. O'Connor and Goodwin may well have harboured personal antipathy towards us. Some years earlier, the university centre they then led was amalgamated with what was the School of Management: they thus went from heading a small unit to becoming 'subsumed' within a larger one, before being elevated to their superordinate positions at the head of the College.[14] As we also noted elsewhere in the book, O'Connor and Goodwin were sociologists and had written approvingly of Critical Management Studies.

The university's deputy vice-chancellor, Edmund Burke, was one of *Shaping for Excellence*'s architects and oversaw its execution on a day-to-day basis. Several of us who were also officers of Leicester UCU – in addition to being staff members fighting for our own jobs – spent many hours in meetings with Burke. Moreover, he convened and chaired all the panels hearing appeals concerning academic freedom, none of which were successful. It's likely that Burke's interest was not solely professional: recall his 'I won't forget this' comment at the conclusion of a previous redundancy dispute.

Whatever their personal investment in our dismissals, the above individuals, with one quite notable exception, all behaved with the dispassionate professionalism one would expect of a senior executive.

Some have suggested that Nishan Canagarajah, the university's president and vice-chancellor, arrived at the University of Leicester in 2019 with a sympathetic view towards the School's critical approaches and that he certainly did not want the bad publicity which came from the redundancies. According to this view, he was forced by others' actions into backing the dismissals. We must remember, however, that acting with 'firmness' in the face of opposition is seen by some local and national political entities as a welcome sign of strength and resolve, of good leadership.

Although Canagarajah attracted considerable opprobrium as a result of *Shaping for Excellence*, in some quarters he will have gained kudos.

The extent of the involvement of Gary Dixon, the Chair of Council, the university's supreme governing body, is unclear. As we mentioned above, we suspect he may have provided Devlin and Ladley with a 'list of names'. As with Henrietta O'Connor and John Goodwin, we suspect he harboured some personal animosity against at least some of us. As with Edmund Burke, we suspect he took personally Leicester UCU's ability to challenge managers' right to manage. What we know for certain is that Dixon was (and remains) an employer-appointed director of USS, the pension fund with which we were in dispute and that he both convened and chaired all panels that heard our appeals against redundancy. None of these appeals were successful, of course.[15]

The other senior individual who played a key role in bringing about our redundancies was Kerry Law, then the university's chief marketing and engagement officer and now one of its deputy vice-chancellors. It's likely that it was Law who ordered and oversaw the systematic monitoring of our public pronouncements on social media. (Other, less senior, administrators played active parts in surveillance too – though we have chosen not to name them.)

Finally, so-called Human Resources business partners played active parts throughout the redundancy process. Despite proclamations that they were neutral, at every turn they appeared to be acting as agents of management. For instance, the minutes of meetings that they are credited with authoring rarely bore any resemblance whatsoever to actual events and speech therein.

There were, of course, many individuals both named and not named in this book who acted in solidarity and extended care to those of us targeted for dismissal. But in keeping with our rejection of neoliberal politics, we acknowledge them as a group for whom community, rather than individual notoriety, was always the motivating factor.

In summary then, there were many identifiable elements or forces that made up the constellation that surrounded us and eventually overwhelmed us. Some we could have done more about, some appear to be beyond our control but not our understanding, some we were ignorant of. It is a salutary warning that organisational forces, albeit arranged in certain ways, can overwhelm intellectual and emotional resources. Some of these elements were unique to the University of Leicester, its School of Business or the particular conjuncture we found ourselves in. Others are more general to the sector; they are likely to be familiar to many others working in universities – different names, but familiar types and roles.

And the struggle we fought is a part of a more generalised one. In 2021, University of Leicester bosses decided that our scholarship no longer had any value to the university – that's the meaning of 'disinvestment'. Many other universities have made multiple staff redundant or threatened multiple redundancies in recent years. We hope that by writing this book, we encourage readers everywhere to reject the 'values' of neoliberal institutions and to reimagine higher education as a space for learning, criticism, and creativity for its own sake. We may have lost our jobs, but the struggle for our university – universities – is still to be won.

Two months after our dismissals, UCU reported that university staff pay had fallen by one-fifth in real terms over the preceding twelve years, 'a "stark reminder" of just how little university bosses value their staff'.[16] In 2020/21, almost one-third of academic staff were employed on fixed-term contracts.[17] In June 2022, another UCU report 'detail[ed] sky-high levels of overwork across all sectors in post-16 education that would breach Working Time Regulations of a maximum 48 hour working week', with 68% of university staff saying their workload had increased significantly over the previous three years.[18] There are many other indicators of the university managers' disdain for scholars and scholarship, of the low value they ascribe to scholars and scholarship. None of this would be the case were the university ours. None of this would be the case were we the university.

The question of whether the university has *ever* been ours is moot. It is certainly the case that, when Margaret Thatcher launched her assault on higher education in the 1980s, academic salaries were significantly higher. Faculty played a central role in university governance and they also enjoyed, via the rights of tenure, almost absolute job security. Workloads were almost unimaginably light by today's standards. But faculty were even less diverse than they are today – and today significant inequalities remain. The faculty who enjoyed such favourable working conditions were overwhelming white men, and they were disproportionately privately educated. While these faculty had ample freedom to pursue their scholarship and to 'question and test received wisdom', their backgrounds and experiences of course shaped the questions they typically chose to ask and their mode of questioning. The university was *theirs* – but since *we* were probably not the same as *them*, the university was not *ours*.

Universities and the future of critical thinking – against the slow cancellation of the future

Critical thinking – in universities, but not only in universities – is essential to our future, essential to our ability to create a liveable world for ten billion people.[20] In his best-known book, *Capitalist Realism*, Mark Fisher writes:

> [E]mancipatory politics must always destroy the appearance of a 'natural order', must reveal what is presented as necessary and inevitable to be a mere contingency, just as it must make what was previously deemed to be impossible seem attainable.[21]

At their best, the critique of political economy (which was the type of political economy that is now redundant at University of Leicester) and Critical Management Studies are both strands within this emancipatory politics. The critique of political economy questions the naturalness of markets and the neoliberal common sense that markets are the best way of ordering every aspect of our lives. Critical Management Studies (at least the type of CMS that University of Leicester managers found problematic, a danger) questions the fairy tale that managers are moral and wise – even the very necessity of managers and 'management' in the ordering of our lives.

We have not abandoned the university. But we have no fidelity toward it, we do not 'worry about the university', nor 'call for its restoration [… or] its reform'.[22] For most of us, our incomes, our livelihoods still depend upon it. Whilst we might dream of escape, or even plot it, where would we escape to? Moreover, as we noted above, more than half of 18-year-olds continue into higher education – and perhaps one sixth of those study business, management or a related subject. We do not wish to abandon them. The university, for most of us, is simply the terrain upon which to do our thing – intellectual work, critique. Important here is the 'critical distinction' Stuart Hall makes 'between intellectual work and academic work: they overlap, they abut each other, they feed off one another, the one provides you with the means to do the other. But they are not the same thing.'[23] Or more directly: 'I was going to be – dirty word – an intellectual. Academia was just how I made my money.'[24]

Critical thinking continues in the university. It even continues at the University of Leicester, despite bosses' concerted attack of 2021. But, to the extent that it does, it does so despite the university – if by 'the university' we mean its senior managers and their state overseers. But the conditions for critical thinking are being undermined – by governance reforms and the financialisation of the university, by the subordination of 'academic freedom' to managerial prerogative and the generalisation of precarity, by the turn to authoritarian leadership. Bosses' attack on critical thinking at the University of Leicester was perhaps exceptional in its suddenness. Across the sector, over the past decades the undermining of the conditions for critical thinking – its cancellation – has been slower.

Comparing his 'Covid generation of graduates with the preceding one', activist and recent graduate Olly Haynes writes, 'I don't think our generation even has expectations of anything beyond collapse. Even the paltry expectations of the Millennials who were young adults pre-crash seem fanciful.'[25] This sense of futurelessness – of the future having been cancelled – has now spread to university staff: in a recent UCU survey, 88% of respondents expressed pessimism about the future, at least of higher education.[26] It might seem then that, as Stefano Harney and Fred Moten argue, 'the only possible relationship to the university today is a criminal one', that we can only steal–just as 'the university' – or its bosses – steal from us: our time, our energies, our creativity.

And yet…

We have not – yet – abandoned hope. The question *could the university be ours?* at the present moment seems a ridiculous one. It is not. For us, it's productive for the other questions it calls into being, the other questions it opens onto. It is a question that is best answered in practice, by *acting* – as best we can – as though the university is already ours. After all, we can only measure the distance between what is possible and what is desirable by travelling its length.[27]

In December 2013, the Centre for Philosophy and Political Economy hosted a conference to mark its tenth anniversary. The mood of the preceding months was wearied. In the UK, we were three years into post-crash austerity – including the tripling of university tuition fees. At the University of Leicester Vice-Chancellor Bob Burgess was approaching retirement and something seemed be shifting there, too. We were starting to feel beleaguered in the School of Management. We held our conference at various city-centre venues, a decision that sparked a row with university managers, who had demanded instead that we use the university's new conference centre – a pricey venue beyond the means of many participants, especially those without generous institutional funding.[28]

Despite the inauspicious circumstances, the conference proved to be a space for participants to decompress and an occasion for renewal. We chose for the conference's strapline a well-known quotation from Samuel Beckett. It seemed to capture the way in which conditions (not of our choosing) both make critical thinking difficult and sometimes impossible, but also absolutely essential. Another decade later the Centre for Philosophy and Political Economy exists only in our memories and various ghostly traces, such as author affiliations from old articles and derelict websites. But the quotation – slightly adjusted to reflect the collective nature of critique and critical thinking – remains apt and a fitting way to end our book: 'You must go on, we can't go on, we'll go on.'[29]

POSTSCRIPT

AFTER 2021

In this brief postscript, we look at what's happened since the redundancies of 2021 were completed. First, we briefly recount events within the School of Business, which show that there was no genuine strategy underpinning the redundancy cases in that School. Second, we look at what has happened to some of the key players. From these, sadly, we learn that (most) of the managers have fallen upwards.

The case changes

In early 2022, members of the School of Business were invited to a meeting to discuss the development of a new School Strategy. To help the School's new Dean, Daniel Ladley, in this process, Paul Baines (juggling his role at the university with his responsibilities as Conservative Mayor of Charnwood Borough Council) was appointed 'Deputy Dean for Strategic Projects'. In an initial all-School briefing about the process, the somewhat considerable elephant in the room was that no one still employed in the School, other than Ladley himself, knew what the old strategy was, that is, the strategy from 2021. This was because, as we have seen, the 'strategic plan' was embedded in the redundancy paperwork and was, therefore, confidential.

Of course, staff knew that the previous strategy had targeted sixteen colleagues for redundancy. Indeed, 'strategy' had become a synonym for 'redundancy', and Ladley was forced to spend considerable time reassuring staff that the School would now be growing, without further redundancies. At an initial briefing for staff, colleagues were told that they should feel free to offer forward any suggestions they had for the School's strategic direction. One person quipped, "what if we want to invest in CMS and political economy?" But they didn't say it too loudly.

After a set of initial workshops designed to get general input from staff, the process moved into a series of strategy workshops. Mimicking the curriculum of a fairly unambitious 'business environment' module, these workshops involved 'SWOT analysis', 'Resource and Capabilities', 'PESTLE Analysis', and a 'Portfolio Analysis'.[1]

The final product of the process focused on development. It noted that Leicester had no distinct teaching approach. It had had one, based around Critical Management Studies – but this approach was explicitly targeted for elimination in the redundancy process. The elimination of CMS (and political economy) left not so much an opportunity for a new strategy, but a void where old values and approaches had once existed, but which could no longer be discussed. But as 2022 continued, memory of the void faded: another forty or so members of academic staff left the School and new starters were seemingly oblivious to the battle that had taken place not many months before. Many of these joined during the global academic boycott. Perhaps they will read this book.

Still, it was not all bad news. Whereas we had been told that reducing the provision of education in management studies was necessary because of declining student numbers, the new strategy's recruitment targets were to hold steady with regard to on-campus teaching, with a vast increase in distance learning/teaching.

The final product was the first strategic plan which all members of the School had seen since 2016.

Where are they now?

In early September 2021, just three weeks after the dismissal by redundancy of nine colleagues, remaining staff were informed that James Devlin was also leaving, in his case to establish a research centre at Nottingham Trent University. The wording of the announcement, with no mention of 'resignation', implied that Devlin's departure was not unwelcome to the institution. On arrival at his new employer, Devlin was given a shared office with two members of staff who had been vocal opponents of the redundancies at Leicester, which Devlin had helped to engineer. We hope they made him welcome. In June 2023, Devlin was named as a founding member of his local branch of Academics for Academic Freedom. (Seriously.)

In the wake of Devlin's departure, Daniel Ladley took over as interim Dean of the School of Business and was confirmed in that post in November 2021. A year later, in December 2022, the Company of Entrepreneurs, an 'aspirant Livery Company of the City of London' whose 'Master' is University of Leicester's Chair of Council Gary Dixon, announced that it was grateful to the School of Business for sponsorship of its 'Entrepreneurs Award for Social Innovation' scheme. 'A significant donation' was reported on the Company's LinkedIn page. When commentators on social media pointed out that this was likely a very strong conflict of interest, the LinkedIn page was swiftly edited to remove reference to the donation.

Gary Dixon remains as Chair of the University of Leicester's Council – alongside his role as Master of the Company of Entrepreneurs, of course. Dixon also remains a Universities UK-nominated board member of the USS pension scheme. Needless to say, the university has not issued any statement that has contradicted

USS or Universities UK on pensions matters whilst Dixon has been a member of the USS board.

In September 2022, Edmund Burke was appointed as the Vice-Chancellor of Bangor University, no doubt leveraging on his 'strong leadership' on industrial relations. One of Burke's first appointments was Martyn Riddleston, to the post of chief financial officer. Riddleston had apparently been side-lined in the University of Leicester senior leadership team: in May 2022, Canagarajah appointed Kerry Law, formerly Chief Marketing and Engagement Officer, to a newly created post of Deputy Vice-Chancellor, Professional Services. Following Riddleston's departure, his Leicester portfolio was incorporated into Law's office.

As Riddleston was in the process of packing up his office, the shiny new Freemen's Common facilities were being officially opened. Meanwhile, back on main campus the estate is almost literally collapsing. One building has had its occupancy levels cut for fear that its structure cannot support the weight otherwise. Another is wrapped in a sort of builder's swaddling to prevent bits of its cladding hitting passers-by when it crumbles. And the main administration building in which Riddleston's office was located, the Fielding Johnson Building, had a two-metre exclusion zone around it to prevent people being hit by falling masonry chipping off the internal gutters.

In the wake of Burke's departure, Henrietta O'Connor was given responsibility for trade union relations at Leicester and, in April 2023, was appointed to Burke's old role, Deputy Vice-Chancellor.

In January 2023, the Vice-Chancellor's moratorium on redundancies – accepted by Leicester UCU in November 2021 in exchange for lifting the global academic boycott – came to an end. The first staff to be targeted in a new round of dismissals are those who work at the university's on-site nursery, which is to be closed.

In March 2024, an employment tribunal found that David Harvie, Geoff Lightfoot, and Simon Lilley were unfairly dismissed from their jobs at the University of Leicester. University bosses did not appeal.

APPENDIX

EXTRACTS FROM REVIEW GROUP OUTCOMES

In March 2021, the research publications of those of us targeted for redundancy were reassessed by a 'Review Group', chaired by Henrietta O'Connor, head of the College of Social Sciences, Arts and Humanities. This Group included four other members: James Devlin and Daniel Ladley, the School's dean and deputy dean, who were responsible for drawing up the original list of targets; Richard Thomas, the College's dean of research and a professor of archaeology; and Professor Philip Baker, the University's pro-vice-chancellor for research and enterprise. Below we reproduce extracts from this group's assessment of each of our 'research outputs'. The text we've reproduced is the entire text for each output and it appears exactly as it was presented to us, though we have made the alignment clearer, such that the Group's assessment of a book, book chapter or article appears next to that output's title. All typographical, grammatical and other errors that appear below were in the original documents.

For Gibson Burrell	
Chapter Burrell G Routledge Handbook of Interpretive Political Science 2015 Organizational sociology	Organizational sociology is a chapter in a handbook on Interpretive Political Science that highlights the "importance of politics and of power to the study of organisations" which aligns with the PE definition of the case.
Journal article Burrell G Global Discourse 2017 The role of coal-mining towns in social theory: past, present and future	The article The role of coal-mining towns in social theory: past, present and future looks at the subject through a CMS/PE lens across countries and commonality of experience.
Chapter Burrell G Organization 2666: Literary Troubling, Undoing and Refusal 2020 Machismo as a mode of organizing	The chapter Machismo as a mode of organizing is a work inspired by reading a particular book (2666) and considers the lack of consideration of certain aspects of social and organisational life (gender violence in this case) and aligns with a CMS approach.
Book Parker M, Burrell G 2015 For Robert Cooper Collected Work	Gibson co-edited a book For Robert Cooper Collected Work. Cooper was one of the first to introduce key critical management themes such as post-structuralism and post-modernism into management and organisation.
Journal article Reed M, Burrell WGG Organization Studies 2019 Theory and Organization Studies: The Need for Contestation	The article Theory and Organization Studies: The Need for Contestation focus on a critique of the emerging orthodoxy within organisational theory and would fall within the definition of CMS for this case.

For Ronald Hartz [*See note 1 below*]	
Chapter Hartz R Martilla, Tomas (Ed.): Discourse, Culture and Organization: Inquiries into Relational Structures of Power. 2018-11 'The People' and it's Antagonistic Other: The Populist Right-wing Movement Pegila in Germany	The chapter 'The People' and it's Antagonistic Other: The Populist Right-wing Movement Pegida in Germany is based on post structuralist approaches and the work of Laclau and is aligned with a CMS/PE approach.
Journal article Kranz O, Steger T, Hartz R Organizacija 2016 The Employee as the Unknown Actor? A Discourse Analysis of the Employee Share Ownership Debate with Special Emphasis on Central and Eastern Europe et	The article The Employee as the Unknown Actor? A Discourse Analysis of the Employee Share Ownership Debate with Special Emphasis on Central and Eastern Europe carries out a semantic analysis of employee share ownership. This article lists CMS as one of the author's areas of work.
Journal article Hartz R Managementforschung 2017-09 Von anderen Organisationen	The paper *Von anderen Organisationen* is subtitled *"An essay on perspectives in critical organization studies"* and falls under CMS/PE

Journal article Hartz R Zeitschrift für Diversitätsforschung und -management 2017	The paper *Geschlecht und Gemeinschaft* translates as and focuses on forms of discrimination (especially gender discrimination) in the context of far right political organisations in Germany. In particular, the article emphasises the importance of these topics for critical management and organisational research. As such the research is related to CMS/PE. Ronald also lists Critical Management studies as an area of focus in the author bio.
Chapter Hartz R Handbuch Organisationssoziologie 2019 Postmoderne und Poststrukturalismus in der Organisationsforschung	The output *Postmoderne und Poststrukturalismus in der Organisationsforschung* concerns *Postmodernism and Poststructuralism in Organizational Research* and displays the profound questioning of the authority and relevance of mainstream management thinking and practice associated with CMS scholarship.

For David Harvie	
Journal article: Barthold C, Dunne S, Harvie D *Critical Perspectives on Accounting* 2018 Resisting financialisation with Deleuze and Guattari: The case of Occupy Wall Street Journal article Harvie D, Lightfoot G, Lilley S, Weir K *Critical Perspectives on Accounting* 2020 Social investment innovation and the 'social turn' of neoliberal finance	David has published two articles in a journal (*Critical Perspectives on Accounting)* that, as the name suggests offers "critical perspectives". Articles by David in this journal include *Resisting Financialization* which has *Critical Finance studies* as a nominated key word/phrase and addresses aspects of the political economy of finance. The more recent article on *Social investment innovation* considers social investment bonds from a political economy perspective.
Chapter Milburn K, Harvie D, Watts D The Aesthetic of Our Anger. Anarcho-Punk, Politics and Music. 2016 The Kids were just Crass	The Chapters *Aesthetic of Our Anger* and *The Commons* are in other areas of research that are not aligned with future strategic direction. *[See note 2 below.]*

For Geoff Lightfoot	
Journal article Harvie D, Lightfoot G, Lilley S, Weir K Critical Perspectives on Accounting 2020 Social investment innovation and the 'social turn' of neoliberal finance	Geoff's co-authored article in *Critical Perspectives on Accounting* (a journal that offers "critical perspectives") *Social investment innovation and the 'social turn' of neoliberal finance* entitled focusses on Social investment innovation considers social investment bonds from a political economy perspective.
Journal article Lilley S, Harvie D, Lightfoot G, Weir K Journal of Urban Affairs 2019 Using Derivative Logic to Speculate on the Future of the Social Investment Market	Likewise Geoff's co-authored article in the *Journal of Urban Affairs* entitled *Using Derivative Logic to Speculate on the Future of the Social Investment Market* which according to the authors investigates a model which "fuses and extends a number of existing trends or developments in the political economy of the public sector."
Journal article Lilley SD, Lightfoot G Organization 2017 Organising destruction: A derivative logic?	Geoff's co-authored article *Organising destruction: A derivative logic?* appears in the journal *Organization* which has been identified as a journal targeted primarily by those writing from a CMS perspective (Swann and Stoborod, 2014) whilst the article itself offers a wide-ranging exposition of war and finance through the lens of derivative logic, which is a research output which is not aligned with future strategic direction of research in the School.

Lilley, S. and Lightfoot, G. (2014), The embodiment of neoliberalism. Sociol Rev, 62: 68-89. Lightfoot, G. and Lilley, S. (2020) 'Markets and Machines: The Magic of Predicting, Obscuring and Securing Value', in H. Letiche, S. Linstead and J-L Moriceau (eds) The Magic of Organization, Cheltenham, Edward Elgar, pp. 143-159.	The article The embodiment of neoliberalism is an analysis of entrepreneurship and finance from a sociological perspective which is not aligned with School strategic priorities in the area of research and neither is The magic of predicting which draws parallels between magic and trading.
Journal article Letiche HK, Lightfoot G, Lilley S Revue Française de Gestion 2017 Classements Capitalisme Academique et Affects des Chedrcheurs en Gestion	The article *"Classements Capitalisme Academique et Affects des Chedrcheurs en Gestion"* looks at the political condition that has created ranking systems (academic) through *the* lenses of *"performativity"* and *"academic capitalism"*. The article itself is in French it is apparent that it does little to contribute to research in School strategic priority areas. [*See note 1 below*]

For Simon Lilley	
Journal article Lilley SD, Parker M Ephemera: theory and politics in organization 2016 Management knowledge in the mirror: Scholarship, fashion and Simmel	The article "*Management knowledge in the mirror: Scholarship, fashion and Simmel*" appears in the journal *Ephemera,* a journal identified as closely associated with CMS perspectives (Rowlinson and Hassard 2011). The article itself has a media/cultural studies orientation and not mainstream Business studies. As such it does little to contribute to future School strategic priorities
Journal article Gasparin M, Brown SD, Green W, Hugill A, Lilley S, Quinn M, Schinckus C, Williams M, Zalasiewicz J Academy of Management Learning and Education 2020 THE BUSINESS SCHOOL IN THE ANTHROPOCENE: PARASITE LOGIC AND PATAPHYSICAL REASONING IOR A WORKING EARTH	The multi author output in *AMLE* looks at the Anthropocene, which although a contested concept highlights the impact of human activity on the climate and ecosystem. Although elements of the article are somewhat esoteric the article makes suggestions for management education and suggests a move towards slow craft. It is not directly a CMS or PE linked output
Journal article Lilley SD Sociology 2014 Material Returns: Cultures of Valuation, Biofinancialisation and the Autonomy of Politics	The article *Material Returns* is mainly a sociological perspective which does little to contribute to debates connected to mainstream business and management understanding or to contribute to future School strategic priorities.

Lilley, S. and Lightfoot, G. (2014), The embodiment of neoliberalism. Sociol Rev, 62: 68-89.	The article *The embodiment of neoliberalism* is an analysis of entrepreneurship and finance from a sociological perspective which is not aligned with School strategic priorities in the area of research and neither is *The magic of predicting* which draws parallels between magic and trading.

Note 1. In the assessment column, the Review Group referred to '*The Commons*', but did not mention this research output at all in the left-hand column. They are referencing a book chapter Harvie co-authored with Massimo De Angelis, included in *The Routledge Companion to Alternative Organization*, edited by Martin Parker, George Cheney, Valérie Fournier and Chris Land (London: Routledge, 2013). The publication date means that this output fell outside of the period supposedly being considered, which had a start date of 1 January 2014.

Note 2. Some of the 'research outputs' assessed were not published in English, those of Ronald Hartz, in particular. These were not translated into English and ignored in the initial screening exercise, which was flagged as a potential breach of the DORA agreement (the University of Leicester is a signatory of this agreement) in the first individual consultation. The judgement of the review group is based on translations of the titles and abstract. Another article (co-authored by Lightfoot and Lilley) published in French, which was deemed problematic due to the word '*capitalisme*' – an easy translate – being in its title.

ENDNOTES

Preface

1. Published in New York by Vintage International, 2011. The quotation is on p. 73.
2. To readers unfamiliar with the UK's geography, Leicester is a city of 370,000 people in the English midlands, 90 miles north of London. It's pronounced *Lester*.
3. *Warwick University Ltd: Industry, Management and the Universities*, edited by E. P. Thompson (Harmondsworth: Penguin, 1970).
4. We have archived on this site many of documents (and videos) referred to in this book: https://ulsb16.com/SfM/
5. John Holloway, *Change the World Without Taking Power: The Meaning of Revolution Today* (London: Pluto, 2002), p. 144.
6. E. P. Thompson, *The Making of the English Working Class* (Harmondsworth: Penguin, 1968), p. 8.
7. University of Leicester, 'University of Leicester supports Government pledge to end victim NDA use', 1 March 2022, https://bit.ly/SfM-P01; University of Leicester (@uniofleicester) 'We are proud to sign the @ educationgovuk pledge to end the use Non-Disclosure Agreements (NDAs) when dealing', Twitter, 1 March 2022, https://bit.ly/SfM-P02.

Introduction

1. Gareth Brown refers to eleven individuals being 'in scope' for redundancy: at the time of this exchange two of the original sixteen had accepted 'voluntary' redundancy and three had been removed from 'scope'.
2. Gwilym Croucher and Peter Woelert, 'Institutional isomorphism and the creation of the unified national system of higher education in Australia: an empirical analysis', *Higher Education*, 71 (2016), pp. 442–43.
3. Thomas Docherty, *The New Treason of the Intellectuals: Can the University Survive?* (Manchester: Manchester University Press, 2018), p. 103.
4. Since the public case for our redundancy was a plan to divest from scholarship and research in Critical Management Studies and political economy, it is perhaps apt to quote from the founding figure of political economy. In *The Wealth of Nations*, Adam Smith is blunt about the role of trade associations: 'People of the same trade seldom meet together, even for merriment and diversion, but the conversation ends in a conspiracy against the public, or in some contrivance to raise prices.'
5. Steven Jones, *Universities under Fire. Hostile Discourses and Integrity Deficits in Higher Education* (Basingstoke: Palgrave Macmillan, 2022), p. 36.
6. Stuart Hall, 'The Great Moving Right Show', *Marxism Today*, 23(1), January 1979. Reprinted in Stuart Hall, *Essential Essays*, Vol. 1, edited by David Morley (Durham and London: Duke University Press, 2019).

Chapter 1

1. Canagarajah made this remark to striking members of Leicester UCU, whom he stopped to speak to on a picket line in November 2019, shortly after his arrival as vice-chancellor.
2. Office for National Statistics, 'Labour disputes in the UK: 2018', 17 May 2019, https://bit.ly/SfM-101.
3. USS is the privatised pension provider to the majority of academic and other more senior professional services staff (i.e. staff represented by UCU) at pre-92 universities, i.e. those institutions that were universities prior to the Education Reform Act 1992. As we mentioned in the Introduction, in 2019 employers' body Universities UK named Gary

Dixon, chair of University of Leicester Council, as one of its four nominated directors of USS. Employees of the UK's post-92 universities (mostly former polytechnics) are typically members of The Teachers' Pension scheme (TPA).

4. Richard Hall, 'On the University as anxiety machine', 19 March 2014, https://bit.ly/SfM-102; Liz Morrish, 'The university has become an anxiety machine', Higher Education Policy Institute blog, 23 May 2019, https://bit.ly/SfM-103.
5. Ben R. Martin, 'What's happening to our universities?', *Prometheus*, 34(1) (2016); Thomas Docherty, 'The boiled frog and the dodo', *Prometheus*, 34(1) (2016).
6. Thomas Docherty, 'The boiled frog and the dodo', p. 35.
7. Data are from Sean Coughlan, 'The symbolic target of 50% at university reached', BBC News, 26 September 2019; at https://bbc.in/41TfeeH, and Paul Bolton, 'Education: Historical Statistics', Standard Note SN/SG/4252, House of Commons Library, 27 November 2012, https://bit.ly/SfM-104.
8. The terms are Martin Trow's. Trow, *Problems in the Transition from Elite to Mass Higher Education* (Berkeley, CA: Carnegie Commission on Higher Education, 1973).
9. Data are from the Higher Education Statistics Agency: https://www.hesa.ac.uk/data-and-analysis/staff. International diversity didn't play a role in the 'business case' for redundancies at the School of Business, which targeted EU staff in a disproportionate way. What we see here is a strong correlation between the ignorance of the international outlook and reputation of the school and its international migrants.
10. See, for example, Hélène Mulholland, 'David Willetts blames feminism over lack of jobs for working men', *The Guardian*, 1 April 2011.
11. Hans Speier, 'Wit and politics: an essay on laughter and power', *American Journal of Sociology*, Vol. 103, no. 5 (March 1998), p. 1358. There is some evidence this is changing. As Marcus Barnett and Chris Webb write in their article about the Communication Workers Union, 'There is potential in taking the piss out of your opponents, and the resonance it'll have with working people. The fact is, humour cuts through.' 'Why we need fighting trade unionism', *Tribune*, 1 May 2021, https://bit.ly/SfM-105.

12. It's important to acknowledge that School of Business employees were not the only ones putting their scholarly expertise to work for the union. The group which uncovered the 'manufactured' nature of 2016's 'crisis' in the University's finances included more faculty from the medical school than the business school, for instance.
13. There should be nothing peculiar about our applying our scholarly expertise in order to make sense of our own situation and struggles. In fact, Liz Morrish has suggested that the emerging interdisciplinary field of Critical University Studies is itself 'informed by a paradigm previously established in Critical Management Studies'. Morrish, 'Academic Freedom and the Disciplinary Regime in the Neoliberal University', in *Neoliberalism in Context: Governance, Subjectivity and Knowledge*, edited by Simon Dawes and Marc Lenormand (London: Palgrave Macmillan, 2020), p. 238.
14. In such documents, we took care to emphasise the necessity of a 'just transition': no redundancies and encouraging staff to move from one area to another, with paid-for retraining.
15. All of the five features concern collective organisation. During this period Leicester UCU, like all union branches, also continued supporting individual members via one-on-one case-support. And, during this period, we believe Leicester UCU's caseworkers were particularly effective in supporting members facing individualised problems with managers. That is, these caseworkers were particularly successful in limiting managerial prerogative. Three of Leicester UCU's six most heavily worked caseworkers were targeted with redundancy in 2021.
16. We know from Data Subject Access Requests that, in another harbinger of the redundancy struggle to come, university bosses debated whether one of us could be disciplined for the offence of challenging advice that, in seminars held in lecture theatres (to facilitate distancing), one should raise one's voice to be heard – an action that would negate the effects of the distancing.
17. Email to staff from Vice-Chancellor Nishan Canagarajah, 13 October 2020.

Chapter 2

1. Letter to Vice-Chancellor Nishan Canagarajah
2. ITV Central East News broadcast, on 9 June 2021.
3. The letters are available at the website ULSB16.com.
4. An external examiner is an experienced academic from an outside institution, who comments on curriculum, assessment questions, student work and associated marks. In the absence of centralised curricula or examination boards – as with secondary education – their role is to ensure some sort of consistency of standards, without imposing uniformity of content, across British universities. In British universities it is standard practice for all student credit-bearing work to be first-marked, moderated (by a second 'internal' examiner) and then reviewed by an external examiner.
5. Professor Clarke shared her resignation letter in a tweet. Catherine Clarke (@CathAMClarke) 'Today I have resigned as incoming External Examiner for the MA #English Studies @uniofleicester', Twitter, 29 January 2021, https://bit.ly/SfM-201.
6. Priyamvada Gopal (@Priyamvada Gopal) 'This is your annual reminder, just incidentally, that "diversity" and "decolonisation" are not the same thing. If the RW wants to blame the Leicester cuts on', Twitter, 24 January 2021, https://bit.ly/SfM-202.
7. According to the Data Protection Act 2018, where we find the UK's general data protection regulations, an individual has the right to ask any organisation for the information that organisation holds on them. According to the legislation, the organisation must respond to the request 'as soon as possible, and within one month at most'.
8. Sara Ahmed, *Complaint!* (Duke University Press: Durham NC, 2021), p. 35.
9. Sara Ahmed, *Complaint!*, p. 2. We are not seeking here to co-opt narratives or vocabulary that people more marginalised than us within the academy use to describe their experiences. Rather, we have included this reader's observation to acknowledge that patriarchy informs all of our interactions with institutions to open up paths to solidarity with others who know the effects of managers' violence.
10. Sara Ahmed, *Complaint!*, p. 5.

11. Sara Ahmed, *Complaint!*, p. 27, quoting Ahmed, *What's the Use? On the uses of use* (Duke University Press: Durham NC, 2019), p. 212.
12. Our suspicion is based on the fact that, when offered the position, Devlin became very curious about Gareth Brown, quizzing former colleagues (of Brown) about him.
13. Sara Ahmed, *Complaint!*, p. 1.
14. Sara Ahmed, *Complaint!*, p. 87.
15. Sara Ahmed, *Complaint!*, pp. 91–97.
16. 'Global boycott of University of Leicester begins today', University and College Union, 4 May 2021, https://bit.ly/SfM-203.
17. Louise Thornthwaite, 'Chilling times: Social media policies, labour law and employment relations', *Asia Pacific Journal of Human Resources*, 54(3) (2016), p. 332.
18. Anna McKie, 'Leicester drops promotion of work by academics facing redundancy', *Times Higher Education*, 12 March 2021, https://bit.ly/SfM-204.
19. Posting 'a nonsensical, irrelevant, or deliberately provocative message, image, comment, etc., on social media, esp. with the intention of amusing an in-group, eliciting a reaction, subverting a discussion, or distracting from the main conversation.' This definition from the *OED*, only appeared in its December 2021 update.
20. Alex Moffett-Bateau and Jenn M. Jackson, 'Moving beyond Niceness: Reading bell hooks into the Radical Potential for the Discipline', *Journal of Women, Politics & Policy*, 43(3) (2022), p. 409.
21. Though, as we noted in the previous section and elsewhere in the book, the University of Leicester's most powerful figures were themselves frequently unable to behave even with the surface manifestations of professionalism and respect – such as addressing interlocutors by title and surname.
22. Professor emeritus is an honorary title granted to a retired professor.
23. Sally Weale and Rachel Hall, 'University of Leicester threatens to strip professor of title over social media barbs', *The Guardian*, 8 April 2021.
24. In April 2023, Peter Armstrong received the lifetime achievement award of the British Accounting & Finance Association (BAFA). In his acceptance speech, he addressed the events at the University of Leicester.

25. Such a reframing also operates to shore up the narrative that equates 'the University' and its 'interests' with those of the Vice-Chancellor and senior leadership. These leaders then arbitrate the possibly competing claims and passions of those below them: unions and dissenters versus 'ordinary' staff, 'concerned' colleagues. See our discussion in the previous chapter where we explain why *We are the university!* is such an important affirmation.
26. University of Leicester, 'VC & Executive Board Live Q&A February 2021', YouTube, 24 February 2021, https://bit.ly/SfM-205. (Also archived at https://ulsb16.com/SfM/)
27. In July 2022, the university confirmed the monitoring of student's and staff's social media accounts as well as the engagement of WPR Agency in a FOI request. at https://bit.ly/SfM-206.
28. Three of us, all prominent in the UCU branch as organisers and/or case workers, submitted DSARs for the 12 months up to 18 January 2021, requesting correspondence to and from various employees within the School, the College and the University.
29. We were particularly interested in Chair of Council Gary Dixon, Vice-Chancellor Nishan Canagarajah and his deputy, Edmund Burke. As we mentioned above, we learned much later – whilst we were writing the book – that Devlin, before taking up his position, was encouraged to engineer Gareth Brown's removal, presumably by Dixon or Burke or someone acting for them. (Canagarajah arrived after Devlin's appointment, so it couldn't have been him.) The testimony of our informants confirms Brown's speculation in his exchange with Devlin during his redundancy consultation that there existed 'a list of names'.
30. We know it was routine for these individuals because emails from us were typically forwarded up the managerial chain without any covering note or comment.
31. Anna McKie, 'From Richard III to boycott: where did it go wrong at Leicester?', *Times Higher Education*, 1 July 2021, https://bit.ly/SfM-207
32. Thomas Docherty, 'Citizen, Denizens and Cosmopolitans', in *Universities at War* (Thousand Oaks, CA: Sage, 2014), p. 90.

33. Five years earlier, then-vice-chancellor Paul Boyle made the decision to close the university's respected and award-winning bookshop. Again we wrote to the organisers of that year's Literary Leicester festival – and also some of its guest speakers – suggesting that they call out Boyle's plan. Again the response was negative. Again a literature event passed with no mention made of the act of literary vandalism then taking place in its sponsor institution.
34. The 50% threshold is stipulated by the Trade Union Act 2017. The 56% turnout was especially auspicious, given that the ballot took place over a period of just two weeks which included the Easter weekend, and given the constraints of the pandemic, which not only precluded in-person *get out the vote* activities but also meant many members were not regularly collecting mail from workplace mailboxes or were not, especially in the case of migrant staff, even in the United Kingdom.
35. The Trade Union Act 2016 stipulates that a trade union must give an employer 14 days' notice of any industrial action.
36. Nick Hartell (@nickhartell), 'And here the blame for a marking boycott @uniofleicester college of life sciences is laid squarely on the shoulders of those bullied into redundancy, VSS or tea', Twitter, 16 June 2021, https://bit.ly/SfM-209. The story was reported by Rachel Hall, 'Concern for students' grades as Liverpool and Leicester universities respond to strikes', *The Guardian*, 18 June 2021.
37. Toby Cray, 'University denies using algorithms for students' grades', *Leicester Student*, 29 June 2021, https://bit.ly/SfM-210.
38. Sally Weale, Richard Adams and Rachel Hall, 'London South Bank staff sound alarm over drop in courses', *The Guardian*, 25 May 2021.
39. Sam (@0151Sam64), 'My son almost went to Leicester Uni, had the grades. Very glad he didn't.', Twitter, 14 May 2021, https://bit.ly/SfM-211.
40. We're quoting Civil-War era Spanish anarchist Buenaventura Durruti.

Chapter 3

1. Unreserved minutes of a University of Leicester Council meeting, held on 25 February 2021, https://bit.ly/SfM-301.

2. Steven Jones, *Universities under Fire. Hostile Discourses and Integrity Deficits in Higher Education* (Basingstoke: Palgrave Macmillan, 2022), p. xxiii.
3. Thomas Docherty, *The New Treason of the Intellectuals: Can the University Survive?* (Manchester: Manchester University Press, 2018), p. 21.
4. See, for example, Benjamin Ginsberg, *The Fall of The Faculty: The Rise of the All Administrative University and Why it Matters* (New York: Oxford University Press, 2011), Randy Martin, *Under New Management: Universities, Administrative Labor, and the Professional Turn* (Philadelphia: Temple University Press, 2012), Stefan Collini, *What are universities for?* (London: Penguin, 2012), Peter Fleming, *Dark Academia: How Universities Die* (London: Pluto Press, 2021), pp. 50–65, and Liz Morrish and Helen Sauntson, *Academic irregularities: Language and neoliberalism in higher education.* (London and New York: Routledge, 2020).
5. Peter Fleming, *Dark Academia*, p. 55.
6. Robert Spillane and Jean-Etienne Joullié, 'The decline of authority and the rise of managerialism'. In *Organization*, 30(5) (2021). Spillane and Joullié are referring to Carl J. Friedrich, *Tradition and Authority* (New York, NY: Praeger, 1972).
7. Rosemary Deem, 'New managerialism in higher education', in *The International Encyclopedia of Higher Education Systems and Institutions*, edited by Pedro Nuno Teixeira and Jung Cheol Shil (Dordrecht, The Netherlands: Springer, 2020).
8. Liz Morrish and Helen Sauntson, *Academic irregularities*, p. 31.
9. David West 'The Managerial University: A Failed Experiment?', *Demos*, 3, 14 April 2016.
10. Liz Morrish, '"Don't frighten the students": the crisis of academic freedom in the managed university', Council for the Defence of British Universities blog, 20 April 2020, https://bit.ly/SfM-302.
11. Benjamin Ginsberg, *The Fall of The Faculty.*
12. Our figures are from Peter Fleming, *Dark Academia*, pp. 51–52, and Paul Jump, 'Academics in the minority at more than two-thirds of UK universities', *Times Higher Education*, 3 September 2015, https://bit.ly/SfM-303.

13. Benjamin Ginsberg, *The Fall of The Faculty*, p. 2.
14. University of Leicester Financial Statements 2020/21, p. 59, https://bit.ly/SfM-304.
15. David West 'The Managerial University', p. 3. It's worth noting in passing that business schools, even those wedded to the mainstream, do not typically endorse authoritarian management, instead teaching quite different forms of leadership.
16. Thomas Docherty, *The New Treason of the Intellectuals*, p. 22.
17. David West 'The Managerial University', p. 4.
18. Mark Learmonth and Kevin Morrell, 'Leadership as a Project: Neoliberalism and the Proliferation of Leaders', *Organization Theory*, 2(4) (2021), p. 3.
19. Mark Learmonth and Kevin Morrell, 'Leadership as a Project', p. 10.
20. Tom Keenoy, 'HRMism and the languages of re-presentation', *Journal of Management Studies*, 34(5) (1997), p. 835.
21. Peter Fleming, *Dark Academia*, p. 5.
22. 'Efficiency', 'effectiveness' and 'relevance' were all invoked in various University of Leicester documents elaborating on Shaping for Excellence and in the 59 pages of the 'Case for Change' that justified our redundancies *excellence* or *excellent* appeared no fewer than 52 times.
23. Bill Readings, *The University in Ruins* (Cambridge, MA and London: Harvard University Press, 1996), pp. 22 & 23.
24. Bill Readings, *The University in Ruins*, p. 33.
25. Thomas Docherty, *The New Treason of the Intellectuals*, p. 114.
26. Marina Warner, 'Why I Quit', *London Review of Books*, 36(17), 11 September 2014; at https://bit.ly/SfM-305.
27. Managers first justified this refusal on the ground of the confidentiality of participants. Later, and following a FoI request, 'commercial sensitivity' was invoked: apparently publication of staff assessment of the School's strengths and weaknesses could damage its competitiveness. The only 'raw' information managers consented to disclose was the number of participants: forty, out of a faculty more than three times this size.
28. Martin Parker, 'University, Ltd: Changing a business school', *Organization*, 21(2) (2014), p. 284.

29. Managers practised the art of stretching time. One reason for managers' presentations taking so long is that they read every slide, point by point, articulating their words slowly. (One shudders to think what it must be like to be a student subjected to these individuals as lecturers.) We were also subjected to monologues about 'technical difficulties'.
30. The term is cultural historian Joe Moran's. See his 'The scourge of managerial blah', *Times Higher Education*, 19 August 2021, https://bit.ly/SfM-306.
31. Cited in Leo McCann, Edward Granter, Paula Hyde and Jeremy Aroles, '"Upon the gears and upon the wheels": Terror convergence and total administration in the neoliberal university', *Management Learning*, 51(4) (2020), pp. 431–451.
32. Thomas Docherty, *The New Treason of the Intellectuals*, p. 114 f/n 8.
33. Naomi Klein, *The Shock Doctrine: The Rise of Disaster Capitalism* (London: Allen Lane, 2007).
34. Joe Moran, 'The scourge of managerial blah'.
35. *Game of Thrones*, created by David Benioff and D. B. Weiss, HBO (2011–2019).
35. Martin Parker, 'University, Ltd', p. 287.
36. John Goodwin and Henrietta O'Connor, 'A critical reassessment of the "complexity" orthodoxy', in *A Critical Youth Studies for the 21st Century*, edited by Peter Kelly and Annelises Kamp (Leiden: Brill, 2015), p. 38. We are grateful to a former colleague who shared this passage with us anonymously soon after we were put at risk of redundancy.
39. Lewis Carroll, *Alice's Adventures in Wonderland* and *Through the Looking Glass* (Oxford: Oxford University Press, 2009), p. 190.
40. Early in Orwell's novel the protagonist Winston Smith speculates: 'In the end the Party would announce that two and two made five, and you would have to believe it. It was inevitable that they should make that claim sooner or later: the logic of their position demanded it.' Thus, as he writes in his diary: '*Freedom is the freedom to say that two plus two make four.* If that is granted, all else follows.' Towards the novel's end Winston and Julia have been taken into custody in the Ministry of Love and Winston is being re-educated by O'Brien, a member of the Inner Party and agent of the Thought Police. 'O'Brien held up his

left hand, its back towards Winston, with the thumb hidden and the four fingers extended. "How many fingers am I holding up, Winston?" "Four." "And if the Party says that it is not four but five – then how many?" "Four." The word ended in a gasp of pain.' George Orwell, *1984* (Harmondsworth: Penguin, 1983), pp. 72–3 & 215.

41. Martin Parker, 'University, Ltd', p. 290.
42. David West, 'The Managerial University'.
43. Yes, it's really called that. According to its LinkedIn page [last accessed 7 January 2024], Validium (now part of HealthHero) is 'an employee assistance and wellbeing consultancy. ... Customers work with us because our clinical expertise and flexibility means bespoke solutions that quantifiably increase the value of people to the business. Impressive returns have been achieved with regard to raised productivity, reduced staff absence, reduced litigation and improved staff morale and engagement.' Validium/HealthHero is also the outsourced contractor providing mental health counselling at several other universities, including Manchester and Essex.
44. Perhaps to remind us just how far the University of Leicester has strayed from normal standards of academic conduct, the text itself appears to have been plagiarised from a University of Bath training manual. Indeed, the text seems to be travelling around various UK universities, for we also found it on the University of York website. You can't find the Leicester version when you search the internet, but we have kept a local copy.
45. David West, 'The Managerial University'.
46. University of Leicester, 'We are Citizens of Change', 24 February 2020, https://bit.ly/SfM-307.
47. Mike Marinetto, 'Modern universities are not neoliberal – but many academics are', *Times Higher Education*, 16 May 2019, https://bit.ly/SfM-308.
48. Cited in Chris Havergal, 'Is 'academic citizenship' under strain?' *Times Higher Education*, 29 January 2015, https://bit.ly/SfM-309.
49. Peter Fleming, *Dark Academia*.
50. Gibson Burrell: 'Dialogue is actually the weapon of the powerful' (Interview with Gislene Feiten Haubrich), *Journal of Openness, Commons and Dialogue*, 1(1), 2022, 24–30.

51. E. P. Thompson (ed.), *Warwick University Ltd: Industry, Management and the Universities* (Harmondsworth: Penguin, 1970), p. 159.

Chapter 4

1. Martin Parker, *Shut Down the Business School: What's Wrong With Management Education* (London: Pluto Press, 2018), p. 83.
2. This seems to be one of those phrases widely attributed to an individual but for which the original source remains elusive.
3. Published in New York, London and elsewhere by Vintage Random House, 1999. The quotation is from p. 2.
4. Stuart Hall, 'The Great Moving Right Show', *Marxism Today*, 23(1), January 1979. Reprinted in Stuart Hall, *Essential Essays*, Vol. 1, edited by David Morley (Durham and London: Duke University Press, 2019).
5. William Taylor, 'The James Report Revisited', in *Teacher Education, the University and the Schools*, edited by David Phillips (Abingdon, Oxon: Routledge, 2010), p. 25; and quoting Margaret Thatcher, *The Path to Power* (London: Harper Collins, 1995).
6. Margaret Thatcher, Interview with Brian Walden for *Sunday Times*, 8 May 1988, https://bit.ly/SfM-401.
7. Baroness David, House of Lords Debate on Education: Expenditure Cuts, 18 March 1981, https://bit.ly/SfM-402.
8. Prior to the Further and Higher Education Act 1992, which allowed them to become universities (hence 'post-92s'), polytechnics were (under-)funded by local education authorities.
9. Department for Education, 'Crackdown on rip-off university degrees', 17 July 2023, https://bit.ly/SfM-403.
10. *White Paper: Higher Education: Meeting the Challenge* (London: HMSO, 1988), at http://www.educationengland.org.uk/documents/wp1987/1987-higher-ed.html; Education Reform Act 1988, https://bit.ly/SfM-404.
11. Martin Parker recounts this history in 'Between Sociology and the Business School: Critical Studies of Work, Employment and Organization in the UK', *Sociological Review* 63(1) (2015), pp. 162–80.

12. Stefano Harney and Stephen Dunne, 'More than nothing? Accounting Business and Management Studies, and the research audit', *Critical Perspectives on Accounting* 24(4–5) (2013), p. 346.
13. A further seven months later, in November 2021, a two-minute video was released in which these themes and their diagramming became somewhat more animated. University of Leicester, 'The University of Leicester launches its 10 year strategy', YouTube, 9 November 2021, https://bit.ly/SfM-405.
14. Peter Armstrong (@PeterAr18228396), 'Never mind what they say, Nishan, I think it's lovely. Did you colour it in by yourself?', Twitter, 14 April 2021, https://bit.ly/SfM-406.
15. Bill Readings, *The University in Ruins* (Cambridge MA and London: Harvard University Press, 1996), p. 39.
16. These are commodities that Marx mentions in his analysis of value in the opening chapter of *Capital.* Karl Marx, *Capital: A Critique of Political Economy*, volume 1, translated by Ben Fowkes (Harmondsworth: Penguin, 1976).
17. Noam Chomsky and James Kelman, *Between Thought and Expression Lies a Lifetime: Why Ideas Matter* (Oakland: PM Press, 2021), p. 4.
18. The three founding members were Stefano Harney, Campbell Jones and Sverre Spoelestra.
19. It's worth naming some of the scholars, who include: George Caffentzis, Nick Dyer-Witheford, Graham Harman, Philip Mirowski, Arkady Plotnitsky, Isabelle Stengers, Gayatri Chakravorty Spivak, Tiziana Terranova and Alberto Toscano.
20. 'Leicester to host business "Utopia"', *Times Higher Education*, 11 April 2003, https://bit.ly/SfM-408.
21. Gilles Deleuze and Felix Guattari, *A Thousand Plateaus: Capitalism and Schizophrenia*, translated by Brian Massumi (Minneapolis: University of Minnesota Press, 1987), in Plateau 12: '1227: Treatise on Nomadology – The War Machine', pp. 351–423.
22. J.K. Gibson-Graham, 'Introduction to the new edition: ten years on', *The End of Capitalism (As We Knew It): A Feminist Critique of Political Economy* (Minneapolis, MN: University of Minnesota Press, 2006), pp. vii–viii.

23. Stefano Harney and Howard Thomas, *The Liberal Arts and Management Education: A Global Agenda for Change* (Cambridge: Cambridge University Press, 2020). Gerald Hanlon, *The Dark Side of Management: A Secret History of Management Theory* (London: Routledge, 2016). Both Harney and Hanlon worked at the Management Centre in its early years, before moving on to Queen Mary, University of London, where they attempted to do something similar. In the business-school soul-searching in the years immediately following the 2008 financial crash, the president of Babson College in Massachusetts was reported as saying that 'concrete business skills tend to expire in five years or so as technology and organizations change. History and philosophy, on the other hand, provide the kind of contextual knowledge and reasoning skills that are indispensable for business students.' David Glenn, 'The Default Major: Skating Through B-School', *New York Times*, 14 April 2011.
24. Don Antunes and Howard Thomas, 'The competitive (dis)advantages of European business schools', *Long Range Planning*, 40 (2007), pp. 382–404.
25. Andrew Jack, 'Business schools work towards a better world', *Financial Times*, 21 October 2019, quoting Ann Harrison.
26. We use positive student feedback as evidence of the popularity of our critical approach while recognising that such feedback can perpetuate inequalities for teaching staff within the university.
27. Francis Fukuyama, *The End of History and the Last Man* (New York: The Free Press, 1992).
28. Whilst writing the book we used Google to search for images carrying the new strapline. Entering "distinctive and relevant" yielded more than a quarter of a million results (text and images). None of the first fifty mentioned the University of Leicester, after which we gave up looking. By contrast "Management is too important not to debate" produced fifty-six results, all of them related to the University of Leicester School of Management. None of the authors of this book is a marketing scholar but we know which strapline is more distinctive.

Chapter 5

1. University of Leicester, 'About the University of Leicester – Gary Dixon', https://bit.ly/SfM-501.
2. Hilary Mantel, *Wolf Hall* (London: Fourth Estate, 2009), p. 365.
3. The exceptions are the colleges and halls of Cambridge, Durham and Oxford, which are registered with and regulated by the Commission, as are universities in Wales. The situation is different again in Scotland and in Northern Ireland.
4. Mary Synge, 'Regulation of universities as charities: One step forward, two steps back', *Legal Studies*, 41(2) (2021), pp. 214–33.
5. Mary Synge, 'Regulation of universities as charities'.
6. Mary Synge, 'Regulation of universities as charities'.
7. Martin Parker, *Shut Down the Business School: What's Wrong With Management Education* (London: Pluto Press, 2018).
8. University Grants Committee, *A Strategy for Higher Education into the 1990s* (London: UGC, 1985), p. 40.
9. All its members *were* men.
10. This story relates to 'old' universities. But the Education Reform Act 1988 transferred ownership of polytechnics and colleges from local authorities to new higher education corporations, whilst the Further and Higher Act 1992 abolished the 'binary divide', allowing the old polys to become universities. Thus, by the mid-1990s, 'old' and 'new' universities shared similar governance structures, though new universities' governing boards contained a maximum of twenty-four members, making them smaller than most old universities' councils.
11. One concrete figure is that 'the utilisation of teaching space is currently about 20 to 30 per cent', while a rate of 35% would be 'efficient'. But there is no explanation of what these numbers mean.
12. 'Some institutions, especially those which began as teacher training colleges, have a denominational and charitable basis'. This is incorrect: as far as we are aware, *all* universities in the UK are, and were in 1997, charities.
13. In much of what follows in this chapter we draw on data publicly available in various iterations of the University of Leicester's annual financial statements, which, like all universities, it must publish on its

website. Universities' financial year runs from 1 August until 31 July and the statements for that year must usually be published by the end of the following January.

14. University and College Union, *Transparency at the top?*, various years, https://bit.ly/SfM-502.
15. As it happens, the School of Management was the single largest contributing department, often the *only* contributing department, to this surplus.
16. The eye-watering salaries of vice-chancellors are now well-documented and University of Leicester – as ever – has followed the trend. What's received less attention is the remuneration of other senior managers – the 'armies of functionaries' including 'deans, deanlets [and] deanlings' that we mentioned in Chapter 3. In 2002/03 no one at the University of Leicester, apart from the VC and a few 'top' medical professors employed on more generous NHS contracts earned more than £70,000 per year. By 2014/15, there were thirty-three individuals – senior managers and some professors – on salaries of £100,000 or greater, a number that had doubled to sixty-six by 2021/22, with eight earning more than £150,000 and one – presumably one of the deputy vice-chancellors – more than £250,000.
17. The two categories that have both been squeezed are 'Technical' and 'Clerical, Manual and Ancillary'.
18. David Graeber, 'On the phenomenon of bullshit jobs: a work rant', *Strike! Magazine*, 3 (August 2013), https://bit.ly/SfM-503; *Bullshit Jobs: A Theory* (London: Penguin, 2018).
19. University and College Union, *UK higher education: A workforce in crisis*, March 2022, https://bit.ly/SfM-504.
20. University of Leicester, Financial Statements, 2020/21, p. 9; at https://bit.ly/SfM-304.
21. We acknowledge that there are complicating arguments around the use of 'lecture capture' systems such as Panopto. Recorded lectures may, for example, open up lecture provision to students unable to attend classes for disability reasons. We do not, however, think that software named for Jeremy Bentham's infamous 'panopticon' surveillance system is necessarily the answer to creating more equitable teaching and learning conditions.

22. István Örkény and Andrea Rossi, 'The green and the unseen', 2 May 2018, Leicester UCU, https://bit.ly/SfM-505.
23. 'University of Leicester: Professor Paul Boyle to become new vice-chancellor', *Leicester Mercury*, 6 March 2014.
24. During the 2018 USS pension strikes, a group of student supporters did visit this executive corridor. They occupied it for several days. Despite the expense of its refurbishment, the executive corridor remains poorly accessible, with someone unable to use stairs required to take a labyrinthine route.
25. Or possibly £265 million. The uncertainty arises due to a discrepancy in the statements for 2019/20, over which there is other controversy. In that year, according to consolidated statement of cash flows, payments made to acquire fixed assets totalled £63,334,000 (on p. 49). In the summary financial review on pp. 20–21, in contrast, the boast is: 'We have invested £93 million ... in our estate and infrastructure.'
26. Council meeting of 16 November 2016; Minute16/M86, https://bit.ly/SfM-506.
27. A prospectus is a formal disclosure document that contains detailed information to prospective investors about the financial asset (share, bond, or whatever) that is being offered.
28. This escrow account is reported in note 27 to the University's 2018/19 financial statements. An escrow account is an account held by a third-party, which mediates between the two transacting parties, in this case the University of Leicester and financial investors.
29. Few details have been made public and the university leadership has consistently refused to share with students, staff or other potentially deeply impacted stakeholders the pertinent minutes from any of the committees that might have been responsible for decision-making and oversight.
30. We know this from Companies House records.
31. 'Assured Guaranty Wraps University of Leicester Bond Issuance', 8 May 2019, https://bit.ly/SfM-507.
32. Lorna Finlayson, 'How universities tricked students into returning to campus, *The Guardian*, 2 October 2020.

33. Peter Bearne, 'Student blames "squalid" university accommodation for severe skin rash', *ITV News*, 24 June 2021, https://bit.ly/SfM-508.
34. The Edinburgh and Sussex bonds were both offered on the Irish stock exchange. Some of our speculations on the shape of the Leicester deal are informed by details in the prospectuses associated with those offerings. Subsequent to these deals, employees at both Sussex and Kingston have faced redundancy schemes. In a report prepared for Sussex UCU in 2020, Andrew McGettigan, an expert on university finances, suggested that covenants on that university's borrowing – notably the requirement that a financial surplus be generated *every* year – represent 'a restrictive imposition on the university's ability to navigate the [COVID-19] crisis'. Andrew McGettigan, 'Scoping report for union branches, University of Sussex', 26 May 2020, p. 1; at https://bit.ly/SfM-509.
35. Data are from the Higher Education Statistics Agency: www.hesa.ac.uk.
36. This was reported by Martyn Riddleston, the Chief Operating Officer. University of Leicester, 'VC & Executive Board Live Q&A – October 2020', YouTube, 27 October 2020, at https://bit.ly/SfM-510. The segment of interest starts at 31:20. (Also archived at https://ulsb16.com/SfM/)
37. University of Leicester Council, Unreserved Minutes of a Special Meeting held by 'Teams' on Thursday 25 February 2021, https://bit.ly/SfM-511.
38. The costs of audit certainly increased dramatically, from £74,000 in 2018/19 to £194,000 in 2019/20.
39. The Covid Corporate Financing Facility was a means by which the state, via the Bank of England, supported large companies during the pandemic by providing cheap loans.
40. Recall earlier concerns regarding the inadequacy of the Office for Students filling of the governance gap left by the 'exempt' status of universities, despite their formal charitable status.
41. In February 2020, Riddleston was appointed Chief Operating Officer. In September 2022 he followed Edmund Burke to Bangor University as that institution's chief financial officer.
42. The quotation is on p. 22.

43. Making at least the unreserved minutes of such committees public is, we believe, essential to enable the transparency that tends to keep bad decision making under control.
44. University of Leicester, Annual Report and Financial Statements, 2021/22, p. 45 and note 17, https://bit.ly/SfM-512.
45. This is partially obscured in the 2021/22 accounts because short term debt in 2020/21 was inflated by a £60 million government loan – the Covid Corporate Financing Facility mentioned above. This was repaid during the financial year so that it looks at first glance that short term debt has actually *decreased*. Ironically, it is possible that it was this repayment which caused the breach of covenant.
46. University of Leicester, Annual Report and Financial Statements, 2021/22, p. 45 and note 18. Auditor fees are reported in note 10; at https://bit.ly/SfM-512.
47. University of Leicester, Meeting of Senate, 8 November 2017 (Minute 17/M12(e)), https://bit.ly/SfM-513; University of Leicester, Meeting of Council, 22 November 2017, Minute17/M102, https://bit.ly/SfM-514.
48. University of Leicester, Meeting of Council, 21 November 2018, Minute18/M116, https://bit.ly/SfM-515.

Chapter 6

1. Section 202. At https://bit.ly/SfM-601.
2. Approved and launched in 2011. At https://bit.ly/SfM-602.
3. Joan Wallach Scott, *Knowledge, Power, and Academic Freedom* (New York: Columbia University Press, 2019), p. 108.
4. European Court of Human Rights, Guide on Article 10 of the European Convention on Human Rights, 31 August 2022, https://bit.ly/SfM-603.
5. Randy Martin, *Under New Management: Universities, Administrative Labor, and the Professional Turn* (Philadelphia: Temple University Press, 2011), pp. 82 & 84.
6. Randy Martin, *Under New Management*, pp. 84 and 85.
7. Randy Martin, *Under New Management*, p. 85.

8. 'Report of the Committee on Academic Freedom and Civil Liberties', *The American Economic Review*, vol. 48, no. 2 (1958): 651–53.
9. Quoted by Joan Wallach Scott, *Knowledge, Power, and Academic Freedom*, p. 5.
10. Polly Curtis and Martin Hodgson, 'Student researching al-Qaida tactics held for six days', *The Guardian*, 24 May 2008; Hicham Yezza, 'Rod Thornton's suspension is a serious attack on academic freedom', *The Guardian*, 11 May 2011; Mark Townsend, 'Nottingham University films students suspected of extremism', *The Guardian*, 11 June 2011.
11. Liz Morrish, 'Academic Freedom and the Disciplinary Regime in the Neoliberal University', in *Neoliberalism in Context: Governance, Subjectivity and Knowledge*, edited by Simon Dawes and Marc Lenormand (London: Palgrave Macmillan, 2020).
12. Terrance Karran, 'Academic freedom in Europe: a preliminary comparative analysis', *Higher Education Policy*, 20 (2007), pp. 289–313.
13. Dennis Farrington and David Palfreyman, *The Law of Higher Education*, 2nd edition (Oxford: Oxford University Press, 2012), para. 13.08.
14. Mark Davies, 'Academic freedom: a lawyer's perspective', *Higher Education*, 70 (2015), p. 989.
15. The Higher Education (Freedom of Speech) Act became law in May 2023, as we were finalising this book.
16. All quoted in Sally Weale, 'Proposed free speech law will make English universities liable for breaches', *The Guardian*, 16 February 2021.
17. Joan Wallach Scott, *Knowledge, Power, and Academic Freedom*, p. 114.
18. Joan Wallach Scott, *Knowledge, Power, and Academic Freedom*, p. 5, and quoting from Adam Sitze, 'Academic Unfreedom, Unacademic Freedom', *Massachusetts Review*, 58(4) (Winter 2017).
19. Joan Wallach Scott, *Knowledge, Power, and Academic Freedom*, p. 5, and quoting from *The Future of Academic Freedom*, edited by Louis Menand (Chicago: University of Chicago Press, 1996).
20. Joan Wallach Scott, *Knowledge, Power, and Academic Freedom*, pp. 114 & 118. In an argument we struggle to comprehend, political scientist Norman Finkelstein – who has himself been repeatedly embroiled in disputes about academic freedom – has suggested 'that Holocaust denial should be taught in university and preferably by a Holocaust denier'.

Aleks Phillips, 'Finkelstein: students should be taught about Holocaust denial by a Holocaust denier', *The Jewish Chronicle*, 23 October 2020; at https://bit.ly/SfM-604.

21. Joan Wallach Scott, *Knowledge, Power, and Academic Freedom*, p. 19.
22. Ben Fine, 'The new revolution in economics', *Capital and Class*, 61 (Spring 1997), pp. 143–48.
23. The 'deal' was a largely implicit one between capital and the working class, managed by the state, trade unions and employers' organisations, and underpinned by the political economics of John Maynard Keynes. In a nutshell, workers delivered rising productivity in exchange for rising wages and greater social spending. In the 1970s this Keynesian deal was forced into crisis by a combination of workers' 'unmanageable' demands and the social struggles of marginalised groups who had been excluded from its 'benefits'.
24. The Ordinance is available at https://bit.ly/SfM-602.
25. Letter from Gavin Williamson MP to Sir Michael Barber and Lord Wharton of Yarm, 8 February 2021, https://bit.ly/SfM-605.
26. Bethan Staton, 'English universities face upheaval as financial strains hit jobs', *Financial Times*, 23 May 2021.
27. Bethan Staton, 'Real-world economics gains ground in business studies', *Financial Times*, 1 June 2021.
28. 'The Conservatives' war on free speech', *Owen Jones Show*, episode 71, 18 February 2021; at https://bit.ly/SfM-606.
29. Thomas Docherty, 'On academic and other freedoms', in *Why Academic Freedom Matters: A Response to Current Challenges*, edited by Cheryl Hudson and Joanna Williams (London: Civitas, 2016), p. 98.
30. Thomas Docherty, 'On academic and other freedoms', p. 109.
31. Sarah Hawkins and John Routledge, 'What were they thinking? A statistical analysis of the ULSB controversy', 23 March 2021; at https://bit.ly/SfM-607.
32. Joan Wallach Scott, *Knowledge, Power, and Academic Freedom*, p. 41.
33. Committee of Vice-Chancellors and Principals, Report of the Steering Committee for Efficiency Studies in Universities (Jarratt Report), March 1985; at https://bit.ly/SfM-608.

34. Karl Marx, *Capital: A Critique of Political Economy*, Volume 1, translated by Ben Fowkes (Harmondsworth: Penguin, 1990), p. 344.
35. These numbers are from the Higher Education Statistics Agency (https://www.hesa.ac.uk) and a UCU report drawing on these data, *Precarious work in higher education* (October 2021 update), https://bit.ly/SfM-609.
36. John Higgins, 'Abstract Human Right or Material Practice? Academic Freedom in an Unequal Society', in *State of the Nation: Poverty and Inequality: Diagnosis, Prognosis and Responses*, edited by Crain Soudien, Ingrid Woolard and Vasu Reddy (Cape Town, SA: Human Sciences Research Council Press, 2018), quoted by Joan Wallach Scott, *Knowledge, Power, and Academic Freedom*, p. 12.
37. Kathleen Lynch and Mariya Ivancheva, 'Academic freedom and the commercialisation of universities: A critical ethical analysis', *Ethics in Science and Environmental Politics*, 15(1) (2015), p 77. In this spirit, Julia Schleck connects the decline of academic freedom (and its obfuscation with free speech) to the rise of the neoliberal university and its precarious working conditions: Julia Schleck, 'Dirty knowledge: Academic Freedom in the Age of Neoliberalism' *Freedom* (Lincoln: University of Nebraska Press, 2022).

Chapter 7

1. Stefano Harney and Fred Moten, 'The university and the undercommons: seven theses', *Social Text*, 79 (Summer 2004), p. 101.
2. 'Strike threat at University of Leicester', UCU Press Release, 31 March 2021, https://bit.ly/SfM-701.
3. University of Leicester (@uniofleicester), 'We welcome last night's decision of @NCanagarajah, Edmund Burke and Gary Dixon to resign from their respective roles as President & Vice-Chancellor, deputy Vice-Chancellor, and Chair of Council of @uniofleicester', Twitter, 1 April 2021, https://bit.ly/SfM-702. We have replaced Twitter usernames with 'real' names. When Professor Paul Boyle's term as Leicester VC ended after just five years in post, he moved to Swansea University.

4. Kellyanne Conway, then-counsellor to then-US president Donald Trump, coined the expression in January 2017. Like Donald Rumsfeld's 2002 contribution to philosophy with his 'unknown unknowns' remark, we wonder if the concept of 'alternative facts' might be more productive than the liberal denigration would suggest.
5. Three years earlier, the UCU branch at the Open University had forced Peter Horrocks to resign as vice-chancellor of that institution. See Richard Adams, 'Open University vice-chancellor resigns after staff revolt', *The Guardian*, 13 April 2018.
6. In discussing so-called productive labour in *Capital*'s first volume, Marx gives the examples of a school and a sausage factory. *Capital: A Critique of Political Economy*, Volume 1 (Penguin: Harmondsworth, 1976), p. 644. The Really Open University, a vibrant counter-university experiment in Leeds, that existed for several months in 2010, called its newspaper *The Sausage Factory* – https://bit.ly/SfM-703.
7. John Holloway, '*The Red Rose of Nissan*', *Capital and Class*, 11(2) (Summer 1987), pp. 142–64. The 'red rose' of the title refers to the 'new look' of the Labour party, launched the same year, as it began its accommodation with neoliberalism. Of course, despite the shared attire and canteen class and other hierarchies remained in place at Nissan's Sunderland plant – just as they would do in a Nissan-like university.
8. University bosses *expect* a lot. 'Expect' is an extremely useful – and thus much-used – word for a manager. Its double meaning allows a manager to make clear what they want of staff, without issuing a direct instruction, which might elicit resistance – and indeed denying their 'expectation' was anything but a probabilistic one. It's the difference between a carer telling a child, "I expect you to clean your teeth before you go to bed", and looking at the sky and saying, "I expect it will rain tomorrow".
9. We mentioned value struggles in our book's Introduction. Although we have not used the term in the in-between pages, our entire book has been a narration and exploration of a value struggle – a struggle over what values should underpin the university.
10. This is the triumph of 'rational choice theory', as relied upon and taught in so-called Chicago School economics, which begins with the

selfish individual and ends with economic value as the only value worth valuing.

11. Lanre Bakare, 'Government scraps ballet dancer reskilling ad criticised as "crass"', *The Guardian*, 12 October 2020
12. Department for Education, 'Crackdown on rip-off university degrees', 17 July 2023, https://bit.ly/SfM-403.
13. Perhaps the sole exception is the HR business partner whom Gareth Brown first addressed in the exchange we quoted at the beginning of our Introduction. As we reported there 'Alex' resigned their position from the University of Leicester.
14. Since we are discussing individuals, it is worth stressing that almost every other former member of that centre found the School of Management (as it was when they joined it) welcoming and more conducive to scholarship.
15. In some respects, Dixon is a personification of the pressure to promote entrepreneurship now being exerted by government on UK universities. Dixon was himself a successful entrepreneur until he sold out in order to concentrate on a number of non-executive directorships, amongst which are USS, the pre-92 universities' pension fund and the Council of the University of Leicester. His enthusiasm for entrepreneurship is most visibly expressed in his promotion of the Company of Entrepreneurs which he describes as 'an aspirant Livery Company of the City of London'. In a strange fusion of modern go-get and ancient flummery, he is frequently to be seen in the social media posts of the Company, attired in the ceremonial robes of Master of the Company, a post to which he was elected in 2021. It may be through Dixon's influence in this respect that there are currently no less than nine entrepreneurs in residence at the University of Leicester, and it may also be that he saw – and influenced others to see – Critical Management Studies as a hostile presence which needed to be swept aside so that this entrepreneurial turn could proceed. Certainly, the crude misapprehension that Critical Management Studies is anti-business played an important rhetorical part in its purge from the University of Leicester.
16. University and College Union, 'University staff pay cut by 20%, new figures show', 26 October 2021, https://bit.ly/SfM-704.

17. Higher Education Statistics Agency, 'What are their employment conditions?', 21 February 2023, https://bit.ly/SfM-705.
18. University and College Union, 'University & college staff do two days unpaid work every week', 20 June 2022, https://bit.ly/SfM-706.
19. Franco 'Bifo' Beradi coined the phrase 'slow cancellation of the future' in *After the Future* (Edinburgh: AK Press, 2011). Mark Fisher picked up on it in *Ghosts of My Life: Writings on Depression, Hauntology and Lost Futures* (London: Zero Books, 2014). Since then the phrase 'against the slow cancellation of our future' has appeared as a political slogan on banners. See, for example, UCU at IOA (@ucuatioa), 'Our lovely banner "against the slow cancellation of the future" at the UCL-IOA, Twitter, 8 March 2018, https://bit.ly/SfM-707.
20. The predicted global population at the end of the century.
21. Mark Fisher, *Capitalist Realism: Is There No Alternative?* (London: Zero Books, 2009), p. 17.
22. Stefano Harney and Fred Moten, 'The university and the undercommons', p. 101.
23. Stuart Hall, 'Cultural studies and its theoretical legacies', in *Essential Essays*, Volume 1: *Foundations of Cultural Studies*, edited by David Morley (London: Duke University Press, 2019), p. 85. Originally published in *Cultural Studies*, edited by Lawrence Grossberg, Cary Nelson, Paula Treichler (London: Routledge, 1992).
24. Quoted by Zoe Williams, 'The Saturday interview: Stuart Hall', *The Guardian*, 11 February 2012.
25. Olly Haynes, 'The future is cancelled', *epilogue*, 21 October 2021, https://bit.ly/SfM-708.
26. University and College Union, 'Two-thirds of university staff considering leaving sector, new report reveals', 25 March 2022, https://bit.ly/SfM-709.
27. Antonio Negri, Afterword to 'The constitution of time', in *Time for Revolution*, trans. Matteo Mandarini (London: Continuum, 2003), p. 133. Negri writes: 'Is there a difference between the possible and the desirable? How is one to measure it without travelling its length?'
28. Their insistence was an instance of what Mark Fisher called 'market Stalinism', a combination of marketisation and overbearing bureaucracy

and control: while bosses depicted the conference centre as a commercial venture, in reality its commercially viability was only secured by managerial diktat and compulsion. Mark Fisher, *Capitalist Realism: Is There No Alternative?* (London: Zero Books, 2009).

29. Samuel Beckett, *The Unnameable* (London: Grove Press, 1958).

Postscript

1. SWOT analysis is a management tool for identifying and analysing an organisation's internal strengths and weaknesses and external opportunities and threats. PESTLE analysis studies key external factors that influence an organisation: political, economic, social, technological, legal, and environmental.

AUTHOR BIOGRAPHIES

Gibson Burrell is now Honorary Professor of Organisation Theory at the Universities of Manchester, Lancaster and York. He was recipient of the 2014 American Academy of Management OMT Division's biennial Joanne Martin 'Trailblazer' award for lifelong contribution to the area and recipient of the Richard Whipp 'Lifetime Achievement Award' from the British Academy of Management in September 2021. Whilst at the University of Leicester, between 2003 and 2007 he was Head of the School of Management, and from 2003 until 2021 was Professor of Organisation Theory.

Ronald Hartz is Research Assistant at Technische Universität Ilmenau, Germany. He is interested in organisation and management studies, alternative forms of work and organisation, and the discursive constitution of organisations. Recently, he became interested in the critical exploration of the transformation of higher education.

David Harvie is now a deprofessionalised intellectual. Information about his various projects and publications can be found at https://hcommons.org/members/davidharvie/.

Geoff Lightfoot was so dismayed by the behaviour of the management at the University of Leicester that he left academia. He now works for Citizens Advice.

Simon Lilley is Professor of Organisational Studies and Management at Lincoln International Business School at the University of Lincoln. He likes it there. Lincoln's Research and Knowledge Exchange Strategy emphasises 'Respecting academic freedom and valuing excellent research of all forms'. It makes a very pleasant change.

zer0
books

CULTURE, SOCIETY & POLITICS

Contemporary culture has eliminated the concept and public figure of the intellectual. A cretinous anti-intellectualism presides, cheer-led by hacks in the pay of multinational corporations who reassure their bored readers that there is no need to rouse themselves from their stupor. Zer0 Books knows that another kind of discourse — intellectual without being academic, popular without being populist — is not only possible but already flourishing. Zer0 is convinced that in the unthinking, blandly consensual culture in which we live, critical and engaged theoretical reflection is more important than ever before.

If you have enjoyed this book, why not tell other readers by posting a review on your preferred book site.

You may also wish to subscribe to our Zer0 Books YouTube Channel.

Bestsellers from Zer0 Books include:

Poor but Sexy
Culture Clashes in Europe East and West
Agata Pyzik
How the East stayed East and the West stayed West.
Paperback:978-1-78099-394-2 ebook: 978-1-78099-395-9

An Anthropology of Nothing in Particular
Martin Demant Frederiksen
A journey into the social lives of meaninglessness.
Paperback: 978-1-78535-699-5 ebook: 978-1-78535-700-8

In the Dust of This Planet
Horror of Philosophy vol. 1
Eugene Thacker
In the first of a series of three books on the Horror of Philosophy, *In the Dust of This Planet* offers the genre of horror as a way of thinking about the unthinkable.
Paperback: 978-1-84694-676-9 ebook: 978-1-78099-010-1

The End of Oulipo?
An Attempt to Exhaust a Movement
Lauren Elkin, Veronica Esposito
Paperback: 978-1-78099-655-4 ebook: 978-1-78099-656-1

Capitalist Realism
Is There No Alternative?
Mark Fisher
An analysis of the ways in which capitalism has presented itself as the only realistic political-economic system.
Paperback: 978-1-84694-317-1 ebook: 978-1-78099-734-6

Rebel Rebel
Chris O'Leary
David Bowie: every single song. Everything you want to know, everything you didn't know.
Paperback: 978-1-78099-244-0 ebook: 978-1-78099-713-1

Cartographies of the Absolute
Alberto Toscano, Jeff Kinkle
An aesthetics of the economy for the twenty-fi rst century.
Paperback: 978-1-78099-275-4 ebook: 978-1-78279-973-3

Malign Velocities
Accelerationism and Capitalism
Benjamin Noys
Long listed for the Bread and Roses Prize 2015, *Malign Velocities* argues against the need for speed, tracking acceleration as the symptom of the ongoing crises of capitalism.
Paperback: 978-1-78279-300-7 ebook: 978-1-78279-299-4

Babbling Corpse
Vaporwave and the Commodifi cation of Ghosts
Grafton Tanner
Paperback: 978-1-78279-759-3 ebook: 978-1-78279-760-9

New Work New Culture
Work we want and a culture that strengthens us
Frithjof Bergmann
A serious alternative for humankind and the planet.
Paperback: 978-1-78904-064-7 ebook: 978-1-78904-065-4

Romeo and Juliet in Palestine
Teaching Under Occupation
Tom Sperlinger
Life in the West Bank, the nature of pedagogy and the role of a university under occupation.
Paperback: 978-1-78279-637-4 ebook: 978-1-78279-636-7

Color, Facture, Art and Design
Iona Singh
This materialist definition of fine art develops guidelines for architecture, design, cultural studies, and ultimately, social change.
Paperback: 978-1-78099-629-5 ebook: 978-1-78099-630-1

Sweetening the Pill
or How We Got Hooked on Hormonal Birth Control
Holly Grigg-Spall
Has contraception liberated or oppressed women?
Sweetening the Pill breaks the silence on the dark side of hormonal contraception.
Paperback: 978-1-78099-607-3 ebook: 978-1-78099-608-0

Why Are We the Good Guys?
Reclaiming Your Mind from the Delusions of Propaganda
David Cromwell
A provocative challenge to the standard ideology that Western power is a benevolent force in the world.
Paperback: 978-1-78099-365-2 ebook: 978-1-78099-366-9

The Writing on the Wall
On the Decomposition of Capitalism and its Critics
Anselm Jappe, Alastair Hemmens
A new approach to the meaning of social emancipation.
Paperback: 978-1-78535-581-3 ebook: 978-1-78535-582-0

Neglected or Misunderstood
The Radical Feminism of Shulamith Firestone
Victoria Margree
An interrogation of issues surrounding gender, biology, sexuality, work and technology, and the ways in which our imaginations continue to be in thrall to ideologies of maternity and the nuclear family.
Paperback: 978-1-78535-539-4 ebook: 978-1-78535-540-0

How to Dismantle the NHS in 10 Easy Steps (Second Edition)
Youssef El-Gingihy
The story of how your NHS was sold off and why you will have to buy private health insurance soon. A new expanded second edition with chapters on junior doctors' strikes and government blueprints for US-style healthcare.
Paperback: 978-1-78904-178-1 ebook: 978-1-78904-179-8

Digesting Recipes
The Art of Culinary Notation
Susannah Worth
A recipe is an instruction, the imperative tone of the expert, but this constraint can offer its own kind of potential. A recipe need not be a domestic trap but might instead offer escape — something to fantasise about or aspire to.
Paperback: 978-1-78279-860-6 ebook: 978-1-78279-859-0

Most titles are published in paperback and as an ebook. Paperbacks are available in traditional bookshops. Both print and ebook formats are available online.
Follow us at:
https://www.facebook.com/ZeroBooks
https://twitter.com/Zer0Books
https://www.instagram.com/zero.books